Since 1980, the American short story has undergone a renaissance of sorts, as students flock to creative writing workshops, sales of anthologies and writing textbooks mushroom, and large publishing houses overcome their traditional resistance to short story collections. *The Culture and Commerce of the American Short Story* is an account of the birth and development of the short story from the time of Poe. It describes how America – through political movements, changes in education, magazine editorial policy, and the work of certain individuals – built the short story as an image of itself and continues to use the genre as a locale where political ideals can be rehearsed, debated, and turned into literary forms. Although the focus of this book is cultural, individual authors such as Edgar Allan Poe and Edith Wharton are examined. The book also contains a history of creative writing and the workshop dating back a century. Andrew Levy makes a strong case for the centrality of the short story as an American art form and provides an explanation for the genre's recent resurgence and ongoing success.

D0208270

CAMBRIDGE STUDIES IN AMERICAN LITERATURE AND CULTURE

THE CULTURE AND COMMERCE OF
THE AMERICAN SHORT STORY

Books in the series

Continued on pages following the Index

THE CULTURE AND COMMERCE
OF THE AMERICAN
SHORT STORY

ANDREW LEVY

Butler University

To Joel + Annie
(and their kids) —
with much affection —

Andy

PS — read this to Allie + Indy. It'll
make great bedtime reading —

CAMBRIDGE
UNIVERSITY PRESS

Published by the Press Syndicate of the University of Cambridge
The Pitt Building, Trumpington Street, Cambridge CB2 1RP
40 West 20th Street, New York, NY 10011–4211, USA
10 Stamford Road, Oakleigh, Melbourne 3166, Australia

First published 1993

Printed in the United States of America

Library of Congress Cataloging-in-Publication Data
Levy, Andrew, 1962–
The culture and commerce of the American short story /
Andrew Levy.
p.   cm. – (Cambridge studies in American literature and
culture ; 68)
Includes index.
ISBN 0–521–44057–2
1. Short stories, American – History and criticism. 2. Creative
writing – Study and teaching – United States – History. I. Title.
II. Series.
PS374.S5L48   1993
813′.0109–dc20   92–38879
                                                              CIP

A catalog record for this book is available from the British Library.

ISBN 0–521–44057–2 hardback

The astonishing thing about the contemporary short story in America is that there is so much of it.

Katharine Fullerton Gerould, 1924

CONTENTS

ILLUSTRATIONS

PREFACE

I wrote this book in Philadelphia during 1988–92. To say I had help would be an understatement; to say that I wish I could express my gratitude to the people I have listed below, and about twenty others I have not mentioned, in some more compelling way than a brief acknowledgment is an equal understatement. For reading the entire manuscript through every draft, and making formative suggestions throughout, I would like to thank Peter Conn, Myra Jehlen, and Gregg Camfield. For providing advice and background at key times, I thank Michael Gilmore, Shannon Ravenel, Jan Radway, and Drew Faust. For an hour of informal conversation that made me redraft the fifth chapter (and for the pleasure of the conversation itself), I am grateful to Bobbie Ann Mason. Hilene Flanzbaum, Paula Geyh, and Andrew Weinstein provided advice and encouragement; I might have written this book without them, but it would have been a more neurotic proposition. For guiding me through the Johns Hopkins Writing Seminars, and providing me with insight into the spheres of writing workshops and publishing, I thank John Barth and Steve Dixon; for all that and for their friendship, I thank Fred Leebron, Kathryn Rhett, Eberle Umbach, and Julie Fishbein. Richard Burgin taught me how a good magazine is run, and gave me invaluable support. I thank Bill Walker and the Humanities Department of the Philadelphia College of Pharmacy and Science for giving me a job I truly enjoyed. For showing me Iowa's offices, thanks to Connie Brothers; for making Penn's offices less labyrinthine, I thank David Coleman. For their support during the last stages of manuscript preparation and acceptance, I am grateful to Eric Sundquist and Julie Greenblatt. Thanks to Charles E. May for writing the book that got me started, to Patricia Caldwell for inspiring me to be an Am Lit student, and to Phil Baruth and Erik Huber for making literary study at once relevant and irreverent. Thanks also to my friends outside of academia (who should feel understandably slighted here), and thanks lastly and always to my family: This book is dedicated to them.

Currently, the short story is moving faster and evolving more rapidly than this book could be written, a circumstance that justifies my reasons for undertaking this study as it dates my conclusions. In 1991, for instance, the year after I wrote Chapter 4, at least four major publishers released short story handbooks to capitalize on the growth of writer's workshops, and several smaller presses also released offerings. This new wave of creative writing handbooks suggests that my comments on pedagogy may require rapid addendum that, unfortunately, cannot be given here. Similarly, in 1988 I wrote the first draft of the chapter on Bobbie Ann Mason, and discussed the dominance of "minimalism" as a short story style; it is perhaps less dominant now, though it seems likely that Mason has little difficulty publishing her new fiction, and that Raymond Carver has more imitators than ever before. Although literary fashion may date some of the specific observations that I offer within this book, however, I believe in the resilience of the larger themes, just as I believe in the resilience of the short story and its place within American culture. It would not surprise me, in fact, to discover that someone has written this book already, nor would it surprise me if someone wrote it again in thirty years.

INTRODUCTION

The American short story is experiencing a renaissance. "In the last 15 to 20 years," Gary Fisketjon of Knopf Publishing has observed, "some world-class writers have been working in the short story form."[1] Many major publishers have increased their support of short story collections to the point where young writers are no longer automatically encouraged to write novels instead. Meanwhile, American universities now offer 250 undergraduate and graduate creative writing programs specializing in short story and poetry composition,[2] and university-sponsored literary magazines have more than justified Eugene Current-Garcia's claim that "short-story publication appears to have become one of the missions of American higher education."[3] The graduate writing programs have produced an ever-increasing circle of competent and even gifted authors. Just as important, they have been creating a base of short story teachers and *readers*. During this recent period (1983–8), the sales of the yearly *Best American Short Stories* anthology increased from 26,000 to 52,000; the O. Henry collection, the second best-selling yearly anthology, doubled its annual sales rate in 1988 alone.[4]

These recent developments are particularly resonant to any individual familiar with the history of the short story in America. Although it is difficult to support the canonical claim that the genre is a distinctly American art form, it is far easier to document that the conscious birth of the short story as a literary genre was an American product of the mid- and late-nineteenth century. In various contexts, the short story has been derided or celebrated as a major (and distinctly American) transformation of the traditional forms of literary expression – a veritable City-On-A-Hill of a genre. It has been associated with attempts to 'democratize' literature, lauded and attacked as the genre best suited to a mercantile culture, and infused with an astonishing level of extratextual energy and expectation. As Ruth Suckow wrote in 1927, America was not the land of the short story, but the "land of the definition of the short story" – a statement that argues the extent to which the short story has

1

lived, and continues to thrive, for a multitude of culturally charged reasons.[5]

The purpose of this work is to describe the birth and the construction of the short story as a literary form, and to describe the development of the social contract that has guided the writing, teaching, and publishing of the short story in America. This book is, in the strictest sense, a genre study, placing emphasis upon the work of three short story writers whose individual visions of the form's potential possessed particular significance for later generations of short story writers, or for their contemporaries. Emphasis is similarly placed upon the institutional developments and critical movements that have defined what, exactly, a short story is meant to do and to say. Predominantly, the protagonist of this work is the short story itself, not its greatest practitioners, nor their greatest performances. I sought to understand the day-to-day work that a literary genre performed, and how a literary genre responds to the day-to-day pragmatic demands of the individuals who choose to compose within its borders: what Poe thought about literature when he looked at his checkbook, and how his checkbook became the short story.

There are two reasons, I believe, that the short story deserves an institutional study. First, no genre could more benefit from a study of its day-to-day functions. From the time of Poe, the short story has been designed as a culturally disposable artifact – a thing to be read once and enjoyed (academic attention to the form has created a second set of short stories, those that are meant to be read closely, and repeatedly – but even those texts, I would claim, are still founded on the same precepts). A recent anthology preface that spoke ambivalently of the "throwaway effect" of the contemporary short story attests to the continuity of that particular axiom.[6] Without that principle, neither Poe's tales of ratiocination, nor O. Henry's surprise endings, nor the modern *New Yorker* story's careful epiphanies would bear any literary power.

Just because the short story may be a disposable product, however, does not mean that it is trash. Our ability to appreciate short stories, rather, is hampered by the alienation of time that is essential to most of our presuppositions about what constitutes great art. We do not think of literature as something that may serve a powerful function in some immediate present, but fail to interest later generations of readers. On the contrary, we use that as our definition of what does not constitute literature. The short story, from the point that Poe's ideas gained widespread acceptance, has been present oriented. As such, it suffers in our esteem – regardless of the number of short stories that are canonized and made "timeless," in spite of all the novels and poems that have proven forget-able despite their eternal ambitions.

The second reason is more complicated, and more valuable. When we think of the value of a literary genre, we think of its member texts. We do not envision any genre as a construction that produces some extrinsic benefit to the community other than the texts themselves. The short story, however, does immense work. The most striking aspect of the modern workshop system, for in-stance, is the extent to which it ensures the continued health of the short story despite the relative lack of a direct commercial demand for the product. The workshop system, rather, is an alternate econ-omy, enclosed and complete – a network of graduate programs, conferences, and literary magazines that creates and encompasses writers of short stories, readers of short stories, sites of publication, and an economic and philosophical rationale for the network's own existence. It is easy to lament the development of this network, to speak of standardization and the death of the individual voice; but that lament mistakes the reasons why the short story has been so resilient. The workshop system currently provides a remarkable confluence of writerly authority and middle-class respectability – it allows for thousands of individuals to write fiction that deliberately eschews popular values, and to be renumerated for the activity. It institutionalizes the marginal voice.

If there is not always enormous demand for the short story itself, there is enormous demand for this alternate economy. With its admixture of unresolvable aristocratic and democratic values, this vision of artistic activity resonates strongly within American liter-ary history. It is the same vision of the artist in America that Emer-son proferred in "The Poet" with his elaborate economies of sym-bols and value, and his prophecy that the artist who shunned the marketplace would eventually become landlord of the earth.[7] In fact, this vision of artistic activity has lived at the heart of the short story project since the antebellum era. The proliferation of work-shops is merely the latest permutation of the same spirit that in-fused Poe's famous review of Hawthorne's *Twice-Told Tales*, the suc-cess of the slick magazine story in the first half of this century, and the work of the New Critics at mid-century.[8] All these phenomena created institutions that kept the short story indirectly or directly profitable, while preserving a partial foothold in the high culture.

Over the past six generations, what we now call the short story has been written in numerous formal shapes – it is odd, even now, that we describe Donald Barthelme and Raymond Carver (or, more cogently, Donald Barthelme and O. Henry) as practitioners of the same genre, when their endeavors bear so few resemblances to one another. As Joyce Carol Oates has observed recently, "it isn't even true that short stories are necessarily short."[9] Rather, the real and measurable similarities between Barthelme's and Carver's efforts, and the efforts of hundreds of their peers, are largely institutional: They appear in the same magazines, they appeal to the same readership, they fill the same classrooms, they occupy the same cultural turf. The short story is best understood, perhaps, if we regard it less as an immutable and natural category for literary discourse, and view it more as a societal junction, like Wall Street, Washington, or Academia – a place that offers certain forms of cultural capital in certain amounts, and attracts individuals to the extent that they seek that particular algorithm.

As described earlier, this book is devoted to individual and institutional visions of the short story. If Chapters 1, 3, and 5 describe how individuals responded to communal rules and expectations, Chapters 2 and 4 describe how the community itself transformed those individual responses into the foundations of new consensuses on the genre. As I worked through early drafts, it became clear that this symphonic call-and-response between the community and the individual was becoming a central organizing principle and theme. It also became clear that I was creating an interpretive framework for understanding the short story that was partly developed as the result of scholarly research, and partly produced by a personal search to understand the literary legacy that my peers and I have inherited – an attempt to interpret personal history, and to *publi*cize it.

Before I entered a graduate literature program, I attended the Johns Hopkins workshop for a year. I gave up a Wall Street job, my critical aspirations, and even my novel, and joined the short story cottage industry. Everything good that was supposed to happen in a creative writing workshop happened to me, in pleasantly diluted doses: I met charismatic teachers, befriended young fellow writers, drank and danced with them, published modestly, learned (somewhat) to self-edit, and got my degree. And yet, despite the fact that I remember so many individual aspects of the experience with warmth, I also remember that, by the end of the year, the fun had gone out of writing. I had simply been too loaded down by institutional structures – not just the rules of writing, but the rules of the game. When I left for a literature program, I left with a feeling of relief – a feeling, strangely enough, that I was finally going to get to do some really creative writing.

In retrospect, it occurs to me that the manner in which each of us in that workshop chose to respond to the institution provided an independent paradigm for how young adults respond to socialization. One friend observed that the entire workshop simply "fluffed away" after graduation: She currently lives like Thoreau on the outskirts of a ranch in Idaho. Another friend chose the opposite path: He became master of the rules of short story success, publishing regularly, acquiring an agent (who, like most good agents, dissuaded him from writing short stories), and ambivalently attending two more workshops. I chose a third response: post facto analysis. Because the rules of the game required that a young writer reside within the short story, I decided to find out how the rules were written. I tried to figure out how history put me at that place.[10]

To the extent that this work discusses the institutionalization of the marginal voice, that focus is the direct result of the workshop. As young writers, the short story and the workshop were the places where we were sent to learn discipline and control. By agreeing to enter a creative writing workshop, we implicitly agreed to write, or learn to write, literature that would be socially sanctioned – if for no other reason than that we ourselves had been approved by, and would be funded by, a socially sanctioned institution, the university itself. Further, by entering a community of writers, and by exchanging ideas with them, we tacitly accepted the idea that our writing could be done in groups. In short, we were not loners. We wanted to be writers where people could see us being writers.

There was another side to this sociality, however. There is a widely spread, probably fictitious anecdote about Flannery O'Connor's stay at the University of Iowa's Writers' Workshop.[11] The essence of the story, which has been told to me several times with slight variations, is that the then-unknown O'Connor sat politely during classtime while her stories were ravaged by her fellow students. When O'Connor submitted her stories in thesis form, however, she had not changed a word. Her thesis advisor thought she had been lazy, and returned the stories to her on the condition that she consider carefully the suggestions offered by her peers, and revise her stories accordingly. O'Connor did, and re-resubmitted her stories a short time later, without altering a word. These same stories eventually earned O'Connor her fame.

This anecdote is powerful because it expresses the tension that many workshop students feel about their responsibilities to the community they have joined. If we became writers in part to reject the more mainstream career paths that had been allotted to us (we mockingly referred to ourselves as the "runaway children," and made jokes that our faces should be on the backs of milk cartons), then the content of the O'Connor story, and its obvious appeal to wish fulfillment, suggests that we made interesting ideological stuff of the workshop itself. We transformed it into a metonym of the society that we repudiated by going to the workshop. Because we weren't Company Men and Women, the workshop itself became the rule-making structure against which we rebelled, while continuing to participate: the measure of our almost congenital ambivalence.

By contrast, O'Connor's refusal seemed brilliant: the mark of the utter self-confidence of the artist who does not need workshops. The fact that she continued to attend the workshop while refusing to participate only completes the circle of the metaphor. If O'Connor does not become famous, after all, then she is merely a kook: Her right to refuse, rather, is sanctioned by the fame eventually bestowed upon her. And that is what we wanted. We did not seek to withdraw, nor did we seek a complete exaltation of the alienated individual; we wanted an exaltation of the alienated individual that would be socially approved.

If the workshop provided an inspiration for many of the ideas that frame this book, magazine work has provided an inspiration for its methodology. For the last four years, I have worked for a literary magazine, *Boulevard.* Over those years, I read approximately one thousand short stories. At the same time, I studied for my Ph.D. in American literature. Working for a magazine and studying contemporary literary theory at the same time is, I think, a revelatory experience. When you work for a magazine, you see the text in all its phases – you see it move from anonymous manuscript through the first phases of acceptance, you see it appear in print, and see it evaluated by readers, and perhaps you see it canonized. More significantly, you see other texts fail to reach these steps – texts that often (though not always) differ only very slightly from the texts that make it into the loop. In sum, you see – alive and vital – all those forces that deconstructionists call "the margins" envelop and transform that original anonymous manuscript. More important, you participate. The experience forces you to think about issues of evaluation in an immediate, partisan sense. The literary theory of historicism, in particular – which dwells on the extrinsic factors that affect a text – comes alive in the most visceral sense.

The magazine experience divided my sympathies between the story, the writer, and the magazine. It also compelled me toward the understudied places on the loop of canonization, by sheer force of numbers. For *Boulevard,* I read short stories by prominent authors, by moderately successful, professional writers, by ambitious beginners, and by individuals who seem to have missed the boat entirely – ranchers, computer programmers, and housewives completely unaware of the in-language of workshops and little magazines. My book work acted in concert with these labors. I avoided reading the 'great' short stories of great authors, many of whom I had read already anyway. Instead, I pored through Best Of- collections from the last ten years, and earlier periods. I also read through hundreds of short stories that were not remembered and likely never will be, but nevertheless filled the magazine pages of decades past. I wanted to know why *Boulevard*'s office was flooded by manuscripts, and why so many individuals wanted to write short stories; I wanted to know why I was writing them myself. And that meant understanding what rewards the short story was offering, and at what costs. It meant exploring the day-to-day work of a literary genre, and leaving the evaluation of canonical short stories for others.

It only remains to be said that being a "critic" adds a final ideological spin to the complex of sympathies I have already acknowledged. When you cross from a creative writing program to a literature program, you cross a small Rubicon. Anyone even remotely familiar with English department dynamics is also familiar with the uneasy mix of symbiosis and condescension that exists between literary scholars and their counterparts in the creative writing department (Marjorie Perloff, in a canny phrase, has called them the "A Team" and the "B Team"). It is the latest permutation of an aged tradition of animosity and mutual dependence between writers and critics. As Wallace Stegner has observed, critics often condescend to the intellectual capacities and lack of erudition of the authors with whom they share office space. Author-teachers, inversely, speak of their sense that analysis kills creativity; in blunter moments, they simply call critics frustrated writers.[12] In between these poles there exists much room for mutual respect; there exists more room for ambivalence. As a Ph.D. student and workshop veteran, and as a dissertation writer and writer of short stories, I had a clear stake in finding that interstice of mutual respect.

As suggested earlier, the modern short story is a cultural item that might benefit from a critical intervention – in particular, an intervention conducted by way of a historicist approach. For better or worse, the short story has always been a genre in which the institutional structures have been especially visible – the magazine editors, textbooks, workshops, et al. I have read convincing historicist interpretations of the growth of the short story circa 1920 that attacked the genre simply because a historicist interpretation was possible – because its growth could be linked to the growth of the magazine publishing industry, for instance.[13] The historicist viewpoint, however, harms a text only if the tension we feel between respecting community and respecting individualism is simplified and codified, rather than being utilized as a focal point from which to enrich our comprehension of what it means to be free. If we simply assume that the best literature is written by the most alienated individuals, then a critic can only be a publicist – and a genre such as the short story must inevitably suffer in our esteem, because of the extent to which it has been a communal production.

It is my belief that the historicist viewpoint tells the story of the genre in the most sympathetic manner possible. To state that the workshop system propounds standardized and academic values, for instance, is to utter the obvious. To make that statement as a criticism, however, is to overlook the enormous benefits that the workshop system provides; it also means ignoring the rather plain fact that participation in a workshop is entirely voluntary. Similarly, when Andre Dubus says (pre-*glasnost*) that "publishing in the *New Yorker* is like publishing in the Soviet Union," he attests to the fact that certain magazines are powerful enough to require even established short story writers to submit to severe editing.[14] He does not, however, say why it is important to publish in the *New Yorker* – or who granted the *New Yorker* the same powers of censorship as a totalitarian state. In sum, we have no right to speak of institutions that we have granted enormous power in the same terms that we would describe repressive institutions with which we have signed no compact. By the same lights, we have no right to assume that the historicist viewpoint is hostile to the individual artist simply because it recognizes the power of such voluntarily constructed regimes. Rather, it is ideally poised to explain how such regimes evolved.

Similarly, the historicist approach is ideally poised to unearth the short story from cultural expectations that have become hard facts. In preparing this work, I was consistently struck by the extent to which the rhetorical patterns and systems of value that evolved in the nineteenth century to discuss and judge the short story have remained predominant, with slight variations, throughout the twentieth – and the extent to which this continuity is not recognized in contemporary discussions. This circumstance is most evident in the treatment of the short story as an apprentice genre. Since the nineteenth century, the short story has been simultaneously lauded and denigrated by critics and authors invoking a pair of contradictory and yet complementary assumptions: first, that the short story was a practice field best suited for beginning authors, or authors whose ability to compose a sophisticated narrative was otherwise impaired; second, that the short story required greater discipline and skill than longer forms. Although it may be possible for individual short stories to exhibit the signs of great authorial discipline or immature simplicity, of course, it is not possible for the entire genre to represent both sides of the formulas: The length of the short story itself simply does not determine whether the individual short story is harder or easier to write than a longer fiction. What is noteworthy, however, is that both assumptions about the short story converge in the classroom, by providing powerful justifications for the use of the short story in either creative writing workshops or in formalist-oriented literature courses.

This circumstance might be less relevant, if one of those aforementioned rhetorical patterns did not persistently dwell on describing the short story as a 'brash, new form,' or as a form that was continually undergoing renewal. But the fact is, the short story does have a tradition. When an anthology such as Peregrine Smith's *Sudden Fiction* (1986) celebrates itself as the declaration of an "explosive new literary form" – the short-short story – it is impossible for the student of the short story's development to forget that critics and editors fifty years ago were equally excited about a spin-off of the short story that they too called the "short-short story."[15] For that matter, it is impossible to ignore the degree to which *Sudden Fiction*'s claim to have founded a newer, quicker art form resembles claims about the short story itself proferred by Poe in his famous review of Hawthorne, by Brander Matthews in his influential "Philosophy of the Short Story" (1885),[16] by the authors of short story textbooks throughout the 1920s, and by every rising generation of short story writers. The packaging of the short story to the American public and to its young practitioners has been entirely contingent upon a voluntary pan-cultural amnesia – an amnesia that allows short story writers to repeat the fascinations of past generations while telling themselves that they are breaking barriers. This book has been written in rebellion against that voluntary amnesia, and as a reminder that the short story has a substantial heritage.

1

POE'S MAGAZINE

Naming is how the world enlarges itself. We might try the same with the thing at hand, calling it *poe,* for instance. "Me, I write poes," one could say.

Russell Banks, "Toward a New Form," *Sudden Fiction,* ed. Shapard and Thomas (1986) 245.

Any history of the development of the short story in America must begin with Edgar Allan Poe's review of Nathaniel Hawthorne's *Twice-Told Tales* in 1842. This is not because Poe necessarily invented the short story; but rather, because later generations of short story writers, editors, and students invented Poe as the founder of the genre. From perhaps 1885 to 1950, Poe's words were "universally quoted" and imitated with what H. S. Canby once called a "servility which would have amazed that sturdy fighter."[1] His review, in turn, was retrospectively canonized as the birthdate of the short story in America. And although this literary-historical reconstruction spent itself by mid-century, it was nevertheless so powerful that Poe's words remain easily the most pervasive in the history of the genre. He was, and continues to be, both the patron saint and the neighborhood bully of the American short story.

As Canby suggests, Poe's words have been so persuasive to later generations of short story writers that his case represents a rather extraordinary example of literary influence. It is tempting to say that later generations used Poe, or constructed a version of his literary philosophy that was convenient to their purposes. But the most intriguing fact about Poe's presence is the degree to which his words have not been distorted, but taken with a dead seriousness that has had the effect of distortion. Ruth Suckow spoke in 1927 of "poor hounded Poe," who would have found "even his monstrous craving for power . . . daunted by the spectacle of the awful success of his own struggle." More recently, Charles E. May has written that the development of the short story in this country was profoundly affected by the fact that Brander Matthews, in his "Philosophy of the Short Story" (1885), simply took seriously Poe's somewhat doubtful account of the writing of "The Raven" in "The Philosophy of Composition" – and was in turn taken seriously by generations of short story practitioners.[2]

I have chosen to preserve the discussion of the retrospective canonization of Poe for later chapters; the purpose of this chapter is to reconstruct the moment of "invention" – Poe's moment. The most visionary aspect of Poe's review of Hawthorne is that it demarcates an ideal genre – a fantasy field for discourse, where uncertain assumptions about readership and authorship were accepted as facts of human nature. In part, Poe was responding to the same ideological currents that were affecting other American intellectuals, both North and South. More significantly, however, Poe composed his review in the context of a set of personal ambitions, which existed in symbiosis with his vision of the short story. To understand why Poe wrote and praised the short story, we must first examine the single project that most dominated his professional life: his desire to found a ground-breaking literary journal that would free him from economic necessity, as well as assure him a position of privilege within the mercantile culture that he openly repudiated.

It was this journal, after all, that would house his ideal genre. As William Charvat has written, Poe was "essentially book-minded" during the early part of his career; it was during the Depression of 1837 that he began to envision "the magazine, rather than the book, as the appropriate expression of American culture," and developed an editorial posture hostile to the traditional prestige of bound volumes and the literary forms they contained. Although these statements appropriately frame Poe's transformation into a "magazinist," however, they suggest only the theoretical depth and precision with which Poe adopted the periodical as the home of America's literary future. For Poe, the Journal itself became a central paradigm of communication and human contact: He used the model of periodical circulation as a basis for the structural philosophy of art he propounded in his review. In seeking to explain why Poe's words have developed such currency within a genre dominated by the influence of the magazine establishment, in particular, the fact that he created a system of value that exalted the short story for the traits it shared with the magazine itself (i.e., disposability, space conservation) is a good place to begin.[3]

Ultimately, however, Poe's review of Hawthorne, and its place within cultural history, are deeply entwined with the figure of Poe himself, and the issues of personality and ideology that have dogged and defined that figure for the past century. It would be inappropriate to equate Poe with the protagonists of his stories. But it has been long recognized that many of his tales developed the theme of the "perverse," and contained protagonists whose conscious machinations were undermined by vague but powerful unconscious impulses – "William Wilson," "The Tell-Tale Heart," and most directly, "The Black Cat."[4] Similarly, many biographers and critics have written in depth about the more sensationalist aspects of Poe's own self-destruction: most notably, his alcoholism, and the still ambiguous but suggestively sordid details of his early death. It sounds, perhaps, like a trivialization of Poe's work to observe that the same admixture of overarching ambition and sudden (and often destructive) self-abnegation that weaves through his protagonists' psyches also weaves through his literary philosophy; but within the context of a discussion of the American short story, a genre that adopted Poe as its patron saint, this observation is essential. If we can begin to understand *both* the ambitious and self-depreciating reasons why Poe wrote short stories, then we can begin to understand why later writers have gravitated toward an art form that has been notoriously undervalued, and yet associated with ideological projects of incredible and even messianic scope. One hundred and fifty years later, Poe's review of Hawthorne remains the best explanation for why individuals in America write short stories, and what they expect in return for writing them.

Apostleship: 1837–1849

A haggard, inspired-looking man now approached – a crazy beggar, asking alms under the form of peddling a rhapsodical tract, composed by himself, and setting forth his claims to some rhapsodical apostleship. . . .

Herman Melville, *The Confidence Man*,
ed. Herschel Parker (1971) 167.

In itself, the review of Hawthorne is a slim document upon which to found a genre. Poe's review of Hawthorne's *Twice-Told Tales* was printed in the April and May 1842 editions of *Graham's Magazine*, and many of its major points were reiterated in his review of *Mosses from an Old Manse*, published in *Godey's Lady's Book* in November 1847.[5] Interestingly, the "leading document in the history of the short story"[6] begins with a strong endorsement of the lyric poem. For Poe, "the fairest field for the exercise of the loftiest talent" is, "without hesitation – in the composition of a rhymed poem, not to exceed in length what might be perused in an hour."[7] Poe's praise of the lyric poem, however telling, is merely a preface for his more detailed exaltation of the short prose tale: "We have always regarded the Tale (using this word in its popular acceptation) as affording the best *prose* opportunity for display of the highest talent." The short forms are supreme, according to Poe, because "in almost all classes of composition, the unity of effect or impression is of the greatest importance." Poe's belief in "unity" as perhaps the highest of literary values was among the most consistent of his credos: In its defense, he attacked *Paradise Lost* and Dickens's novels. In his reviews of Hawthorne, Poe describes two kinds of unity: the effect on the reader, and the intention of the author. For the reader, unity is the result of an uninterrupted engagement with the text: "Worldly interests intervening during the pause of perusal, modify, annul, or counteract, in a greater or lesser degree, the impressions of the book." Hence, "the ordinary novel is objectionable" for purely generic reasons; the "short prose narrative, requiring from a half-hour to one or two hours in its perusal," can be read in one sitting, and is capable of producing "the immense force derivable from totality."[8]

For the author, unity is the dominant principle of composition. Nor is unity an organic or intuitive property. Poe describes the creative process as a conscious, analytical exercise:

> A skillful literary artist has constructed a tale. If wise, he has not fashioned his thoughts to accommodate his incidents; but having conceived, with deliberate care, a certain unique or single *effect* to be wrought out, he then invents such incidents – he then combines such events as may best aid him in establishing this preconceived effect. If his very initial sentence tend not to the outbringing of this effect, then he has failed in his first step. In the whole composition there should be no word written, of which the tendency, direct or indirect, is not to the one pre-established design.[9]

In the central document in the history of the form, this is the central passage. Nor can it be said that Poe did not intend that it receive such emphasis. He repeated the passage, almost verbatim, in the review of *Mosses from an Old Manse,* four years later. He devoted "The Philosophy of Composition" to a precise (and probably fraudulent) description of the writing of "The Raven," in the hope of rendering it "manifest that no one point in its composition is referrible [*sic*] either to accident or intuition – that the work proceeded, step by step, to its completion with the precision and rigid consequence of a mathematical problem." Although Poe's tales are rife with ecstatic and frenzied protagonists, his criticism seems designed to repel the "autorial vanity" that writers "compose by a species of fine frenzy – an ecstatic intuition."[10]

It is, in most respects, an audacious claim. Poe seems aware that he is threatening to deprive authorship of much of its cultural power: "Most writers . . . would positively shudder at letting the public take a peep behind the scenes . . ." But Poe's attack is not on authorship per se. Having repudiated traditional notions of the artist's intuitive gifts ("there is a radical error, I think, in the usual mode of constructing a story"), Poe introduces himself as the exemplar of the new method: "It will not be regarded as a breach of decorum on my part to show the *modus operandi* by which some one of my own works was put together."[11] It is comparatively easy to see, in retrospect, why Poe was considered arrogant by many of his contemporaries, and praised by later writers such as William Carlos Williams for his desire to "clear the ground."[12]

Unlike Melville's rather cruel portrait of him in *The Confidence Man,* however, Poe was no mere rhapsodist; even his most fantastic literary ambitions were moored to earth by pragmatic underpinnings. Searching for consistency in Poe's critical canon is a discouraging approach to understanding his beliefs about the nature of literature. Much of his critical commentary was 'shop talk' designed to respond to personal rivalries and alliances, or to address what he perceived as corruptions and inadequacies in the American literary establishment. A survey of his essays, reviews, and letters suggests that his faith in short prose forms was consistent. However, such a survey also suggests that Poe's belief in the short story was secondary to, and a supplement of, his greater ambition to be the founder and editor of a popular, ground-breaking literary journal.

Poe's efforts at founding such a magazine constituted his chief professional ambition from 1837 to his death in 1849. In the prospectus for the "Penn Magazine," circulated in 1840, Poe described the importance of the project in terms he was to repeat to potential sponsors until his death: "In founding a magazine of my own lies my sole chance of carrying out to completion whatever peculiar intentions I may have entertained."[13] A letter to Charles Anthon in 1844 suggests the continued importance of the project to Poe, and how it subsumed all his other endeavors:

> holding steadily in view my ultimate purpose – to found a magazine of my own, or in which at least I might have a proprietary right – it has been my constant endeavour in the meantime not so much to establish a reputation great in itself as one of that particular character which should best further my special objects, and draw attention to my exertions as Editor of a magazine. Thus I have written no books and have been so far essentially a magazinist . . .[14]

Poe may have been exaggerating for Anthon's benefit – he was, after all, requesting money for the project – but the contents of the letter clearly suggest that Poe's affinity for the short story had important institutional and professional motives that went unmentioned in the review of Hawthorne. Poe did not necessarily write (and praise) short stories because he considered them superior to novels, but because he considered the operation of a magazine a superior pursuit to writing what the next century would call the Great American Novel. In this event, Poe's celebration of short forms was part of an effort to enhance the status of the magazine as a site of high-culture discourse by enhancing the status of its most visible and exclusive contents.[15]

For this reason, examining Poe's vision of magazine editorship is a necessary step in understanding how his preference for the short story addresses demands at the root of his culture. The "watchword" of his magazine, as Poe claims, will be "a vigorous independence": Specifically, the magazine will be the seat of "an absolutely independent criticism," "self sustained." The magazine itself will be printed on "superior" paper, and will contain "pictorial embellishments" of the highest quality, sketched by "the leading artists of the country." The text will be provided by "the loftiest talent," who will be employed "not necessarily in the loftiest way." If this last claim seems odd – it is not clear why the loftiest talent would accept working at less lofty tasks – Poe quickly alters his terms. His writers will not be employed at the "pompous" or "Puritanical" forms that have previously been considered lofty, but rather, will work at the tasks deemed newly lofty by Poe's independent criticism. In sum, every aspect of the magazine will be strictly high-class, and trendsetting: "It is proposed to surpass, by very much, the ordinary Magazine style . . ."[16]

The economics of Poe's magazine perform similarly. Poe adamantly insisted throughout his life that the magazine should sell for five dollars, although most magazines of a like class sold for three.[17] This added cost was expected to finance the higher quality of the paper, and also allow Poe to attract "the loftiest talent" and "the leading artists" by offering above-standard wages. Despite the added cost of the magazine, however, Poe consistently anticipated an enormous circulation within two years of inception: While 20,000 was the figure he most commonly quoted, on other occasions he wrote hopefully of subscription rolls of 50,000, and even 100,000.[18]

In turn, Poe's marketing strategy explains how he expected to charge more for his magazine and still outsell his competitors. He hoped to unite the highest class of Americans in subscribing to, and sponsoring, his magazine: "What I need for my work in its commencement . . . is *caste*. I need the countenance of those who stand well, not less in the social than in the literary world."[19] Specifically, Poe believed that the Southern planters (whom he considered to be a disenfranchised group within a Northern-dominated literary world) would form a financial base for his magazine:

> I knew from personal experience that lying *perdus* among the innumerable plantations in our vast Southern and Western Countries were a host of well-educated men, singularly devoid of prejudice, who would gladly lend their influence to a really vigorous journal . . .[20]

Having united that class, Poe believed that the next lower class — the middlebrow — would follow their lead. In this manner, the magazine would receive financial support by virtue of its status as an upper-class literary icon; that financial support, in turn, would allow Poe to employ what he considered to be the loftiest talent, forming them into a united literary elite. The appearance of the loftiest talent on Poe's pages would assure, in turn, that his magazine would develop a critical reputation commensurate with the social positioning of its subscribers. In both the social and literary worlds, Poe's magazine was to represent a unified aristocracy – and it is fitting that he hoped to turn to the Southern planters, as "men devoid of prejudice," to form the economic substructure of his ambition.[21]

During the 1840s, however, Poe was not the only journalist to seek this particular ideological alliance. As Drew Faust has described in *A Sacred Circle*, a group of Southern intellectuals during this decade was exploring the possibilities of utilizing periodical literature to catalyze the development of an independent Southern character. Working through already existing or newly formed reviews, authors such as William Gilmore Simms, Edmund Ruffin, and George Holmes sought, in Faust's words, to "establish intellectuals as an indispensable social class," and "provide a formal structure for the activities of the Southern mind."[22] These intellectuals spoke of their journal endeavors in terms greatly similar to Poe's; James Hammond wrote of "uniting our minds," while Ruffin spoke of the *Southern Magazine* as being the central mouthpiece through which the "people of the region might be 'organized and disciplined.'"[23]

If the activities of this Sacred Circle of five Southern literati (Faust also included Nathaniel Beverly Tucker within their ranks) place Poe's endeavors in historical perspective — Poe and Simms were correspondents, and Tucker wrote for the *Southern Literary*

Messenger at the same time Poe was its editor – they also provide a significant comparison.[24] While Simms et al. sought to use the public press as the means by which to create an intellectually unified and independent South, Poe conceived of an intellectually unified South as the means by which he could establish his magazine's authority. Contrarily, this circumstance did not necessarily mean that Poe was simply a journalistic hack – a "Magazinist," in his own words – and that his desire to run a magazine was a self-serving, callow ambition to which he would subsume broader political movements. During the period of Poe's professional life, hacks, poets, and scholars alike were already running their own magazines all along the eastern seaboard; only Poe wanted to run the magazine upon which would be founded a magazine-based high-literature.[25]

In the letter to Anthon, for instance, Poe observes that his magazine plan was a literary aspiration that was unusually attuned to American life – particularly in the manner in which it emphasized the bond that might exist between a rapidly paced, rising mercantile culture, and short literary forms in an easily circulated package.

> I perceived that the country from its very constitution, could not fail of affording in a few years, a larger proportionate amount of readers than any upon the earth. I perceived that the whole energetic, busy spirit of the age tended wholly to the Magazine literature – to the curt, the terse, the well-timed, and the readily diffused, in preference to the old forms of the verbose and ponderous and the inaccessible . . .[26]

In many ways, this letter reveals as much about Poe's literary philosophy as the review of Hawthorne, and deserves to be read as closely – Arthur Quinn observes that the manuscript draft "was prepared with the greatest care, giving it the appearance of a literary composition."[27] The letter is no more than an impassioned plea for funds; yet that plea is made with rhetoric that resounds with classic American political ideology. Poe is not merely proposing to commence another magazine. The New World, by its "very constitution," offers an opportunity for a new kind of literature and a new kind of readership. "Old forms" exist, but are decadent and elitist ("inaccessible"), and outmoded by the "spirit of the age." The spirit of that new age is "energetic, busy" – unabashedly mercantile. The new form will reflect that mercantile spirit, both by respecting the fact that time is a limited commodity (a fact that the novelist, practicing a European form, does not respect), and by taking advantage of new technologies of production (as described in the review of

Hawthorne) and publication (the magazine). Poe himself appears to appreciate the visionary quality of these ambitions:

> I saw, or fancied that I saw, through a long and dim vista, the brilliant field for ambition which a Magazine of bold and noble aims presented to him who should successfully establish it in America . . .[28]

For Poe, the magazine project was an ideological end, not a means; the magazine's success per se would constitute a revolution, or the culmination of one.

Of course, the triumph of that revolution would also conclude with Poe's personal coronation: It is impossible to ignore the *to him* that forms the core of his fancy, or the extent to which even his nationalist visions center on his example and his private benefit. Poe wanted to run a magazine in part because he recognized it as a vehicle for his literary ambitions, but also because he believed that he could make money at it. This statement is not made glibly: Poe himself wrote in the letter to Anthon that "even in a pecuniary view, the object was a magnificent one."[29] Any reader of Poe's letters will quickly see how much his life was dominated by economic necessity. Notes requesting loans ("of course I need not say to you that my most urgent trouble is the want of ready money"), or calling in loans, recur with depressing frequency.[30]

Similarly, the entire magazine project amounted to one long and ultimately fruitless exercise in fund-raising. To Anthon, Poe wrote that he had borne "not only willingly but cheerfully sad poverty & the thousand consequent contumelies and other ills which the condition of the mere Magazinist entails upon him in America" in order to be taken seriously as a potential magazine founder – a strategy for success reminiscent of Emerson's reminder that the true artist must pass for a fool before becoming landlord of the earth. Poverty was one of Poe's less sensational obsessions, perhaps, but it was an obsession nevertheless.[31]

However, for Poe – gifted with the ability to merge his self-interest with national political visions – even his personal poverty had global ramifications for the realm of literature. Throughout his life, he conducted private (and unfulfilled) crusades, devised literary forms, and envisioned models of creative activity that represented hard, structural responses to the poverty of the American artist. Some of these responses were direct and specific: During the mid-1840s, for instance, he conducted an intensive campaign against the international copyright laws that created penurious conditions for American authors by allowing publishers legally to pirate British work.[32] In 1843, he proposed that instead of running the magazine himself, it might be run by a coalition of artists, in the hope that "if we do not defend ourselves by some such coalition, we shall be devoured, without mercy."[33] In each prospectus, he consistently proposed that agents will be eliminated; that no publishing cliques will generate "a pseudo-public opinion by wholesale"; and that critics will be unable to interfere for personal reasons because they will be proscribed by the bounds of an "absolutely independent criticism," the guidelines of which will be published in Poe's magazine.[34] In certain versions of the magazine project, Poe even suggests that he will write the material (under pseudonyms) as well as select material to be published, edit that material, and design the magazine's appearance.[35] Williams wrote that Poe's "attack was from the center out," but a phrase resonates from Poe's personal writings that addresses the magazine project in the mercantile terms it deserves: He sought to claim the "proprietary right" for the written word, from all the other parties who might claim it, transform it, interpret it, profit from it, or make it different from what Poe – or any other artist – intended.[36]

Superficially, Poe's magazine plan appears like a fantasy. He promises huge circulations in spite of high circulation costs, and guarantees that the best and most respected writers will not mind the subservience that he attempts to free himself from by devising the plan in the first place. He proposes this in the early 1840s, in the midst of a severe economic depression and an increasingly egalitarian society interested less and less in his overt social constructions of the many and the few. He was aware, as he notes to Anthon, that similar efforts had not succeeded: "Now, I knew, it is true, that some score of journals had failed."[37] He had, for instance, attentively watched James Russell Lowell's similarly ambitious (though less anthemic) *Pioneer* rise and fall after a few short issues.[38] He was further aware that the social elite to which he hoped to appeal for sponsorship – the Southern planters – were content to read Northern literary journals, in the rare cases that they had read literary journals at all.[39] The Sacred Circle members were not succeeding in their endeavors; it was not clear what Poe believed he would do differently, or better.

Overall, Poe's entire plan seems contingent upon the existence of an imaginary, and oddly docile, America. The chief irony of Poe's magazine project is that he makes his own success, and the success of his aristocratic ideal, dependent upon the resources that can be provided only by a rising mercantile culture: a large literate class and, of course, the magazine technology itself. In that sense, Poe's search for the ideal sponsor reflected, in metonymic form, his search for the ideal relationship between art and business:

> I have managed at last to secure, I think, the great object – a partner possessing ample capital, and, at the same time, so little self esteem, as to allow me entire control . . .[40]

Poe wrote that he needed caste to make his magazine succeed, but what he really needed was insecurity: not a culture that already believed in class (for Poe sought, after all, to clear the ground), but a culture that would accept his construction of class because it lacked the self-esteem to establish its own.

Whether or not this was a fantasy is a difficult question to answer. Poe did, in fact, work for three journals during his brief career as an editor, and in two of the three cases – the *Southern Literary Messenger,* and *Graham's Magazine* – the journal experienced a rapid rise in circulation during his short tenure, commensurate with the estimates he presented for his own magazine. And although these circulation increases probably had more to do with Poe's ability to generate high-publicity intermagazine feuds than with either his (much-debated) competence as an editor or his possible implementation of elements of his ultimate magazine plan, Poe's success in these earlier venues also suggests that his thoughts on magazine stewardship had a significant pragmatic basis.[41]

His circulation strategy also justifies careful evaluation. It was during this period, after all, that Alexis de Tocqueville observed in *Democracy in America* that the consciousness of equality made Americans acutely aware of minute class differences, and that this oxymoronic circumstance caused them to be restless even amidst great wealth.[42] Poe's circulation strategy, which preys directly upon the insecurities of a rising middle stratum, seems designed to attack his audience at precisely this point of weakness. Further, that strategy was profoundly similar to one of the most successful of the twentieth century. As Theodore Peterson describes in *Magazines in the Twentieth Century,* the *New Yorker* was designed to appeal to those social elites in each town and city that considered themselves "honorary New Yorkers" – representatives of a wealthy, cosmopolitan class. The magazine would then appeal to advertisers, who would recognize that the *New Yorker* was a venue in which they could communicate to the wealthiest percentile of Americans in every location. More important, it would appeal to a large portion of the middlebrow audience who would consider a subscription to the *New Yorker* a status symbol, even if the magazine itself went unread.[43]

Almost a century passed between Poe's death and the founding of the *New Yorker*, and the conditions of American magazine publishing changed substantially during that period – most notably, in that industry's approach to advertising, and technologies of circulation. Nevertheless, the relationship between Poe's prospectuses and the marketing strategy of the *New Yorker* is so substantial that the success of the latter suggests that Poe was not deluded, nor out of touch with the American cultural mainstream. Specifically, that marketing strategy has appeal because it maintains the illusion of an elite class, while making the qualifications for membership to that class (i.e., subscription to the magazine) easily attainable. The *New Yorker* succeeds, and Poe might have succeeded had he lived, by acquiring the authority associated with the social and literary elite, and placing it in a site of discourse that was not at all elite – the magazine subscription.

The Curt, the Terse, the Well-timed

Amidst this amalgam of aristocratic desires, self-destruction, poverty, and acute cultural perception, Poe 'invented' the short story. The celebrations of the short story and the magazine were, first and foremost, symbiotic projects. His preference for short forms over longer forms, of course, was also an implicit exaltation of the modes of publication that were most likely to contain short forms – magazines – over more established publishing forms; in particular, the heavy emphasis Poe placed upon the unity of the reading experience virtually disqualified epic poetry or novels (which could appear in journals in serial but disunified form) from the field of literature.[44] For Poe, however, the bond between the magazine and the short story extended beyond the essentially pragmatic observation that the genre could be the literary flagship of a burgeoning magazine establishment. In every sense, the blueprint of ambitions and anxieties that Poe encoded into his magazine project was also inscribed into his definition of the short story.[45]

There are three major ways to read Poe's magazine project into his review of Hawthorne. The first concerns his affinity for disposability. As Donald Pease observes, "Poe insists on his cultural expendability" throughout his fiction: "Indeed, Poe elevates the procedures of cultural obsolescence into a necessary criterion for taking the measure of his literary merit."[46] Poe's magazine project furnishes an ideal illustration for Pease's statement: Its success was entirely contingent upon Poe's ability to transform the magazine into a site for high-culture discourse. But the magazine was, then as now, more cheaply and quickly produced and distributed than its main competitor within the cultural marketplace, the bound volume. Then as now, consumers were far more likely to throw out their magazines than their books; exceptions to that rule – magazines such as the *New Yorker* or contemporary literary journals such as *Antaeus* – resisted their expendability by simulating 'bookness' by utilizing expensive paper and artwork (the same strategy Poe sought to use to establish the cultural importance of his own magazine). The magazine's main strength in contrast to the bound volume was its ability to respond more rapidly to contemporary events, but even that strength only increased its eventual expendability.[47]

In a similar manner, Poe also insisted that the ideal short story be constituted as a disposable artifact. Just as he wrote that the magazine was better suited to a fast-paced mercantile culture than was the bound volume, Poe founded his belief of the superiority of short forms on the claim that the average reader was too distracted by worldly events to devote more than one-and-a-half hours at any given time to the act of reading.[48] More significantly, by emphasizing a "single effect" toward which every aspect of the composition must contribute – a single effect that must necessarily be communicated in the story's climax – Poe designed a short story that was to be read once, and only once, with great impact. And by exalting that single effect as the most intense of reading experiences, Poe explicitly linked the superiority of the shorter form to the very fact of its expendability. Like the magazine within which it was published, Poe's short story was meant to be thrown away and revered at the same time.

The second way to read Poe's broader literary ambitions into his definition of the short story is to examine the role of economic necessity in both venues. Where the magazine project was a concrete professional choice that offered Poe the possibility of literary respectability and affluence, the review of Hawthorne presented a model of creative activity that corresponded to the behavior of individuals who were constricted by economic limitations. The pre-established design upon which he insisted was a labor-saving device; unlike an intuitive design, or no design at all, a preconceived design allowed the writer to allocate his or her resources according to the thriftiest plan possible. For Poe, artists should conserve their resources, and utilize only what was necessary for the "single effect": "There should be no word written, of which the tendency, direct or indirect, is not to the one pre-established design."

Finally, Poe's definition of the short story reflects his magazine project in the relationship it posits between the artist and the audience. Poe's definition of the short story is the generic expression of his attempt to claim the "proprietary right" for the written word for the artist. In particular, his insistence upon "unity" and "pre-designed effect" relies upon the faith that the artist's intention can be communicated completely uncontaminated to a kind of tabula rasa reader. Every element of the text is subservient to the "preconceived effect," which has been selected before composition has even begun. Abiding by this effect, the writer consciously selects every word in the text. The text, read in a single sitting, exists in a pure, inviolate space: "There are no external or extrinsic influences," Poe writes – including those the reader might bring to the work in the form of opinions, expectations, or memory. The cooperative reader, agreeing to peruse the text in one sitting, is duly seduced: "The soul of the reader is at the writer's control."[49] Similarly, Poe wrote more than once in "The Philosophy of Composition" that he was capable of *intentionally* producing a work of art that would be simultaneously popular and critically acclaimed: "I kept steadily in view the design of rendering the work *universally* appreciable."[50] Poe offers the possibility that the author's intent is all that matters in *the entire literary transaction:* Critics, audience, and publishers all disappear from the loop of creation, publication, dissemination, and canonization.

Whether or not Poe himself believed in this vision of literary production, or even recognized its potential appeal, is difficult to gauge. Just as the success of Poe's magazine project was dependent upon the resources of a wealthy but strangely insecure mercantile culture, his definition of creative activity rests upon the assumption that audiences (and, just as significant, the author's own unconscious) will behave predictably, and can be easily controlled. Poe's literary philosophy, as expressed in his review of Hawthorne, owes much to Aristotle's *Poetics* for its discussion of unity, but it also rests firmly within the tradition of the confidence man (another American invention of the 1840s), who attempts to manipulate an audience directly for the purpose of personal profit.[51]

Unlike the confidence man, however, Poe rarely won over his audience. If Poe's theories about literature and class were ideologically astute, and at least indirectly seductive, they were enacted within a framework of self-destructiveness and an almost willful refusal to respond to *real* audiences in any way that ensured lasting success (this was, after all, the same Poe who wrote in "The Black Cat" that "perverseness . . . the unfathomable longing of the soul to vex itself," was "one of the primitive instincts of the human heart").[52] He feuded with other editors, and then expected them to publish his material. He circulated droll but condescending hoax news reports, and expected his audience to ask for more. He wrote crushing book reviews, and then supplicated the authors for money. He spent his entire life insistently trying to market his tightly knit, economical tales to an audience that, as Nina Baym documents, had already embraced the novel as "*the* literary art form of the nineteenth century."[53] If all Poe wanted was to be an insider – if all he wanted was to be solvent – there were easier ways.

Similarly, at the heart of Poe's literary philosophy lies an element of self-deprecation that simply cannot be dismissed. As his affirmation of disposability indicates, every aspect of his ideal short story was dependent upon the oxymoronic belief that what was most valuable would also be most forgettable. Further, his praise of both the magazine and the short story contained a corollary act of literary insecurity: Poe assumed a priori the existence of an audience that would be too busy to pay more than passing attention to art and literature. In doing so, he voluntarily surrendered the traditional authority ascribed to literature: He placed it within the cultural marketplace as just another necessity competing for the time and money of a potential consumer, when it already possessed cultural capital as a luxury good. Most significantly, however, he attempted to do this while novels and other literary forms continued to compete for the attention of the literary consumer, using for themselves the authority associated with being "literature." Even his specific celebration of the short story in the review of Hawthorne explicitly ranked it below the lyric poem. Poe created a genre that would be considered inferior to other genres, until the categories of culture changed – and, perversely, even after.

The element of self-displacement (and, just as important, the element of poverty) makes it virtually impossible to judge the ideological bias of Poe's ideas by their surface content. Poe played with the tropes of aristocracy and democracy, testing how they could be defined and used within a literature that he would associate with the "*New* World," but not necessarily with "America." For Poe, however, these political terms – unity, aristocracy, democracy – were not inert, and cannot remain inert in any discussion of Poe, or his legacy for the short story. If it is easy to condemn Poe for penning a simplistic authorial power fantasy, it is worth noting that his desire for control is also the expression of great vulnerability that would eventually be shared by thousands of authors as authorship became a middle-class pursuit. Poe became devoted to the idea of removing all spontaneity from the narrative transaction because he simply could not take the chance that his audience would respond with enough self-esteem to claim its share of his proprietary right. Rather, he wrote literary theory for the author who, like him, possessed aristocratic ideals (and even literary vision), but no outside income – the author for whom rejection means starvation or death.

In this event, Poe's legacy within the short story might lie less with
those authors who have consciously imitated his literary style, and
more with those who best understood the bond between the genre
and the life of the economically restricted but aspiring individual.
Raymond Carver, for instance, has explained both his affinity for
short forms and what one critic has called the "violent economy" of
his prose by describing the penurious early period of his career,
where he focused on "short things" that he could "write quickly
and have done with" before "having the chair yanked out from
under me, or one of my kids smarting off about why supper isn't
ready on demand." In his essay "Fires" (1983) – in many ways, a
fitting modern companion to Poe's review – Carver described his
preference for short stories over novels as being directly correlated
to poverty and the habitual self-deprecation impoverishment produces. To write a novel, Carver observed, "a writer should be living
in a world that makes sense." He chose the short story as his medi-
um, rather, because

> I couldn't see or plan any further ahead than the first of next
> month and gathering together enough money, by hook or by
> crook, to meet the rent and provide the children's school
> clothes

and continued to write in the genre because "I still can't adjust to
thinking in terms of having a great swatch of time to work on
something – anything I want!"[54]

Any attempt to understand the appeal of Poe's vision must recognize all these factors. Poe's words never actually gained currency
with a broad popular audience. Instead, they gained a high level of
popularity within a relatively small but significant subset of America – the short story community of writers, students, teachers, editors, and even readers. As tempting as it may be to say that Poe's
words were popular because they offered an anxiety-free (for the
author, at least) resolution of the writer–audience interaction,
however, it is also possible that his vision was popular in part because it was never truly empowering. For the proponents of the
short story to have adopted the review of Hawthorne as their
founding document, despite the implicit statements of inferiority
that it contains, suggests strongly that those practitioners may have
empathized with Poe's "perverseness" as much as they undoubtedly
identified with his Rasputinlike vision of the relationship between
the artist and the audience.

If men and women chose to become writers, after all, they did so
partially as a repudiation of mercantile values, and partially because being a "writer" offered them a different kind of cultural

authority. In a mercantile, anti-intellectual culture, however, such an exchange can be profoundly self-denying. In response, Poe offered a felicitous marriage of irreconcilable ideals, packaged in an elegant capitalist poetics. His review of Hawthorne speaks directly to the individuals who were most torn by those irreconcilable ideals. Buffeted from above and below, where aristocratic and populist desires presumably existed without ambivalence (though not without contradiction), Poe's words found their home among the class that most felt the tension between upward yearnings and the cultural authority conferred by mercantile success: the middlebrow who, from between 1885 to 1950, transformed him into the George Washington of a revolution to make literature a paying profession.

2

THE LAND OF DEFINITION

First of all (I would say), my young friend, you should choose a truly American subject. All the critics say that this is essential. American-ism is what the age demands; and it must be produced even if we have to invent a machine to do it. Do not go abroad for your theme. Do not trifle with the effete European nightingale or ramble among Roman ruins. Take a theme from the great Republic; something that comes close to the business and bosoms of the Democracy; some-thing unconventional and virile. Take, for example, the Clam – the native, American, free-born, little-neck Clam. We all know it. We all love it. Deal originally and vividly with the Clam.

Henry Van Dyke, from an address delivered before the Periodical Publishers' Association of America, Washington, D.C., April 17, 1904, quoted in Esenwein, *Writing the Short Story* (1908) 41.

If the first peculiar truth of the American short story is that Edgar Allan Poe is its patron saint, then the second peculiar truth is that the genre is a purely American art form. When Peter Prescott, in his introduction to the *Norton Anthology of American Short Stories* (1988), writes simply that the short story is "ours," he invokes a commonplace that evolved in the nineteenth century, and has maintained currency ever since. Modern authors seem to be aware that the statement might be naive, but they continue to use it: A. Walton Litz, in the introduction to *Major American Short Stories* (1980), observes in ironic quotation marks that the short story is the "'national art form,'" but then observes without quotation marks (or irony) that it also "presents the most coherent record of Ameri-ca's literary and social development." Heather McClave, in her in-troduction to *Women Writers of the Short Story* (1980), claims that "it would not be too startling to say that this latter-day short story is virtually an American form." A. Robert Lee, in his introduction to *The Nineteenth-Century American Short Story* (1985), calls the genre "if not uniquely then most markedly American" – ours.[1]

Not every work on the short story discusses its Americanness: Many do not, and many severely criticize the conceit. Nevertheless, it is difficult to find a period or venue in the past one hundred years in which the belief that the short story is an American art form was not widespread. William Dean Howells, in an editorial in *The North American Review* in 1901, wrote that the short story gave him "pride . . . as an American." William Peden, in his full-length treatise, *The American Short Story* (1964), labeled the short story "the only major literary form of essentially American origin and the only one in which American writers have always tended to excel." Archibald L. Bouton, professor in the Department of English of New York University in 1912, wrote that "the short story . . . is thus far the distinctive contribution of America to literature." Walter Pitkin, in his popular how-to short story handbook, *How to Write Stories* (1923), told his readers "there is not the slightest dispute among competent critics here or abroad" that the short story was the supreme American art form. As if to verify Pitkin's claim, Boris Eichenbaum, the famed Russian formalist, wrote in "O. Henry and the Theory of the Short Story" (1925) that "the short story is the one fundamental and self-contained genre in American prose fiction."[2]

The nationalist claim has proven so useful that it has withstood the most vitriolic objections, and even incorporated them. Ruth Suckow, for instance, spoke of the "avidity with which American literary men rushed to the Short Story, and the child-like trust with which they have clung."[3] James T. Farrell, in his equally acerbic "Nonsense and the Short Story" (1945), wrote that "perhaps more nonsense has been written about the short story than any other literary form"; his first example of what constituted that "nonsense" was "Commentators" that had "long ago popularized the conceit that the short story is the typical American literary form."[4] As is the case with many powerful cultural 'facts,' however, these counterclaims have not overcome the initial argument, despite having also received widespread acceptance. Rather, they have merely added an ironic and often schizophrenic tone to its invocations – the use of distancing quotation marks, for instance, or the outright confusion of Johan Smertenko who, in 1923, endeavored to refute the "dictum that the short story is distinctly our literary form of expression" while citing a history of the genre that was thoroughly self-contained and wholly American: "Hawthorne and Irving chose it instinctively; Poe was undoubtedly the first to formulate its principles; and Bret Harte popularized it and made it inherent in American art . . ."[5]

In general, the nationalist claim has had far-reaching consequences for the development of the short story in this country. As Frederic Jameson has observed, genre definitions perform historically grounded and specific social functions: They are "essentially literary institutions, or social contracts between a writer and a specific public, whose function is to specify the proper use of a particular cultural artifact." According to these terms, the claim that the short story is quintessentially American is not a neutral judgment on the nature of the genre; it is, rather, a judgment "clearly implicated in the literary history and the formal production" of the genre itself.[6]

It is, perhaps, tenuous to claim that the nationalist spirit of the American short story has had a *direct* influence on short story writing. If we accept that any audience wants to read about its own fascinations, concerns, and desires – a basic assumption in much, if not all criticism – then we must accept that anything written and published in America contains strains of Americanness, and that these strains have been somehow internalized within the editorial offices of magazines and publishing companies. There is little way – and little reason – to claim that novelists or poets in America do not have to write about America any more than do short story writers. Just as important, it is impossible and undesirable to claim that an immutable set of attributes exist by which we can define what it means to be American: If anything, the nationalist claim has been so powerful because authors can agree that the short story is American, without necessarily agreeing as to what it means to be American.

Rather, the most interesting aspect of the nationalist claim is how it has limited short story criticism to an expressive but strangely restricted debate over whether or not (and how) the short story has performed the one function for which it was apparently designed: to advertise American life, and to advertise a particular set of assumptions about Americans in general. And although the flexibility of the adjective "American" suggests that the debate about the true nature of the short story might be a variegated one, in fact the most significant arguments in the field of short story criticism have been narrow and dialectical, and have been fought by critics who accepted the same underlying visions of how the American political project should be transformed into literature, and who recognized the same set of problems associated with that endeavor.

In this manner, the nationalist claim has framed and transformed short story criticism. It has filled magazine pages in the twentieth century with thoughtful conjecture on what, exactly, it means for a form of communication to be structurally 'American.' It has provided a vocabulary of ideological terms that short story critics, authors, and editors have used to describe the genre and its uses. More significantly, it has provided a set of seemingly undebatable political models that have played a major role in shaping the institutions that have guided the short story through even its current development: The design and editorial policies of anthologies, the commandingly self-conscious tenor of short story pedagogy, and the growth of workshops and graduate programs in short story writing have all been energetically authorized by nationalist rhetoric at crucial points in their respective developments. Lastly, the nationalist claim has created some unusual and intense expectations for what cultural functions the genre, as a whole, was anticipated to perform. For that reason, discussions of the short story in this country have been infused with a millennial spirit. Like the nation it supposedly represented in microcosmic form, the short story was thought to be a pluralistic melting pot, democratically modeled and market-driven: the genre of art that heralded the death of an old, decadent spirit and promised the birth of a new egalitarian and efficient literature.

The National Art Form: 1885–1901

The short story had come not, as many believed, as a result of the American temperament, the American proneness to rush and hurry. Its phenomenal success had been won simply because of the success of American magazines, which is nothing less than prodigious . . .

William Dean Howells, "Editor's Study,"
Harper's New Monthly 74 (Feb. 1887): 484.

The nationalist claim developed during the last twenty years of the nineteenth century, at about the same time that critics began to insist that the short story was a genre of literature. A possible genealogy is suggested by Brander Matthews, who in "The Philosophy of the Short Story" (1885) became the first critic to claim in a major work that the magazine tale or short story (renamed, for Matthews's genre-founding purposes, the Short-story) was an autonomous form, as worthy of literary respectability as its prose cousin, the novel. In his 1885 version of "Philosophy," Matthews wrote that "it is not a little comic to see now and again in American newspapers a rash assertion that 'American literature has hitherto been deficient in good Short-stories'"; in 1901, he appended a footnote to this comment that reminded the reader that "this essay was written in 1885. Although these absurd assertions were not infrequent then, they are unknown now" and added that "for fifty years the American Short-story has had a supremacy which any competent critic could not but acknowledge."[7]

Clearly something happened between 1885 and 1901 that transformed the general perception of the short story: Walter Dyer would write in 1921 that "what were axioms in 1890 had often become outgrown notions by 1900."[8] Prior to the beginning of this period, the short story was recognized as a commercial genre, but not necessarily as a literary one: The title of the 1870 collection *Short Stories For Spare Moments* indicates the extent to which even the name of the genre was designed to emphasize its main selling point.[9] By 1900, though, the genre had a new, literarily respectable name (which would be forgotten in the following century); it had been endowed almost overnight with a fifty-year national tradition ("the history of the Short-story, *la voilà!*" an English critic wrote in sarcastic response to Matthews);[10] and courses in short story writing were attracting students at universities and correspondence schools across the country. Most significantly, so many people were writing short stories, and so many magazines were publishing them, that respectable critics like Howells were questioning "whether a branch of art tempting to such profusion . . . ought to be encouraged."[11]

With the possible exception of Matthews's treatise, it is impossible to ascribe the credit for this transformation to any individual or single document. Nevertheless, several historical factors can be reasonably implicated in the sudden growth of the short story during this period, and the equally sudden recognition that it received. First, and most important, a boom period in the history of the American magazine took place during these two decades. Technological developments in photoengraving – in particular, the invention of the "halftone" – exponentially cheapened the illustration costs of mass-circulated magazines, while the development of national advertising campaigns greatly increased the potential profit margins of those same magazines.[12] At the same time, major newspapers began to run Sunday supplements, which were designed to compete with magazines at a fraction of their cost. This competition, when coupled with the vastly reduced cost of printing a magazine (the halftone lowered the cost of an average illustration – usually the most expensive aspect of the printing process – from $300 to $20), catalyzed the development of a new kind of cheap magazine, which typically sold for five or ten cents per issue, but also encouraged intraindustry competition that caused 'quality' magazines such as *Scribner's* and *Lippincott's* to lower their issue costs substantially.[13]

The consequence of these industrial developments was that, in the words of the *Nation*, magazines were being created and were dying "in numbers to make Malthus stare and gasp."[14] According to Frederick Mott, there were approximately 3,300 periodicals in the nation in 1885; during the next twenty years, 7,500 more magazines were founded. And although half of these periodicals either folded or merged with other periodicals, circulations increased at a rapid pace throughout the period: In 1885, there were 21 magazines that sold 100,000 copies or more; by 1905, that number had increased to 159. Similarly, prior to 1891, no magazine had ever sold more than half a million copies per issue; by 1906, the *Ladies' Home Journal,* the *Saturday Evening Post,* and eight other magazines had passed that mark, and the *Delineator,* the most popular magazine in the country, was selling 1.5 million copies per issue.[15]

For many observers, this explosion represented a major change in the nature of American life – the framework of which was outlined by Poe fifty years earlier in his many magazine prospectuses. As Mott noted in his *History of American Magazines,* the "American Cheap Magazine" of the late nineteenth century was a source of considerable national pride;[16] during its brighter moments, the magazine industry in America seemed to be creating a form of literature, and a mode of circulation, that corroborated the most affirmative view of the possibilities of American life. "There is nothing quite like them in the literature of the world – no periodicals which combine such width of popular appeal with such seriousness of aim and thoroughness of workmanship," wrote William Archer in 1910.[17] What was taking place, according to an anonymous commentator in the *Independent,* was a "revolution" that allowed "cheap magazines" to "compete for" and publish "the most expensive story-writers," a circumstance that threatened the traditional literary caste system, which divided newspapers from magazines, cheap magazines from quality magazines, quality magazines from bound volumes – and, suggestively, newspaper readers from magazine readers, and magazine readers from book readers.[18]

The short story played a major corollary role in this revolution: As these industrial developments took effect, government activity was altering the traditional methods by which American magazine publishers would fill their pages. In the early nineteenth century – most dramatically, during the 1840s, when new printing technologies lowered the cost of publishing – American magazines had been able to answer (and create) periodic increases in demand for fiction with British work, which according to previous copyright laws (or the lack of them) could be legally pirated for American use. This circumstance plagued American authors, who also were forced to endure consistently unflattering comparisons between their own efforts and those of the more established European tradition: Poe, for instance, conducted a fervent editorial campaign against these copyright laws; Irving circumvented them altogether by copyrighting his work simultaneously in England and America, and often interceded with British publishers on behalf of other American authors.[19]

Throughout the century, however, as an increasingly ensconced American periodical industry protected American writers with more stable pay scales and relatively zealous copyright policies, and as solidarity deepened among the writer-editors who frequently operated American journals, the incentive for publishing English material steadily diminished. And, in 1891, the Senate Committee on Patents, after several years of exploring copyright abuses (and with the approval of a Congress inclined toward both trade protectionism and nationalism), arranged a new international copyright agreement that removed for publishers any economic advantage to printing borrowed material.[20] As a result, American magazines that between 1850 and 1885 had embraced and then withdrawn from the serial form of fiction popular in Great Britain ("In other countries the *feuilleton* of the journals is a novel continued from day-to-day," Howells wrote in *Harper's*, "but with us the papers . . . rarely print novels") now had an extra incentive to seek and publish the homegrown product.[21]

This new copyright agreement, when coupled with the growth within the American magazine industry, and the position of respectability occupied by the short story in magazine aesthetics, catalyzed the explosion of national interest in the short story. The short story was already the glamour product among magazine genres: "That magazine is liked best which has the best short stories," the *Ladies' Home Companion* observed in 1882.[22] Competition among burgeoning magazines and newspapers for the most salable fiction (fueled by the influx of capital from spiraling advertising revenues and increasing circulations) encouraged bidding wars and often bizarre publicity stunts, such as S. S. McClure's "one hundred short stories by one hundred authors in one hundred days."[23] And the new copyright agreement ensured that the economic benefits of the magazine boom rewarded American writers; the promise of that reward, in turn, redoubled interest in the short story. Authors who were previously enticed into writing novels or nonfiction now became attracted to the suddenly profitable genre. As "The Lounger" wrote in *The Critic* in 1890:

> There was a time . . . when authors objected to writing short stories. They agreed that as much plot went to the making of a short as of a long story, and that if they took a little more time to elaborate it, they would have a manuscript worth one thou-

sand dollars instead of worth fifty or a hundred. This left most of the short story writing to be done by second rate writers, and the reading public began to complain . . . This aroused the editors, so they offered prices for short stories which brought forth much good work; now quite a good crop of short story writers has sprung up.[24]

The result of these changes was not unexpected: The Arthur Kimball study, published in the *Atlantic* in 1901, reported that the single greatest change that occurred in the magazine industry during the last twenty years of the nineteenth century was the increase in the amount of short stories that reached publication – an increase vastly disproportionate to the amount of extra pages made available by the increase in the number of magazines.[25]

In sum, the collective decision to call the short story "an American form" was catalyzed by an act of trade protectionism (the new copyright law), which freed American literature from an economic subservience to European sources, while creating financial conditions that encouraged American writers to flock to the genre. The keynote of "The Philosophy of the Short Story," it must be emphasized, was that the short story was a separate and implicitly superior form of the novel, the classic form of European fiction.[26] That Matthews intermixes this abstract formal definition with claims of American superiority within actual practice is no surprise; nor is the fact that Matthews was treated with severe condescension by European critics who were perplexed by his lust for definition. The genre-fication of the short story was an informal declaration of independence from an economic and cultural subservience to European literature. The claim that the short story is also quintessentially American is implicit within, and not separate from, the desire to claim that the genre is a self-contained form.

Concomitant with these economic developments, the critical reputations of Poe, Hawthorne, and Irving rose significantly, thus creating in retrospect the fifty-year-old tradition of American short story writing that Matthews describes, and that found its way into college syllabi by 1900. The resurrection of Poe by short story scholars during this period, in particular, provides a central illustration of the ideological vigor that fed this conscious and communal effort to claim a great genre of art for American possession.[27] In every sense, Poe was directly given credit for having founded a literature. References to his work were described consistently in terms such as 'first,' 'leading,' and 'beginning.' Matthews's treatise reiterated Poe's dictum on the subject so closely that he included the review of Hawthorne in an appendix to the 1901 edition and wrote that his sole intention had been to "make explicit what is more or less implicit in Poe's review of *Twice-Told Tales*." Elias Lieberman, in his history, *The American Short Story* (1912), rewrote literary history to imply that Poe was as influential to his contemporaries as he would become to his followers sixty years later: "The short story writer if he is an artist desires to create a definite impression. Since the work of Edgar Allan Poe, beginning with the publication of 'Berenice' in 1835 this has been an accepted canon of short story writing." Frederick Pattee, on the other hand, rejected the assertion that Poe "invented the short story," and wrote instead that he was merely the "first to awake to the situation, the first to formulate this technique into a system." And Eichenbaum, in "O. Henry," stated that "all American stories, beginning with Edgar Allan Poe, are more or less constructed on these principles."[28]

In diluted (or internalized) form, this usage continues to the current day. Poe's stories are among the first read by American elementary students, and excerpts from his literary theory are invariably quoted or paraphrased in short story anthologies and textbooks. The introduction to Mary Rohrberger's Houghton Mifflin textbook, *Story to Anti-Story,* quotes Poe at length. The St. Martin's anthology, *The Story and Its Writer,* mentions Poe in the second sentence, as "one of the first to attempt an analysis of the short story's aesthetic properties." McClave begins her introduction to *Women Writers of the Short Story* by describing Poe as an "incisive and provocative practitioner-critic"; she quotes him in detail before she even cites a single female writer. Lee's *Nineteenth-Century American Short Story* contains a series of essays on individual authors, presented in chronological order; Poe, however, is leapfrogged in front of Irving, so that the essay devoted to him is the first in the book.[29]

And Charles Johnson, asked to describe the "short-short story" for the critical afterword of the 1986 *Sudden Fiction* anthology, wrote that "the likely father of the unusual form called the contemporary short-short story is, I'd wager, Edgar Allan Poe."[30] Spectating at the birth of what the book's editors described as an "explosive new literary form," Johnson cited the name of the man who will probably continue to be given credit for founding new literary movements until people stop reading short stories, or needing literary founders.[31] This does not necessarily mean that Johnson's analysis was unsophisticated, however. It is, in many respects, astute to recognize Poe's presence behind the making of *Sudden Fiction,* an anthology that declares a brash ground-clearing new form, and also contains a lengthy afterword that attempted to define that new form as it lay aborning. Such editorial strategies are a testament not only to the power of Poe's symbolic presence, but also to the continuing seduction, and salability, of his initial gesture: the declaration of newness coupled with the ready-made definition of identity.

And that approach has national ramifications. As easy as it may be to provide quotes that indicate Poe was directly given credit for having "founded a literature," it is a more vital proposition to explain the reason why the genre needed a founder at all. In this context, it is wholly appropriate, and more than coincidental, that the central document in the history of the American short story, Poe's review of Hawthorne, held that the ideal prose tale was a fully self-conscious operation. The creation of the short story as a cultural artifact – that is, as a recognizable genre of communication – was a similarly self-conscious operation, one that exalted Poe by applying his methodology of narration (however indirectly) to the making of cultural history. But literary Americans, perhaps, were particularly attuned to that method of telling cultural history: From Winthrop's sermon on the Arbella, through Jefferson's Declaration of Independence, Franklin's *Autobiography*, Douglass's *Narrative*, Fitzgerald's *Gatsby* et al., America's biographers of self and community have provided no lack of examples of how to repudiate the past and consciously construct a new identity. In essence, Poe simply wrote that stories should be told the way many official Americans had been telling their own story. In return, he was anointed founder of the only form of art in American life that would equate issues of generic definition with national definition – the only form whose participants would be sufficiently fascinated by the issue of generic identity to even need a founder.

Isolation, Color

By the time Edward J. O'Brien published a second edition of *The Advance of the Short Story* in 1931, he was widely considered the nation's foremost authority on the genre: "Mr. O'Brien's position," a *New York Times* reviewer wrote in 1927, "is unique and none the less so because he created it for himself." While editing the *Best Short Stories* (later titled *Best American Short Stories*) annual series from 1915 to 1941, he had developed a ranking system that divided stories into "distinctive" and "not distinctive" classes, railed against the standardization of the short story in *The Dance of the Machines,* created a much-imitated anthology selection style, published short story and anthology parodies, embraced regionalism and the less difficult modernist voices, and annually awarded the title of "Best" to fifteen or twenty magazine stories by both obscure and established authors.[32] Despite the heraldic title, however, *Ad-*

vance is unquestionably a jeremiad that reflects both O'Brien's frustration and hope regarding the genre. In particular, his ambition is to explain the "defeat" of the short story to the forces of standardization and to ask whether "we have the faith" to "reset the balance" between "spiritual . . . and mechanical progress."[33]

More important, O'Brien is interested in seeking an ethnic balance. In the preface to the volume, he writes of a period of change between 1892–1914 marked by the "influx of vast numbers of immigrants . . . who brought with them the utmost variety of different racial traditions." The great problem of the age is the "assimilation and fusion" of this ethnic heterogeneity with the mainstream "Anglo-Saxon body." For O'Brien, America will achieve its greatest strength via this fusion:

> The hope and pride . . . would be its demonstration of the possibility that all the varying and hitherto separate racial traditions of other continents could borrow from each other their richest and noblest memories and experiences, and fuse them into a common eclectic culture purged of national weakness and compact of international strength . . .

This idealized vision of the American melting pot is then extended into a gentle vision of American cultural manifest destiny:

> Such a culture, which would have deep and abiding contacts with all races, if it had a faith and an ideal, could impose that faith and ideal peacefully and almost unconsciously upon the world . . .

All that remains for the execution of this "experiment of fusion" is a means of expression; and on this point, O'Brien is unequivocal, if vague:

> In these new races, whose coming was inevitable, lies the only hope by which America may achieve not only an individual literature of its own, but a literature which could be a unique experiment in the history of the world. Moreover, all indications prove that the chief artistic form of such a literature during the fusing generations is likely to be the short story . . . which is, after all our national literary form and almost our discovery . . .[34]

Although O'Brien's proprietary interest in the short story was unmistakable, he was no extremist concerning the genre's position within American culture. As Suckow wrote, "the whole creed" of short story criticism during this period was "founded upon the . . . assumption . . . that any form of art . . . is moving toward a millenium which will be brought by a savior in the form of a master, a

method, or a movement."[35] Rather, O'Brien's vision presents, in an
abbreviated form, an illustration of how the definition of the short
story as an American art form has introduced unusual ideological
pressures into descriptions of the genre. Just as important,
O'Brien's words indicate the precise point at which the ideological
ambitions of the nation intersected with the short story project:
Both were to be "experiments in fusion" that achieved a perfect
balance between uniformity and diversity, between the desire to
seek consensus and the need to preserve difference. In turn, this
experiment in ethnic fusion was conflated with other experiments
in union, which also possessed democratizing possibilities: between
the civilized culture of the East and the "inchoate poetry" of the
West, as Bret Harte suggested in "The Rise of the Short Story" in
1899; between art and science, as literally hundreds of how-to-
write-a-short-story-handbook authors were claiming in American
correspondence schools and universities throughout the 1920s; or
between literature and the mercantile world, as V. S. Pritchett
stated in 1953 by writing that the ideal short story writer is "a
hybrid" of "the poet on the one hand and the newspaper reporter
on the other."[36]

There is nothing monolithic about this discourse, of course. Isaac
Rosenfeld's left-wing, antibourgeois critique of the American short
story's undue formalism in the *New Republic* in 1941 must necessarily be distinguished from Farrell's more overtly Marxist condem-
nation of the same traits in the same year, or Ruth Suckow's pro-
bourgeois, regionalist critique fifteen years earlier. Similarly, both
Peter Prescott's proprietary defense of the short story's "ours-
ness" in 1990, and William Peden's cold war pride in American
individualism speak for different literary generations than does
O'Brien's Depression-era call for a transfigurative American art
form.

And although it may be ingenuous to yoke together these different voices (by late-twentieth-century standards, of course, they are
in many ways a homogeneous group), this listing nevertheless illustrates two necessary points about the development of the American
short story (and American fiction in general): first, the extent to
which institutions of the short story have made the ideology, and
simple facts such as the site of publication and means of renumera-
tion have been crucial determinants in interpreting the messages
embedded in the texts; and second, the extent to which the short
story developed in the context of assumptions about class and
country that were not (and are only slightly less now) considered
contingent points of debate. Like any resilient cultural axiom, the
effect of the nationalist claim within discussions of the short story

MAGAZINE AVERAGES

AUGUST, 1927, TO JUNE, 1928

The following table includes the averages of distinctive stories in twenty-eight American periodicals. One, two, and three asterisks are employed to indicate relative distinction. "Three-asterisk stories" are considered worth reprinting in book form. The list excludes reprints.

PERIODICALS	No. OF STORIES PUB- LISHED	No. OF DISTINCTIVE STORIES PUBLISHED			PERCENTAGE OF DISTINCTIVE STORIES PUBLISHED		
		*	**	***	*	**	***
American Magazine	47	10	2	1	21	4	2
American Mercury	18	14	10	7	78	56	39
Atlantic Monthly	21	19	12	9	90	52	43
Bookman (N. Y.)	13	13	12	11	100	92	85
Catholic World	31	11	6	5	35	19	16
Century Magazine	35	29	13	9	83	37	26
Chicago Tribune (Syndicate Service)	47	8	1	0	16	2	0
Cosmopolitan	130	64	27	13	49	21	10
Country Gentleman	42	17	6	4	40	14	9
Delineator	41	13	3	3	32	7	7
Dial	25	25	18	14	100	72	56
Forum	13	12	8	5	92	62	38
Good Housekeeping (N. Y.)	57	10	2	1	18	3	1
Harper's Bazar	30	9	6	3	30	20	10
Harper's Magazine	33	33	29	21	100	88	64
Ladies' Home Journal	61	14	6	6	23	10	10
McCall's Magazine	42	10	5	3	24	12	7
MacLean's Magazine	95	18	9	3	19	10	3
Menorah Journal	13	7	4	3	54	31	23
Midland	20	19	15	9	95	75	45
New Masses	12	5	3	0	42	25	0
Pictorial Review	55	22	13	9	40	24	16
Prairie Schooner	13	13	4	0	100	31	0
Saturday Evening Post	334	68	17	8	20	5	2
Scribner's Magazine	43	31	21	13	72	49	30
Transition	57	31	26	16	54	46	29
Vanity Fair	28	18	8	4	64	29	14
Woman's Home Companion.	60	18	5	2	30	8	3

The following tables indicate the rank, by number and percentage of distinctive short stories published, of thirteen periodicals coming within the scope of my examination which have published an average of 50 per cent or more of distinctive stories. The lists exclude reprints, but not translations.

"Magazine averages" from Edward J. O'Brien, ed., *Best Short Stories of 1928*, 379.

has been essentially insinuating: It both transforms, and is transformed by, the particular literary and cultural milieu of the individual speakers within the discourse.

This resilience, however, speaks directly to the nature of the axiom's power. In part, the nationalist claim endures because of the continuing appeal of nationalist rhetoric in general. Within discussions of the short story, however, the nationalist claim endures because it has never been associated with a specific literary school or cultural movement; rather, it has been yoked to institutional and structural aspects of the genre that also endure – its presence in inexpensive and easily disseminated forms of publication, its adaptability to teaching regimens and anthologization, and most important, the perception that it is an easy form within which to compose. These facets of the short story – or rather, the public emphasis upon them – have allowed the short story to be interpreted throughout the twentieth century as a new and radically democratic form of literature, a mouthpiece for and inheritor of the revolutionary energies of the American political project. Oppositely, these facets have also allowed the short story to be viewed as a leveled form of literature, one in which the eccentricities of the individual genius were oppressed in response to the desires of a tyrannous majority.

The canonical explanations for why the short story is 'democratic' are numerous. For one hundred years, authors and critics have routinely observed that the short story required little time to write, and was a less sophisticated endeavor than composing either a novel or developing a working knowledge of poetic forms. At the very least, the short story widened the franchise of potential authors, if for no other reason than writing one seemed to be a far less intimidating task than writing a novel. Mary Wilkins Freeman, for instance, wrote that the short story was "a simple little melody" in contrast to the "grand opera" of the novel, and observed that she selected the form because "the short story did not take so long to write, it was easier, and, of course, I was not sure of my own ability to write a short story, much less a novel."[37] More recently, Margaret Atwood noted in 1989 that the short story was a valuable resource for beginning writers because

> if you're going to be a fiction writer, and you're young, it's unlikely you're going to plunge immediately into a novel. Number one, you don't have the time. And number two, you don't usually have the material and the expertise.[38]

Although the length and supposed simplicity of the short story argued that it could be composed by people who might not be highly educated, nor members of a leisure class, the magazine itself operated within a system of complimentary assumptions. At the very least, the magazine establishment has traditionally offered far greater numerical opportunities for publication than has the centralized publishing industry. As Theodore Peterson observes in *Magazines in the Twentieth Century,* however, the American magazine system has functioned as the "freest of free enterprise":[39] While the organization and operation of a publishing company requires a vast capital outlay, a magazine can be formed on a shoestring budget, an economic factor that was a crucial element in the magazine boom of the late nineteenth century, and the growth of the "little" literary magazine in the twentieth century. Not surprisingly, many of these magazines developed editorial policies that matched the dispossessed quality of their economic resources, and attempted to provide outlets for previously unpublishable voices. *The Guild Pioneer*, for instance, stated in its prospectus in 1923 that it was "an organization of young writers who were meeting the usual coolness on the part of the existing papers, not because they represented any startling innovations in form or content, but because they were not nationally known." *Outsiders*, in 1928, announced its intention to "assist young writers to a more rapid recognition." *Jackass* was organized in the same year to "fill a gaping need and a gaping hiatus in the existing periodicals." In theory at least, the growth of the American magazine catalyzed the increasing dissemination of editorial power to an ever-increasing franchise of interested individuals, who would then presumably choose to publish and circulate an ever-increasing franchise of potential authors. And crucially, the short story was perceived as the literary form most suited for this transformation. Charles Allen, in the *Sewannee Review* in 1943, estimated that 80 percent of the major twentieth-century American novelists first published short stories in 'little magazines'; Stephen Vincent Benet wrote in 1939 that short stories were an invaluable cultural resource because "they give the beginning writer his first important step" toward publication.[40]

In this manner, the structural aspects of the short story, when combined with the economic flexibility of the magazine establishment, created a portrait of a genre that was both easy to read and easy to publish: When Matthews wrote in 1885 that "more than once in the United States a single short story has made a man known," he recognized the degree to which the genre itself seemed to disrupt and loosen the traditional paths of literary advancement and canonization.[41] This perception, in turn, had already been well entrenched within the actual workings of the American magazine industry, where the short story had become a seminal tool for both authors and editors who consciously sought to bring the fringes of American life to mainstream audiences. Much of the early development of the American short story, for instance, took place in the sporting journals and newspapers of the 1830s and 1840s (such as William T. Porter's *Spirit of the Times*), which published brief anecdotes gleaned from small papers and educated readers living in the South and West, for the benefit of urban readers in the more civilized Northeast.[42] The premise was that these earliest of short stories were the place where the spontaneous, vibrant anecdotal material of "real life" could be transformed into a published product for the ages: G. W. Harris, describing his *Sut Lovingood Yarns* to the *London Folklore Journal* in 1867, claimed that "not one of them is cooked, and not one, nor any part of one, is an invention of mine. They are all genuine folklore tales."[43]

This belief in the short story's adaptability to otherwise unpublishable voices has also proven resilient. In an analogous contemporary situation, Eugene Current-Garcia and Bert Hitchcock, in their 1990 anthology *American Short Stories*, wrote that the proliferation of "regional, ethnic, or gender-based" voices within the contemporary American short story had created among its readers a new consciousness of "non-highbrow/non-literary-establishment kinds of writing."[44] Whether or not Bret Harte's (or Current-Garcia's) definition is appropriate, the short story has been, throughout the first hundred years of its history, strongly associated with literary movements such as regionalism, local color, or dialect, which endeavored to bring previously disenfranchised voices in contact with the central machinery of publication and canonization. Mark Twain's "Jumping Frog of Calaveras County," T. B. Thorpe's "The Big Bear of Arkansas," Harte's "The Luck of Roaring Camp," or A. B. Longstreet's *Georgia Scenes* are only a few examples of how the short story became engaged in a magazine-based national project to publish oral folkloric material that would otherwise not be preserved, let alone celebrated as literature.[45]

It was not until the following century, however – until roughly the period when O'Brien began speaking of "ethnic fusion" – that this polyglot of professional, ideological, and formal properties cohered into an explicit politics of the short story. For many twentieth-century observers, the brevity of the short story suggested that the genre was fundamentally better suited than were other forms for chronicling a diverse, heterogeneous culture of equal voices – Poe's emphasis on "unity" turned inside out. William Carlos Williams, for instance, wrote in "A Beginning on the Short Story" that he chose to compose short fiction because he wanted to write about the poor, and that the genre fit "the briefness of their chronicles, its brokenness and heterogeneity – isolation, color." In a famous phrase in *The Lonely Voice*, Frank O'Connor called the short story the genre of "submerged population groups," and reached back to Gogol's *The Overcoat* to illustrate how the short story was infused by an "everyman" spirit. More paradigmatic was Ruth Suckow's allusive statement that the short story was the genre best suited to reproduce the heterogeneity of the American melting pot:

It was the chaos, the unevenness, the diversity of American life that made short stories such a natural artistic experience . . . roving, unsettled, restless, unassimilated, here and gone again – a chaos so huge, a life so varied and so multitudinous that its meaning could be caught only in will-o-the-wisp gleams . . . It was the first eager, hasty way of snatching little treasures of art from the great abundance of unused, uncomprehended material.

For other observers, the link between this model of the short story and the anthology as an opportunity to display the "diversity of American life" was irresistible. Yoli Tannen, for instance, in reviewing the Best Of- collections for 1956, noted the high number of minority voices that had been cited for inclusion; this fact he attributed to the vitality of those voices as compared to a centralized, commercial, white, Protestant mainstream. More recently, John Updike, in the introduction to the 1984 *Best American Short Stories* anthology, observed that the editorial choices of that anthology's founder and first editor, Edward J. O'Brien, were consciously ethnically diverse – as though O'Brien believed that the anthology itself should represent, in microcosm, the kindest possible vision of the American melting pot.[46]

There is, of course, enormous tension between these claims regarding the short story and anything that could be reasonably called 'the actual history of the genre.' In order to justify his claim that the short story was the genre of the submerged population group, for instance, Frank O'Connor was forced to include a catch-all group he identified as "lonely idealists" and "dreamers"; similarly, Tannen included stories told from the points of view of children and the elderly as evidence of the strength of the minority voice within the genre.[47] At the very least, the eagerness with which these two authors associated the short story with an idealized vision of an integrated community bespeaks the seduction of that vision. But it should also remind us of the extent to which the short story is only in theory the ideal genre for the expression of the rich heterogeneity of American life. The link between the 'bigness' of the novel form, its unrestricted length, and the 'bigness' of American life is a natural one: Nina Baym has illustrated how even the earliest American reviews of novels celebrated the form for its "range" and "infinite variety."[48] That link, however, is also a standard of narrative value that has done much to hinder the stature of the short story in this country: F. O. Matthiessen, for instance, celebrated Hawthorne, Melville, Whitman, and Emerson in his canon-making *American Renaissance* for "their devotion to democracy," while rejecting the short story writer Poe's more "narrow" and "factitious" vision.[49]

That Poe's narrow and factitious vision contained democratizing possibilities probably would have shocked Poe as much as it would have Matthiessen. Nevertheless, the short story remains truly democratic only in the ideal that anyone could write it, anyone could read it, and everyone would judge it. But even in its farthest reach "for the million,"[50] the circulation of the short story was still restricted to the highest section of the social pyramid; although the notion that an immensely popular magazine such as the mid-century *Saturday Evening Post* or the turn-of-the-century *Delineator* could circulate through first- and second-hand sources to twenty million people is impressive, it nevertheless indicates the extent to which the magazine was still the icon of middle-class culture – what James Hart calls "the public possessed of enough wealth, education, and leisure to obtain and to read new books as they appear."[51]

The project to capture the oral folktale tradition of American life within the short story is similarly inscribed by a condescension that undercuts its seemingly democratic ambitions. Projects such as regionalism and local color possess radical implications because they deconstruct the notion that universal values exist, redefining them instead as another form of regionalism, one that happens to be centered in a dominant capital of culture:

> the "universal," when healthy, alive, pregnant with values, springs inevitably from the specific fact. This conception of the interpretation of life I would oppose to the idea of cosmic minded people that understanding springs from abstract ideas and images in the mind – in the soul. To such extent regionalism in my judgment, is earth-minded . . .

Harold G. Merriam wrote in "Expression of Northwest Life," in *The New Mexico Quarterly* in 1934.[52] The conservative implication of such projects, on the other hand, is that regional or folkloric material is valuable only to the extent that it is received and appreciated by a middle-class, or educated audience. As both Bret Harte's and G. W. Harris's words indicate, they believed that the goal of the short story project was not actually to create new art, but to find "material" from lower-class and marginalized sources and act as the paid conduit through which that material could reach a mainstream public. In 1931 O'Brien wrote bitterly of local colorists who were "generally Anglo-Saxon," and who "reaped a harvest of esteem for their indulgent and usually uncomprehending chronicles of what they regard as alien quaintness."[53]

These issues of ethnicity and homogeneity also mark the anthology-making process. As Laurie G. Kirszner, coeditor of Holt, Rinehart and Winston's three-genre anthology *Literature: Reading, Reacting, Writing* (1991) observes, ethnic balance is among the selection guidelines most consistently practiced by contemporary anthology editors. But that balance must be achieved within a network of other guidelines that often mute the degree to which even the most conscientious anthology-maker can seek to publish new voices. When combined with the quest to seek ethnic balance, for instance, the similarly powerful obligation to publish "the writers that are in every anthology" often results in anthologies that have the same "core" but different "nuggets stuck on the outside." Similarly, editors must choose among traditional representatives of ethnic groups or "fresh" authors from within those same groups; they must consider sequencing; and, in the instance of anthology-textbooks, they must select which stories are to be featured as objects of critical study, and which are to be merely included. These decisions are further mediated by an external review process in which the publisher invites (and remunerates) outside readers – other anthology editors, experts on cross-culturalism or pedagogy, or individuals possessing institutional power within universities or secondary school systems – to recommend further additions, deletions, resequencing, or alterations to prefatory material or exercises. In sum, the notion that any anthology represents a neutral collection of diverse American voices is deeply undercut by the nature of the editorial process (and the pragmatic financial considerations inscribed therein), which requires the editor to thread his or her way through a variety of conservative and progressive ideological constructions concerning what constitutes true inclusion.[54]

Even the claim that the heterogeneity of the magazine establishment contributed to a similar heterogeneity in the short story requires a careful evaluation. Many commercial magazines of the twentieth century have done far more to enforce centralization than heterogeneity among the kinds of fiction and the authors being published: *See* magazine estimated in 1950 that 90 percent of all fiction published in commercial magazines was supplied by one hundred authors; *Better Homes and Gardens* more charitably guessed in the same year that 50 percent of the published fiction was written by a community of 250 authors. Earlier in the century, *Scribner's* revealed that only 1 percent of the fiction it published was unsolicited material; *American Mercury*, incredibly, placed its own figure at .001 percent.[55]

Nor was this trend toward homogeneity restricted to commercial magazines. As Theodore Peterson has noted, the wild swing between individuality and standardization was virtually a genetic trait of the American magazine.[56] Edmund Wilson wrote in 1935 that

> In its earliest years, a magazine may seem spontaneous, novel, and daring; but by the time it has reached its maturity it has, as the French say, "taken its fold," and it succumbs to the force of inertia against which the youngest and freshest editor is as powerless as the oldest and stalest . . .[57]

The temptation to succumb to an established formula was endemic even among those 'little' magazines that had been organized to offer alternative voices. Marianne Moore, then editor of *The Dial*, told Charles Allen in 1941 that "what had begun as a spontaneous delightful plotting in the interest of art and artists, was becoming mere faithfulness to responsibility"; a decade earlier, the aptly named *Janus* attempted to circumvent this dilemma by including on its masthead a "dissenting editor" whose sole function was to prevent the chief editor from "going fundamentalist."[58]

Last, and most significant, the issue of the short story's 'accessibility' has possessed a notoriously double-edged value within discussions of the genre. To claim that the short story is easier to write and publish than the novel is also to imply that it might be inferior to the longer prose form ("It is ten times as easy to write a short story as it is to write one ten times as long," one late-nineteenth-century academic wrote).[59] As Thomas Gullason observes in "The Short Story: An Underrated Art," the short story has often been treated as an apprentice prose form, a practice field for authors too inexperienced, unsophisticated, or otherwise incapable of composing a novel. Frederick Lewis Pattee, a leading historian of the short story during the 1920s, wrote of Mary Noailles Murfree that

> short lengths of fiction were imperative for her during the uncertain days when she was acquiring a market: most of the young writers of the period were forced to try the currents with skiffs before launching the five-decked galleons of their dreams . . .

This ranking between the short story and novel is then enforced by the publishing establishment. Young writers may develop their early reputation by publishing short stories in the more accessible magazines, but they are discouraged from assembling short story collections by both literary agents and publishing companies, and are instead urged to write and market novels. As Jennifer Rudolph, a literary agent for the Virginia Barber agency, acknowledges, "getting a book of short stories published is still almost the hardest thing to do."[60]

The arguments about the relative simplicity of the short story provide an illustration of how, in Jameson's words, "the history of forms" becomes intertwined with "the evolution of social life."[61] To say that the short story is easier to write than the novel is to make an implicit judgment about the intellectual capacities of those who write short stories. This is perhaps a comparatively harmless judgment when directed toward beginning writers, but it can possess strong ideological overtones when directed toward entire groups who might be deemed restricted to the 'inferior genre':

> The magazine forms were inferior forms, the product for the most part, of youth or the apprenticeship period, or of women who as a rule were restricted to them by reason of their more restricted lives and necessarily narrower outlook on the world . . .

Howells wrote in 1887.[62] In this manner, the short story is eagerly embraced as a site of discourse in which minority groups are abstractly privileged, and that implicitly contains an attack on an abstract ruling class. Concomitantly, the short story itself is perceived as an inferior art form, a skiff among galleons, a simple melody compared to grand opera. When John Cheever anthropomorphized the short story at a 1969 conference as "something of a bum," he not only recognized that the genre had been labeled as a disenfranchised player in the round of literary genres, but he also captured the sense that the bond between the short story's status and the status of disenfranchised participants in the American political project was somehow essential to definitions of the genre. To the extent that the short story is a celebration of the marginal voices of our culture, that celebration is mitigated by the marginalization of the short story itself.[63]

Literary Drugs and Soulless Machines

> Mediocrity should be fostered. That is, it should be given its just due . . . What if a man's novel or short story be a bit feeble or maudlin or perfervid. He himself is the better for the exercise of his talents, the clearer of thought, the more eased of restrained emotion. In truth it is his inalienable right to make fiction if he so desire and by all odds the best thing he can do . . .

> anonymous editorial, "Of Mediocrity and its Excellences,"
> *The Dial* (6 Sept. 1919): 193.

As the above quote (and its slippery tone) suggests, many observers of the American literary scene in the early twentieth century believed that they were spectating upon a radical and uncomfortable shift in the traditional models of authorship and literature. It might be inappropriate to call these developments 'the democratization of authorship,' given the comparatively small and homogeneous groups represented among these numbers. Nevertheless, the *Saturday Evening Post*'s 1950 estimate that they received 60,000–200,000 unsolicited manuscripts yearly indicates the extent to which an increasingly large class of Americans in the early twentieth century had come to believe that authorship was no longer the province of the eccentric or the wealthy, and that the short story was the vehicle of their ambitions.[64]

There are many ways to measure the success of this appeal. This shift in the model of authorship was at the heart of the two most significant institutional developments in the short story in the twentieth century: the creation and popularity of the system of how-to handbooks and courses during the period 1910–35, concomitant with the period during which the short story had its highest value in the commercial market; and the more recent development of the system of academic workshops and graduate programs, concomitant with the near-demise of the short story as a commercial product and its rebirth as an academic genre with second-hand commercial implications (i.e., anthologies). The how-to books became permanent properties for publishing houses, and outsold short story collections (though not, of course, short stories in magazines). The growth of the academic creative writing program is equally noteworthy: At present, one-third of all American high schools have creative writing programs; 250 such graduate programs exist, and every year confer over 1,500 degrees on would-be writers of *literature*, of whom approximately half will attempt to publish short stories.[65]

Perhaps the best indicator of the success of the ideology of accessibility, however, is the depth and nature of the counterresponse that it has generated. For high- and middle-culture authors and critics in the early twentieth century, for Modernists and regionalists and Marxists alike, the short story itself had become strangely undemocratic. At the rate of thirty or more articles and reviews per year (as tabulated in Edward J. O'Brien's annual "Yearbook" of short story activity),[66] these writers cogitated the state of the American short story, and overall circulated the perception that the genre was somehow out of control: catering to the mob, held thrall to commercial purposes, and even threatening the fundamental cultural authority of the American political project that it had otherwise promised to exemplify.

Throughout the 1920s and 1930s, essayists and reviewers used the pages of magazines such as *The Dial, Saturday Review of Literature,* and *Bookman* to promulgate the idea that the short story was a popular form of art that was perverting American audiences and appealing to their worst impulses. Canby, for instance, understood and invoked the sense of national mission associated with the short story during this period when he wrote that

> our defects in taste are slowly but certainly being remedied.
> The schools are at work upon them . . .

The tenor of Canby's statement, and those of his contemporaries, was that the American reading public was essentially passive, and as malleable to the forces of low culture as it would be to the forces of true literature, were they as empowered. It was thus doubly disappointing for Canby that "American editor(s)," playing "safe, constantly and from conviction," were undermining this mission by selecting formula fiction against which "American taste does not rebel."[67] According to Herbert Ellsworth Cory, the short story itself was "an artificially stimulated demand" created for the benefit of a few "hundreds of Grub-streeters" and "teachers" and foisted successfully upon an undiscerning public: "we do not want the short-story – we think we want it."[68]

This portrayal of the American reading public as a dumb, monolithic force gelled with the portrayal of the short story as a potentially subversive art form: If the American public was a body without a brain, then the short story was the "literary drug" that would conceivably inspire the body to rebel. Cory was quite specific on this point when in criticism of the genre he wrote that "I do not say this because the short-story ministers to the mob . . . I say it because the short-story ministers to the mob in its most capricious and hedonistic mood."[69] The spirit of Cory's remarks is present throughout criticism of the genre during this period. It is present, for instance, in essay titles that suggested the short story worked on the body of the American public in a particularly visceral manner (i.e., "The Literary Drug Traffic," or "Short Story Orgy"),[70] as well as in statements about the genre that associated the act of reading a short story with the physical activities that most deprived the intellect of control of the body:

> overindulgence in the short-story is a dissipation which produces an inevitable reaction; it leaves the mind in a jerky state . . . the perfect short story is like champagne, scarcely to be taken in quantity as the sole article of diet . . .

Walter Dyer wrote in *The Dial.*[71] In contrast to this "debauch," the novel was perceived as the standard-bearer for the "literature of cool reflection" that Cory believed we desired "in our healthier moments"; the short story was simply "pathological, and titillates our nerves in our pathological moments."[72]

A second major concern of critics during this period was that the short story, because of its popularity and its presence within commercial magazines, had become an uneasy intersection of the fields of literature and commerce. This concern was expressed most concretely as a fear that advertising considerations were influencing editorial selection of material: Smertenko wrote that "advertising has taken the fiction magazine out of the realm of art and into the field of industry." For these critics, the physical configuration of the commercial magazine, which arranged fiction and advertising on the same page, represented a perfect example of the contamination that had taken place. O'Brien observed that many short story writers also wrote advertising copy and claimed that "even a careless study of a popular magazine will show you how closely the stories, articles, and illustrations fit into the advertising pages." Helen Hull spoke sarcastically of how "a story of a woman stranded on poverty by the death of her husband might well wind between insurance advertisements. The possibilities are infinite . . ."[73]

Although these critics only conjectured that an actual link existed between the content of the short story and its adjacent advertising copy, their displeasure with the idea that the story was "a thin trickle in a deep canyon of advertising" was more tangible.[74] The physical configuration of the commercial magazine created a site of discourse in which the margins of the text, so unintruded upon with the bound volume of a novel, were thoroughly overrun by what seemed to be the expression of a bullying mercantile culture. It did not matter that the short story writer made money; what mattered more was that the short story itself appeared subservient to economic necessity – a conclusion that was further supported by the popularity of Poe's frugal narrative standards during the period. Not surprisingly, one of the chief reforms instituted within the "little" magazines was the elimination of the commingled configuration of text and advertising; advertising (what there was of it) was placed in sections at the front and the back of the journal, leaving a pure field for high literary discourse sandwiched in between.[75]

On a more basic level, however, many twentieth-century observers expressed concern that the short story represented a fundamental threat to the autonomy of the individual. William Dean Howells devoted the entirety of his essay "Some Anomalies of the Short Story" to one particular issue: why the short stories of a given author would succeed (both critically and commercially) when they appeared individually in magazines, and would fail when they appeared in a book-length collection comprised solely of that author's work.[76] In fact, this "anomaly" of the short story has had considerable endurance: William Peden wrote in 1964 that "no one has been able to explain satisfactorily or completely just why collections of short stories by individuals 'don't sell.'"[77] Howells initially sought an explanation for this breakdown that resonated of the vision of the short story as a literary cheap thrill:

> He (the reader) can read one good short story in a magazine with refreshment, and a pleasant sense of excitement . . . but if this is repeated in ten or twenty stories, he becomes fluttered and exhausted by the draft upon his energies . . .

But Howells also recognized, at least implicitly, that the failure of short story collections had more to do with the insistence upon modes of publication that depended upon faith in the Individual Talent:

> Then, what is the solution as to the form of publication for short stories, since people do not object to them singly but collectively, and not in variety, but in identity of authorship? Are they to be printed only in the magazines, or are they to be collected in volumes combining a variety of authorship?[78]

Forty years later, Edith Mirrielees reformulated the problem as to indicate how the canonical American faith in the individual seemed hopelessly conflicted with the short story project. Although granting that "notable individual stories appear," and that "it is not, seemingly, talent itself that is lacking," she nevertheless bemoans the fact that "one story does not make a story writer." According to Mirrielees, even though there is no lack of good short stories, the genre is failing because it is not producing good short story writers: "The very point of the present plaint is that the story writer who began prior to the twenties tended to nourish his talent . . . and that today he does not . . ."[79]

But what if one short story did make a story writer? In other hands, Mirrielees's "plaint" would have been a celebration of the fulfillment of the democratic possibilities of the short story project, of the doors to publication thrown wide open and the happy discovery that everyone had a story worth telling. Instead, Mirrielees states that the short story establishment exerts a kind of pressure on authors that encourages them merely to duplicate their first achievements:

> It requires no Cassandra to prophesy that of half a dozen writers within the allotted period whose first discovered story made your breath catch in your throat, and your mind record the writer's name, five certainly and probably all six are now

appearing with replicas — let us keep to the safety of understatement — with replicas which cause no breath-catching . . .[80]
What is interesting here is that Mirrielees is only tangentially concerned that the short story establishment of teachers and editors
might be encouraging all authors to abide by a single standard. She
is more fearful, rather, that the short story establishment might be
encouraging each individual author to conform to himself or herself with too much precision — essentially, by adopting the editor's
conservative but businesslike desire to go with a proven winner. For
Mirrielees, the short story is an attack on individualism from the
inside out: Rather than deconstructing identity, the short story
turns identity into a strait-jacket.

To some extent, this concern is simply an issue of literary economics. As "The Lounger" reminded us, the short story could
seem to be a bad investment of authorial resources when compared
to the novel: The narrative voice, plot, and characters that might
reasonably sustain a novel-length prose work are instead expended
in the service of a smaller product. Similarly, the "personal style"
that might meaningfully be represented in a single narrative within
an autonomous bound volume instead appears absurd when iter-
ated again and again within that same volume in the form of a story
collection; and since, presumably, the individual author must
spend years evolving a personal style, the short story seems like a
dangerous way to invest that effort. None of these claims would be
meaningful, of course, if a dialogic opposition between the short
story and the novel did not already exist: if, specifically, the novel's
breadth did not seem like a better investment, and a better fit, for
the notion that literature should celebrate the kind of extraordinary lives that could only be described in detail. For O'Connor and
Williams, for instance, the short story possessed appeal precisely
because its length was better suited to the description of lives that
were not extraordinary, but typical, or at best exemplary at epi-
phanic moments.

For the most part, however, the perception that the short story
somehow diminishes the individuality of both its author and its
reader can be ascribed to issues that are intrinsic to the genre's role
in the literary marketplace. When Truman Capote, in 1958, observed in an interview that "whatever control and technique I may
have I owe entirely to my training in" the short story, he proferred
a claim about the genre that has been commonplace in workshops,
anthologies, and conferences since the nineteenth century, and that
has been used from the time of Poe to counteract the notion that
the short story was easy to write: that the form was the place where

an author went to learn discipline, but not inspiration, and that this kind of discipline was particularly attuned to the values of a mercantile, technologically advanced community.[81]

Given this emphasis on technique, the focus of Mirrielees's concern becomes clearer. O'Brien described this concern in explicit terms when he wrote that "in nine cases out of ten I am still unable to recognize the author of a story from its style. It is his formula which usually reveals his identity." For O'Brien, and for other critics of the short story during the 1920s and 1930s, the genre was not an assault upon individualism per se: They rarely disputed the notion that the mark of an individual author was visible in all of his or her work. Rather, what concerned these critics was that the model of identity the short story was propounding encouraged individuals to think of themselves as being constructed of quantifiable, iterable parts:

> This commercial malady is infectious because a sentimental national optimism is rooted in a purely industrial civilization which worships "efficiency" . . . Our literature tends to have a more and more striking resemblance to a soulless machine with a clever mind, and the American short story more and more suggests that the secret of perpetual motion is being fatally discovered . . . This soulless machine is hypnotizing the masses . . .

Henry Ford, clearly, was not the literary messiah that O'Brien had anticipated.[82]

Why Short Stories?

A survey of the essays written on the short story in America over the last one hundred years creates no plausible narrative chronology of the genre's progress. "The Lounger"'s 1890 piece, for instance, begins by telling its reader that "the short story is having its day *again*," five short years after Brander Matthews claimed to provide the form with that name, seven years before Frank Norris would eulogize the genre in "The Decline of the Magazine Story," and a full three decades before the popularity of the "magazine story" would even begin to show signs of decline.[83] It is particularly difficult to evaluate the response to an art form that has been so consistently *and* simultaneously buried and resurrected by its official chroniclers. The essays that have been most quoted in this chapter, however – for instance, those by Canby, Suckow, Smertenko, and Howells – all were designed to be "state of the short story" assessments, and were usually jeremiads. They began with uneasily ironic invocations to the Americanness of the genre (Suckow: "It has been put into the schools, like the salute to the flag"), continued with steady listings of the likely malefactors, and usually contained at least one paean to the potential of the form.[84] To the extent that these essays best capture the full scope of thought on the American short story — both the hope that the genre might legitimately represent a transfiguring art form, and the remarkable confusion and betrayal associated with the failure of that hope — they might reasonably be called the core of American short story criticism.

And they speak with a searching, almost fervent tone of voice, one that often strikes a modern observer as disproportionate to the occasion. What these critics tried so diligently to explain is simply how a community makes itself, and why, in this case, a community so avowedly "American" should have taken such a peculiar form. But despite the listings of potential culprits (Mirrielees, for instance, absolves authors, but blames editors and the audience; Canby absolves the audience, but blames the editors; Suckow blames Poe but then absolves him, and then blames the schools and the writers; Farrell blames them all), what remained undecipherable for these critics is why a community would *voluntarily* enter into a social contract that would unnecessarily inhibit the rights of the individuals who comprised it. The editors could be blamed, but that did not explain why the writers and the audience cooperated. The schools could be blamed, but the schools could not have existed without willing pupils. The short story did not have to be American (an anonymous *New York Times* writer in 1927 spoke laconically of "the official character" that the form had "been allowed to acquire");[85] it did not even have to be a genre. But somehow, all this happened: The interlocking institutions and ideologies of American literary life coalesced to create a genre that could be called their own and then, strangely, devalued it.

There could be only one true culprit. Isaac Rosenfeld, in a jeremiad published in the *New Republic* in 1941, surveyed what he called the "Great American Desert" and, absolving the writers who occupied that Desert, alighted on the guilty party: "I believe the short story itself is at fault." For Rosenfeld, the genre had simply overwhelmed its practitioners (among whom he included such canonical figures as William Faulkner and Katherine Mansfield), who, with their awareness of the rules of composition, were "afloat in a tradition . . . stale . . . bookish . . ." Rosenfeld's approach is a fascinating one: It is as if the culture had literally taken the pen out of the individual's hand and robbed him or her of the free will to choose. The genre itself is actually doing the writing: "The stories in this volume were already written long before they were conceived – an *a priori* category engulfed them."[86]

Other essayists shared a similar fear of this a priori method of literary composition. Canby wrote disdainfully of a "formula" that would not "relax its grip" upon the otherwise "unformed short story." Farrell complained of "literature . . . changed, pieced together, in order to make it fit into an arbitrary structure." Suckow rather pointedly warned that "if America continues to be the land of the Short Story, it will ultimately lose its short stories."[87] Suckow's punning use of capitalization vividly illustrates the particular distinction that these critics sought to identify. It was as though America were producing two 'short stories':

1. a short story *project,* developed by commercial and academic forces, and infused by nationalist expectations of what, exactly, an American art form should be (the *S*hort *S*tory);
2. the natural, spontaneous short stories of freely acting individuals, unconstrained by the definitional fervor of the *project* and, by inference, more truly American (the *s*hort *s*tory).

This was a fine distinction, of course. The commercial and academic formulas of the short story have been so pervasive that even a comparatively narrow and homogeneous group of critics would not even agree on who was writing short stories and who was writing Short Stories. The distinction, rather, was purely theoretical: It was an attempt to retain, or recapture, the cultural power of authorship (and the exaltation of the individual upon which it was dependent) during a period in which the sheer success of the short story project was posing a threat to that power. To blame the *short story itself* for this, recalling Jameson's model, was tantamount to blaming Americans for voluntarily entering into a contract with themselves to restrict their individual freedoms. But that was, in fact, the only explanation that made sense.

And that is how the short story has been written into American literary history. When Suckow wrote in 1927 that "we entertain the fallacy that America is the land of the short story, without too much dangerous inquiry into the possibility of its being the land of the definition of the short story,"[88] she was objecting to the proliferation of how-to handbooks and courses in story writing during the early part of this century, as well as the nationalist rhetoric that had played a major role in that proliferation. But her observation also states the degree to which the short story has been a genre of literature where the rules and demarcations have been particularly visible: As Charles E. May has written recently, "the twentieth century has seen more discussions about how to write the short story than how to read it." This has transformed – at least, within academic discussions – the short story into a model for a kind of narrative transaction, and a kind of community in which the individual is unusually restricted by the laws of the culture.[89]

This model gained currency in the early twentieth century ("the novel may more or less do what it pleases," Katharine Gerould wrote in 1924, "but the short story must mind its p's and q's"),[90] and has maintained vogue ever since. It has generally been used to define the short story as the genre in which "authentic expression" is most stifled, either by excessive academicization or commercialization. Thomas Gullason, May, William Peden, and many major contemporary specialists in the short story have written on the fact that the genre, when opposed to the other major genres of literature, is treated as a perpetual outsider: a "second-class literary citizen," in Peden's words.[91] But the marginalization of the short story has been played out in America against the backdrop of a political ideology that traditionally exalts and simultaneously represses its most marginal constituents, and often views marginality as a heroic virtue, evidence of true individualism. Thus, for other authors, the short story has represented the least conventionalized of genres, the beneficiary of what Nadine Gordimer calls the "healthy neglect" of critics and publishers.[92]

Further, this dialogue between issues of standardization and issues of individualism also dominates short story discourse because it represents the intersection of the nationalist discourse with the institutions of the short story itself, all of which developed within the framework of corollary nationalist projects. Although *Janus's* playful editorial policy makes light of the tension present in the attempts of any little magazine to maintain its dissenting stance, for instance, it also bespeaks the contradiction inherent in any cultural project that declares itself to be perpetually avant-garde and "new." The magazine that founds itself with the purpose of enfranchising marginal voices brings those voices nearer to the center if it succeeds, and upon establishing itself risks succumbing to formulas that might exclude new disenfranchised voices, or eccentric versions of the original.

Any literary form that similarly promises to be eternally new (or "sudden") must in turn respond to the same tensions. Associated with regional and marginal voices in the nineteenth century, the short story became the image of a standardized, commercialized genre in the early twentieth. Disgruntled critics and authors believed that the solution to the standardization of the genre in the early twentieth century was the construction of a system of university-sponsored writing programs and periodicals, which would provide support for writers and their apprentices and allow them to be free from commercial pressures – an attempt to, oxymoronically, institutionalize the marginal voice. Smertenko, for instance, wrote that

> what must be done, then, is to endow a number of magazines – no one periodical, however nobly conceived, can do all of this work – which will publish the best work of our masters and at the same time furnish an opportunity for full expression to our unknown writers; to call forth editors of unquestioned integrity and literary judgment.

Thirty years later, in 1951, Hershel Brickell gave credit for the resurrection of the American short story to "the widespread establishment of courses in creative writing and the mushroom-like growth of writers' conferences." Ironically, this system is now perceived as the institution that enforces formulaic standards and encourages a new kind of mediocrity: "Many critics and editors of short story anthologies," Falcon Baker wrote forty years ago, "have been so concerned with disparaging the formula story that they have in effect created another formula." More recently, Current-Garcia and Hitchcock have noted that "this 'academization' has been decried by some critics as a pernicious new species of elitism that is drying up and debilitating the traditional, vigorous life of the short story."[93]

This is, of course, subtle, demanding language. The phrase "traditional, vigorous life of the short story" posits a previous golden age and suggests a future one; and, like Smertenko waiting seventy years ago for the short story to "carry on its early tradition," it exemplifies how short story criticism has been laden with intense ideological ambition. When Rosenfeld begins his "Great American Desert" by conjecturing "suppose there were no short stories," however, or when Helen Hull begins her "Literary Drug Traffic" by asking "Why Short Stories," these critics illustrate how the voice of short story criticism in this country has also sounded perpetually disappointed, due to the constant failure of those ambitions.[94] The short story is perhaps the only genre in literary history in which critics could be sufficiently disappointed by its progress, and sufficiently aware that the form was a self-conscious cultural construct to question openly and angrily whether we ever needed it at all, and whether or not we should stop using it. That the short story instead thrives is a testament to the continuing appeal of the cultural aspirations that provided a raison d'être for the genre in the first place.

3

EDITH WHARTON

THE MUSE'S STRATEGY

In 1925, the year that F. L. Pattee described Poe's review of Hawthorne as "universally quoted,"[1] Edith Wharton published a chapter entitled "Telling a Short Story" in her *Writing of Fiction*. Wharton's essay has never been widely quoted; in fact, from the opening sentence, in which she turns her back on the nationalist tenor of American short storytelling by observing that "the modern short story seems to have originated . . . in France,"[2] Wharton seems to be consciously reworking many of the established canons of the genre. It was a task for which she was almost ideally qualified. She published eighty-six short stories between 1891 and 1937, a time span that coincides with the short story's period of widest activity and greatest commercial popularity. Like Poe, she was a literary entrepreneur who attempted to control as much of the narrative transaction as possible, and who attempted to make literature into a paying profession. Unlike Poe, she succeeded to a great extent, earning the equivalent of modern six-figure royalties yearly while writing fiction that captured both critical acclaim and popularity with the deliberate ease of which Poe dreamt in "The Philosophy of Composition."[3]

In one sense, Wharton's career is a significant, even archetypal, instance of how Poe's vision took corporeal form on the American landscape, and how it was transformed in the process. But Wharton also brought other, significant resources to her own vision of the genre. As her autobiography *A Backward Glance* indicates, she spent a lifetime consciously and deliberately weighing the relative value of tradition versus the necessity for social change. Her favorite trope for civilization, and the comforts and traps inherent in tradition, was 'enclosure': Indoor metaphors were a leitmotif in her letters, essays, and fiction, and her books on garden architecture and home decor were among her most gratifying labors.[4] It is not enough to say that Edith Wharton understood and explored the aesthetic values of enclosed spaces; she also understood the political implications of those artistic opportunities. Her works on architecture, in particular, possess anthemic resonances. As Judith

58

Fryer explains in depth in her recent *Felicitous Space* (1986), they
are no less than manifestos for how any individual makes the most
of a culture that 'encloses' personal freedoms.[5]

Perhaps no other major author in the last 150 years has been able
to discuss the short story using a richer and more relevant set of
metaphors. At the very least, Wharton's architectural writings (in
particular *The Decoration of Houses*, but also *Italian Villas and Their
Gardens*) provided a complete lexicon of aesthetic standards that
she readily applied to that most enclosed of narrative spaces, the
short story. But significantly, she applied the political ramifications
of her architectural vision to the short story, and subtly transformed the mainstream consensus on the form. While Poe's model
short story writer was an unmoved mover of his audience's emo-
tions, Wharton's short story writer was an interior designer mediating among the concerns of her audience, her artistic integrity, and
an uncaring unmovable Architect − literary tradition itself.

In addition, Wharton's use of visual and decorative metaphors
reminds the reader that one of the modern short story's generic
antecedents was the late eighteenth- and early nineteenth-century
"sketch" − a form that, as the name suggests, owes much of its
aesthetics to the visual arts.[6] It also suggestively links Wharton to
the professional creative writing teachers who plied their trades
during her lifetime, and who doted on architectural metaphors for
the craft of short story writing. It would be wrong to say that
Wharton 'invented' a particular viewpoint on the short story, or
that she anticipated the historicist literary theory of the late twentieth century (literary theory that, as Frank Lentricchia has recently observed, is scarcely "New" itself).[7] More appropriately, she
made use of many of the same Romantic materials that were available to Poe, and made use of Poe's legacy as well, to remind her
reader that short story writing was a social act. Her gesture was not
unique, but it is important; for our purposes, it places her and Poe
at opposite yet symbiotic ends of the spectrum that contains American attitudes toward short story writing, and art in general. Poe
sought transcendence from his audience, and he created a poetics
founded upon that goal; Wharton located the earthboundness that
drove Poe's desire, and instead built a poetics of immanence.

Inherences

As Elizabeth Ammons observes in *Edith Wharton's Argument with
America*, despite a groundswell of optimistic feminism around the
turn of the twentieth century, Wharton remained pessimistic about
the ability of 'new women' to shatter the constricting stereotypes of

a patriarchal culture.[8] Although her fiction consistently and compassionately dealt with the intricacies and tragedies of middle-class women's lives, she steadfastly refused to be associated with those women who were known as the feminists of her time. She avoided meeting the English novelist and reformer May Sinclair on two separate occasions in 1908, for instance, and privately referred to her work in disparaging terms.[9] Much later in her life, in 1928, she refused to be profiled in a documentary film entitled *Woman Marches On,* writing to her associate Rutger Jewett that "I should not be greatly flattered at being associated with some of the ladies named in the list who are to figure in the same series" – the leading female scientists, artists, and entertainers of the 1920s.[10]

According to Ammons, Wharton pursued a different yet still feminist path, one that was parallel to the economic writings of Charlotte Gilman and Thorstein Veblen. Wharton saw a pervasive economic enslavement where women required financial self-sufficiency to establish independence, and continued to possess only one available career path: the business of courtship and marriage, where infantile, reliant women were still far more likely to be 'hired' than any others.[11] Ultimately, bitterly perhaps, Wharton saw the entrepreneurial approach as a way out for some women. If marriage was frankly viewed as a business, then a woman could trade one husband for another, constantly and openly negotiating better terms, like Undine Spragg, the protagonist of Wharton's *Custom of the Country.*[12]

Wharton's own approach was otherwise, only sharing with Spragg an awakening economic consciousness. Wharton chose to make herself an astute, self-reliant manager of her own literary output. In her early career, she called for more widespread advertisement of her work; she attentively demanded royalties when she believed they were due. She regularly requested changes in covers, jacket blurbs, and carefully oversaw the translations of her work for European audiences. She produced short fiction virtually on demand, particularly when one or more new stories were necessary to complete a volume for publication.[13] Her novels, similarly, tended to fit genres that were popular in their given season: "a historical romance in 1902, a society novel in 1905, a problem novel with muckraking overtones in 1907, a picaresque satire in 1913."[14] Her publishers, Appleton and Company, claimed in a promotional pamphlet in 1912 that she was capable of "producing, whenever she feels like it, a best seller."[15] Wharton sought to be, in her own words, "the compleat housekeeper," and was proudly conscious that she had arranged her desk optimally for the most efficient literary output.[16]

What must be emphasized is that she really did not need the

money. Trust funds had long since removed the need for parsimony.[17] There was an intensity to Wharton's 'housekeeping' that can be measured only by her own litmus in *French Ways and Their Meaning* that "money making is interesting only in proportion as its object is interesting."[18] Inherited wealth could earn little independence when, in Ammons's words, "typical women in her view – no matter how privileged, nonconformist, or assertive – were not free to control their own lives."[19] If she was socially imprisoned in a steadily deteriorating marriage (she divorced eventually in 1913), she could at least establish herself as economically free from her husband's support and the strictures of trust funds placed in joint title. With this same sort of fervor she financed, built, and decorated the first house she could call her own (The Mount), haggling for furniture and insisting upon the "newest" home renovations.[20] She exerted similar authority over every aspect of the publication of her own works, attempting to ensure that the published product was distinctly her own. If her pessimism about the condition of women was unshakable, it was scarcely paralyzing. Rather, it appeared to catalyze a strong personal response, the success of which could best be measured in the sales figures Wharton carefully noted in her personal diaries.[21]

In these circumstances, what is most striking is that Wharton spent no more and no less than what she earned: As Lewis documents, Wharton's annual expenses during her years as a professional writer "were almost identical to her income."[22] For Wharton to have annual expenses that match annual income suggests that she was as uncomfortable with unused funds as she was with debt or dependence, and viewed her annual income as the measure of the circumference of her life. It also suggests that Wharton perceived enclosure as something more than a symbol of the social entrapment that she sought to avoid: It was an inevitability at least, and perhaps even a welcome determinant.

Her ambivalence toward the idea of enclosure and its social ramifications was a persistent theme throughout her writing. Her pessimism about genuine social change, after all, also represented faith in the strength of the traditional consensus: "The value of duration is slowly asserting itself against the welter of change," she wrote in 1934, but the value of duration had been evident in even her earliest stories.[23] Her nonfiction, in particular, is full of passages in which she appears to be balancing the relative value of tradition against its disadvantages:

> Caprice is as ruinous as routine. Habit is necessary; it is the habit of having habits . . . that must be incessantly fought . . .[24]

Unsurprisingly, she came to favor habit as she grew older; shocked and debilitated by the loss of friends and relatives and the destruction of her adopted continent during World War I, she wrote *A Backward Glance* as if to commemorate (and insist upon the noncontingency of) the European aristocratic tradition as well as the nouveau colonial aristocracy of her New York parents. Like a true social historian, she accepted the inevitability of inheritance: "I don't mind being called 'cynical and depressing' by the sentimentalists," she wrote in an early letter, "as long as those who see the 'inherences' recognize my ability to see them too."[25] It was, rather, the value of the "inherences" about which she remained ambivalent.

This duality was expressed in Wharton's aesthetic vision as well. For the most part, her books on home decor, architecture, and literature can be perceived as constituting a sophisticated program of corrective responses for the individual seeking livable space. At the same time, however, Wharton vehemently rejected those artists and movements that, superficially at least, most represented change. It is tempting to speak of her as a proponent of 'unmodernism': "You'll tell me that's the old way, and consequently not your way," she wrote to F. Scott Fitzgerald, defending her suggested revisions to *The Great Gatsby*.[26] It is better, perhaps, to speak of Wharton's opposition to one of the more-or-less constant manifestations of modernism: the "hunger to break past the bourgeois proprieties and self-containment of culture," in Irving Howe's words.[27] Although Edith Wharton's hunger to break past the bourgeois proprieties of marriage and economic dependence was genuine (and mostly sated by the time she reached middle age), she remained fascinated by the aesthetic and social possibilities of self-containment throughout her entire life.

The implications for her fiction were numerous. She worked in commercial forms ("all the masterpieces of fiction have been potboilers, I think the name a very honorable one" she wrote in 1906),[28] which simulated containment by requiring the author to acquiesce to a set of predetermined literary conventions. More important, she disliked many of the literary manifestos of those individuals who were most visibly seeking to break through the bourgeois proprieties: the abandonment of the "useful fiction of the common reader," for instance;[29] the use of open, difficult, or "innovative" forms that simulated the failure of art to present closed or coherent visions, and suggested the author's liberation from the closed forms of more mainstream genres; and, in general, what Andrew Ross calls "an extremist modernist politics, phobicly caught between the prospect of an advancing mass culture and the moribund values of the bourgeois mind" – the utopian product of which would be a dissenting community independent of, and elevated from, the need to "think" or perform within the limits of the larger culture.[30] As her fascination with home decor indicates, Edith Wharton preferred to work inside.

The Compleat Housekeeper

Throughout her writing, Wharton freely used images and models from decor, architecture, and visual arts to describe emotional and cultural states. In particular, it is difficult to read *The Decoration of Houses*,[31] Wharton's 1897 collaboration with architect Ogden Codman Jr., without recalling her unusually resonant description in "The Fullness of Life" of wasted human potential as a series of underutilized and senselessly decorated rooms.

> I have sometimes thought that a woman's nature is like a great house full of rooms: there is the hall, through which everyone passes going in and out; the drawing room, where one receives formal visits; the sitting room, where the members of the family come and go as they list; but beyond that, far beyond, are other rooms, the handles of whose doors are never turned; no one knows the way to them, no one knows whither they lead; and in the innermost room, the holy of holies, the soul sits alone and waits for a footstep that never comes.[32]

Her recommendations on home decor in *Decoration* are presented as practical advice for the individual attempting to create a livable space with materials that are "fundamentally ugly" (DH, 30). And yet, when she observes that "the science of restoring wasted rooms to their proper uses is one of the most important and least understood branches of house furnishing" (DH, 22), the specific parallels between her social vision and her decor aesthetic are unmistakable. Her pessimism (and her faith) regarding the force of history takes metaphorical form in the architectural lines that do not make comfortable the individuals living inside the house, the ugly furniture that cannot be replaced, and — as so powerfully described in "The Fullness of Life" — the rooms that go unused. Her solution, because (for Wharton) the house itself cannot be replaced or rebuilt, is to repair whatever she can, using available materials.

Still, as the word "restore" suggests, Wharton is entirely ambivalent about the prospect of social change. In fact, she directs most of her invective in *The Decoration of Houses* toward the mass of Victorian decorators and architects who exalted change for its own sake. She objects to eclecticism, and disputes architects who claim that "a regard for symmetry indicates poverty of invention. . . . Proportion . . . the desire for symmetry, for balance, for rhythm" (DH, 33) are all justified as universal standards for home design by virtue of an appeal to "the most inveterate of human instincts," a set of standards established by "the artistic experience of centuries" – crucially, not the same "artistic experience of centuries" that had transformed Victorian rooms into chaotic, overstuffed museums of world culture.[33] Her theory of home decor, rather, appears to be catalyzed by the insistence that everything "harmonize," a harmony best created by the subservience of all elements to unity and a loosely defined classical tradition (DH, 13).

Given this evidence, one might justifiably expect that *The Decoration of Houses* would be an authoritarian manifesto of home decor. In fact, Wharton's *specific* recommendations are remarkably flexible, and imbued with an appreciation of the limitations confronting any "designer" engaged in renovation or reform. The designer is "hampered by artistic tradition" (DH, 13), equally aware that "it must never be forgotten that every one is unconsciously tyrannized over by the wants of others" (DH, 18). "Hopeless discord" exists between the architect who constructed the house and the designer who is required to live within its confines (DH, 15). Worse, the foundations of Wharton's hypothetical house are rotten, but essentially unalterable; the designer's main goal is to "produce a good design upon the background of a faulty and illogical structure" (DH, 23). The designer, introduced to rigorous principles of order, is in fact instructed pragmatically to "do all that he can" (DH, 24). *The Decoration of Houses* posits an unsympathetically conditioned world, "faulty and illogical" in construction, and challenges the reader-designer to "courageously" improve it, ever mindful ("it *must never* be forgotten," Wharton urges her reader) of economic limitations, and the unconscious effects of external influences upon seemingly private schemes of design (DH, 30).

The villains of *The Decoration of Houses* are those designers who place too much faith in the "new." Only "the most inexperienced architect" imagines that he can slough off the "inheritance" of artistic tradition (DH, 13). That architect, in Wharton's view, produces unlivable spaces in the name of artistic autonomy: "That cheap originality which finds expression in putting things to uses for which they were not intended is often confounded with individuality" (DH, 17). What is crucial here is that Wharton does not ascribe a "use" to every "thing," in authoritarian (or Emersonian) fashion. Rather, she prescribes an active engagement between artist and audience, where the "use" of every work of art is determined contextually: "The individual tastes and habits of the people who are to occupy it must be taken into account" (DH, 17). But not be blindly obeyed, she implies. "True originality," Wharton claims, "is never a wilful rejection of . . . accepted . . . forms," but the ability to "express new intellectual conceptions" within their limitations (DH, 9). In other words, art – and the potential for change – exist *within* the restrictions of the larger culture. The "use" of any work of art, therefore, appears to be double-edged: simultaneously cooperating with, and altering from within, the expectations of the larger culture. In this manner, Wharton identifies herself first with the home's resident, who is trapped (or more relevantly, voluntarily chooses to reside) within the confines of the house, but she also identifies herself more strongly with the "designer," an outside agent who is not obligated to live within the house, but prescribes from outside. Most significantly, however, she refuses to identify herself with the architect; whoever built the foundation is neither completely adversary nor ally, but he is distinctly Other.

Angle, Perspective, Illumination

Wharton's home decor aesthetic readily translates into her theories on the short story. For many reasons, the commercial short story is the literary genre Wharton found most appropriate for a discussion of enclosure. Among prose genres, it is most like an enclosed space, most concentrated in form. Among *all* genres, it is most "locked," requiring the synthetic closure of an impact-filled beginning and a dramatic conclusion. As described in Chapter 2, these limitations were not necessarily viewed as the attributes of some timeless, natural (and therefore justifiable) genre; rather, they were seen as the imposition of either editorial demand or audience expectation. The model short story writer of Wharton's era, William Sydney Porter (O. Henry), for instance, honed his much and easily imitated style of rapid openings and surprise endings during a two-year period from 1903–5, in which he published 113 stories in order to satisfy the kind of voluntarily contracted debts and publication obligations that Wharton consciously avoided. In O. Henry's world – the world of slick magazines and Sunday supplements, specifically, but also the world where middle-class aspiration and authorship in the early twentieth century conjoined – the short story writer plied his trade over prearranged spaces, constantly comprising with uncontrollable (if voluntarily imposed) external demands: "Even the character of a story has rights that an author cannot ignore. The hero of a story of New York social life must dine at least once during the action," the protagonist of O. Henry's "A Dinner At ———" warned his acquiescent narrator.[34]

Crucially, the short story was also considered a "woman's genre" by many critics and writers in the early part of this century. For any literary form to be called a "woman's genre" was, of course, an odd claim. As James Hart writes in *The Popular Book*, "women have always been the great readers of fiction," never more so than in the nineteenth and early twentieth century.[35] Nevertheless, during the first period of conscious appreciation of the short story (1885–1901, when Wharton first began writing stories), much cultural work was devoted to associating the formal aspects of the genre with some immutable definition of femininity. Howells, for instance, noting how Best Of- anthologies during the 1890s were populated by a majority of women, conjectured that "this is because the slighter form lends itself more willingly to their touch."[36]

In a different context – the "Editor's Study" column of *Harper's* in 1887, quoted in Chapter 2 – Howells was more explicit: The short story was simply an "inferior form," best suited for "apprenticeship," or for "women who as a rule" lived "restricted lives" that produced a "necessarily narrower outlook on the world."[37] Frank Norris, in "Why Women Should Write the Best Novels: And Why They Don't" (1901), provided a corollary to Howells's observation. For Norris, "writing a novel" was "by far the most arduous and exacting task within the province of literature": although women had sufficient leisure and education to write "the best novels," they "chafe," "fret," "try to do too much," "fatigue," and finally succumb to "complete discouragement and a final abandonment of the enterprise." Men, on the other hand, could "grind on steadily for an almost indefinite period," and were thus best suited temperamentally to the 'task' of producing great books.[38]

If Howells's and Norris's statements provide allusive indications of the cultural process that allowed the work of women to be privileged in the short story because the genre itself was not, they also concretely illustrate the manner in which the short story (despite the efforts of more 'robust' Westerners like Bret Harte) was equated structurally with women's lives.[39] For Norris, the distinction between novels and short stories matched what he perceived to be the difference between the levels of fortitude ingrained separately within men and women. For Howells, novels were best written by individuals who had broad experiences, which could then be transcribed into the narrative sweep, multitude of characters, and range of situations presumably necessary to sustain a longer prose form. The short story, rather, was a small canvas that rewarded a narrow or restricted outlook; the best short story writers were those individuals who were not allowed outside (or chose not to go outside), metaphorically or literally. By these standards, the short story was an indoor genre – and as such, an icon of the domestic realm, like the Magazine within which it generally resided.

In this event, the cultural links between short story writing and home decor are unmistakable. In a significant letter to Robert Grant in 1907, Wharton described the associations she believed to exist between gender, architecture, and narrative:

> The fact is that I am beginning to see exactly where my weakest point is. – I conceive my subjects like a man – that is, rather more architectonically & dramatically than most women – & then execute them like a woman; or rather, I sacrifice, to my desire for construction & breadth, the small incidental effects that women have always excelled in . . . As soon as I look at a subject from the novel-angle I see it in its relation to a larger whole & I can't help trying to take them in, at the cost of the smaller realism that I arrive at, I think, better in my short stories. This is the reason why I have always obscurely felt that I didn't know how to write a novel . . . it is in such sharp contrast to the sense of authority with which I take hold of a short story . . .[40]

Wharton observes several times in *The Decoration of Houses* that architecture was considered to be a significantly more vital art than home decor, a judgment that frequently resulted in the construction of unlivable and ugly homes. The short story was a woman's work, in the same manner that home decor was a woman's work – it was an art that required the individual to be concerned with working within a predetermined (and often unsympathetic) space, with being obsessed with "small realism" (rather than large structural issues), and with being an expert on the aesthetics of enclosure.

Even a casual glance at *The Decoration of Houses* and "Telling a Short Story" illustrates how fluidly Wharton interchanged narrative and decorative metaphors. Wharton's guidelines for the relation between rooms, for instance, describes house structure in a linearly narrative manner: "Every house should be decorated according to a carefully graduated scale of ornamentation culminating in the most important room of the house" (DH, 24). Her discussion of linear narrative, however, uses the kind of spatial metaphors that readers would more likely expect in her works on architecture and decor: "The short story writer must not only know from what angle to present his anecdote if it is to give out all its fires, but must understand just why that particular angle and no other is the right one" (TSS, xxxvi).

These are, of course, highly impressionistic metaphors. But what these examples suggest is that Wharton's use of decorative metaphors in her literary aesthetic (and vice versa) is more than cosmetic — that, rather, her exchange of spatial and linear metaphors signifies an attempt to unearth the short story of 1925 from the most fundamental terms of its already over-codified critical pedagogy. When Poe wrote that a short story should produce a given "effect," in particular, he created a model for economical narrative that was not explicitly linear, but that early twentieth-century critics had defined as such. Because every word in the story must contribute to the overall design, the "effect" must necessarily be presented (or revealed) at the climax of the story, as a culminating moment. Poe's insistence on both unity and economy creates a scenario in which the would-be author is easiest taught to chip away at any little scene, statement, or description that does not prefigure or otherwise explain the ending. The author-student's task in this pedagogical model, essentially, is to draw the straightest possible line, from "the very first sentence" to the climax.[41]

Wharton, too, speaks of economy and effect: Many passages in "Telling a Short Story" illustrate more than anything the pervasiveness of Poe's terminology throughout the early part of this century. When she writes of "the precious instinct of selection" (TSS, xxxviii), for instance, or insists that "every phrase should be a signpost" (TSS, xxxiii), or when she uses the word "economy" seven times in three short paragraphs (TSS, xxxix), Wharton seems to be invoking Poe's consensus without irony. More significantly, however, she also comments on that consensus: She places the phrase "economy of material" in distancing parentheses, and continually reworks the term throughout her essay (TSS, xxxix). "Repetition and insistence," for instance, are "excusable" (TSS, xxxviii). The unalloyed celebration of economy, rather, has caused "critics, in their resentment of the dense and the prolix" (TSS, xxxviii) to "overestimate the tenuous and the tight" (TSS, xxxix); and writers have responded by "leaving out" narrative details that would have "enriched the subject" (TSS, xxxix). For Wharton, economy in the short story is useful only to the extent to which it produces the effect of "illimitable air within a narrow space" — a metaphor that illustrates Wharton's affinity for spatial models for literary conduct, as well as her acceptance of artifice (TSS, xxxix).

One paragraph, in particular, illustrates how effectively Wharton distances herself from Poe's narrative models, and the significance of that act. Any reader of "Telling a Short Story" will be struck by the number of fiduciary metaphors for literary conduct that Wharton uses; when contrasted to Poe's review of Hawthorne, where Poe used models of economic necessity as standards for aesthetic conduct ('not a word to be wasted'), it initially appears that

Wharton has simply adopted (or spontaneously shares) Poe's affection for narrative frugality:

> There is a sense in which the writing of fiction may be compared to the administering of a fortune. Economy and expenditure must each bear a part in it, but they should never degenerate into parsimony or waste. True economy consists in the drawing out of one's subject of every drop of significance it can give, true expenditure in devoting time, meditation and patient labor to the process of extraction and representation (TSS, xxxix).

In fact, Poe's and Wharton's uses of fiduciary models are radically different. Poe seems simply to dislike expense, and preaches frugality.[42] Wharton, rather, treats the transaction between author and story as a two-way exchange – she defines economy as the net sum of narrative decisions that both add and excise text from the story itself. And in this context, it is impossible to miss the similarity between Wharton's fiduciary metaphor for literary conduct and her handling of her own expenses: Just as she refused to spend any more or any less than her income, she refuses to accept the notion that narrative frugality is, in itself, an authorial virtue. Poe defined the individual short story as a utilitarian product; the author was its producer, and his object was to create the product by expending as little of the authorial capital as possible. Wharton treated the individual short story as a space within which a subject resided, and used the exact standards with which she created her personal enclosure as a guide for literary conduct – as though she sympathized with the subject, as well as the writer.

Not unexpectedly, Wharton wavers between these two different visions of the short story throughout her essay, maintaining her divided sympathies throughout. "Every subject must necessarily contain within itself its own dimensions," she writes twice, suggesting an idyllic world where the enclosed subject, "*ab ovo*," organically generates its own natural enclosure, rather than having that enclosure enforced from outside (TSS, xxxvii, xxxiv). This theory neatly conforms to Wharton's own fiduciary behavior, of course; as a subject of history, she created the dimensions of her enclosure. Similarly, it owes much to the aesthetic theory of her close friend Henry James, who in turn owed much to Romantic theories of creative activity. It is, however, only one part of the theory of short story writing contained in Wharton's essay; given the larger context of Wharton's artistic philosophy, "Every subject must necessarily contain within itself its own dimensions" is almost exactly the kind of idealistic rumination that Wharton usually derided. The *ab ovo*

theory of artistic production implies that no extrinsic forces interfere with the artist's labors. Wharton's affinity for artifice stemmed
from the fact that she preferred to accept the idea that art is produced when the artist recognizes and identifies the flaws and
strengths of the literary tradition that he or she has inherited, and
expresses a personal vision in interaction with those parameters. In
this context, "Every subject must necessarily contain within itself its
own dimensions" appears to be (whether or not it was intended as
such) a narrative trick of the very kind that Wharton prescribes in
other locations in her essay – a theory of literary production that
convincingly creates the illusion that the author works within an
illimitable space when in fact she does not.

For the most part, however, "Telling a Short Story" dwells on
artifice. Describing the process of composition, Wharton turns to
metaphors from the visual arts, all of which suggest aesthetic
choices dictated by the compromises of a predetermined enclosed
space. The writer concerned with "optics of the printed page" must
consider the "angle" of presentation, "perspective," and "illumina-
tion" (TSS, xxxvi–ii, xl). The subject may contain within itself its
own dimensions, but the writer does not appear to choose the
subject; and tellingly, Wharton offers no advice on that matter. The
writer, rather, is a passive "mirror," who controls only the angle of
its reflection, but not the subject, nor the distortion of the reflected
subject (TSS, xl).

In a Romantic aesthetic, this last metaphor could be read as a
paradigm of the artist's enrapture by higher spiritual forces, but
read against Wharton's personal history, it is also a striking metaphor for the artist delimited by external forces. Any perspective on
Edith Wharton's aesthetic of fiction must account for both of these
possibilities – as well as account for the variety of sympathies present in her essay, and how they appear to parallel her own multi-
roled method of literary production. If the *ab ovo* theory of literary
production has real significance within Wharton's writing, in particular, it is because it implies that the individual author can somehow internalize outside forces and make them part of an otherwise
spontaneous creative process: The author can save outside forces
the trouble of intruding within her writing by embodying those
forces herself.

This is, to some extent, exactly what Wharton did. What is noteworthy about her method of production, for instance, is the degree
to which she took upon herself the roles of designer, agent, and
especially editor. In turn, this reflected her uneasy but powerful
relationship with the idea of tradition itself: Wharton spoke so
frequently of creating the illusion of freedom in limited spaces (i.e.,

"It was by such means that the villa-architects obtained, with simple
materials and in a limited space, impressions of distance, and sensa-
tions of the unexpected")[43] that it is difficult to tell whether she
had simply given up on attaining personal freedom, or believed (as
a social historian) that 'personal freedom' was neither definable nor
practicable.

Her solution was to mediate between these options, and to make
a poetics of mediation. An early short story, "The Muse's Tragedy,"
illustrates how complex the play of subversive and authoritarian
roles becomes in Wharton's poetics. In "Telling a Short Story,"
Wharton insists upon the classical unities, in particular, unity of
voice. In her early stories, however (written well before "Telling a
Short Story"), she rarely obeys this dictum. These stories are full of
switches in voice from third to first person, or from one first person to another. A story begins in one voice, but is focused upon
another, presumably unvoiced, character; a formal switch occurs
when that unvoiced character speaks up, wrenching the story out
of its traditional form and destroying the unified authority of the
original voice.

"The Muse's Tragedy" is told in third person omniscient, focused
within the mind of a young man pursuing a woman thought to
have been the mysterious muse of a great poet. At a point where
the successful consummation of the courtship seems assured, the
narrative is abruptly broken off and resumes in the form of a letter
from the woman to the man, ending their romance and lamenting
that she has been cast as a muse. She was not a muse, she explains,
but an intellectual companion, whose love for the poet was frustrated by his infantilization of women, and specifically his affection
for another woman whose "mind was . . . 'all elbows.'"[44]

The effect of this formal shift has more than formal implications. The female muse speaks, breaking off both narrative and
closure-providing courtship, to inform both reader and protagonist that her miscasting has had tragic consequences – her entrapment in a role as a silent, spoken-for resource, and the consequent
frustration of healthy relations between men and women. Although the story is alert to the artistic stereotyping of women, it is
also sensitive to the economic implications that underpin those
stereotypes. The entity that is supposed to provide unvoiced inspiration for the artist develops its own voice, and ceases to speak
through an intermediary. The story, aptly, shifts from third to first
person at that moment, diminishing the illusionary existence of any
mediator between muse and reader. If the artist is somehow entrepreneurial, using the natural resources of life to produce a commodity for market, in this story the manipulated resource recovers

its own voice, and exposes the gap between 'authorized' and 'un-authorized' versions of the same tale. In doing so, of course, the muse becomes authorized; ironically, it is the poet character in "The Muse's Tragedy" who becomes the unvoiced resource that provides inspiration. The story seems wholly subversive, paradigmatic of Wharton's own insistently independent and economically astute literary conduct: The traded commodity claims voice and turns trader in the narrative marketplace.

And still, Wharton herself was unsure what to make of such narrative and social strategies. In the letter in which she refers to herself as the "compleat housekeeper" (written shortly after "The Muse's Tragedy"), she notes that the "housekeeper" is only one of her "two souls," the temporarily ascendant one.[45] It is that second soul, unnamed and unvoiced, who appears to reject the thoroughness and ease of the housekeeper's regimen, and seeks alternate, less disciplined responses to imprisoning conditions. "As to the old stories of which you speak so kindly," the housekeeper writes to her editor in 1898,

> I regard them as the excesses of youth. They were all written at the top of my voice, and "The Fullness of Life" is one long shriek. I may not write any better, but at least I hope that I write in a lower key, and I fear that the voice of those early tales will drown all the others; it is for that reason that I prefer not to publish them.[46]

Eighteen ninety-eight was early in Wharton's career; many of her letters during this time reflect an insecurity about her abilities as a writer that eventually disappeared within a decade. And still, this letter reflects many of the tensions that were present throughout her writing career. Wharton's self-censorship does not appear to be based on explicit standards of literary quality; she admits openly that she "might not write any better." Rather, she appears to be suppressing an internal voice she fears might speak too uncontrollably, and subvert more conservative efforts. The relationship between herself and her editor also seems paradigmatic; the editor, representative of the external forces that would in theory restrict her literary endeavors, appears less concerned with suppression than does Wharton herself.

Only the stories got published: Identifying with both the muse and the poet, she blessed each with her sympathy. And ultimately, she incorporated both into her poetics. A late story, "Roman Fever," illustrates how she finally resolved her divided sympathies into a working literary aesthetic. Written shortly before Wharton's death in 1937, "Roman Fever" describes a late afternoon conversation between "two American ladies of ripe but well-cared-for middle age"[47] at a Rome restaurant. For the most part, the story is about the misinterpretation and reinterpretation of the past. The Roman landscape upon which the two characters gaze between dialogue is described by Wharton as a "vast Memento Mori,"[48] a landscape of ruins built upon ruins that both reflects and affirms Mrs. Ansley's and Mrs. Slade's increasing apprehension that their own lives have been constructed upon layers of buried misunderstandings: "'I've come to the conclusion that I don't in the least know what they are,'" Mrs. Ansley says of their two daughters, "'and perhaps we didn't know much more about each other.'"[49]

Despite this somewhat caustic theme, however, there is no "shriek" in "Roman Fever." Rather, "Roman Fever" is striking precisely because, unlike "The Muse's Tragedy," multivocality provides the story with what Wharton herself describes as "a sort of diffused serenity."[50] Like many of Wharton's later stories, "Roman Fever" contains point-of-view switches, but not voice switches: The story is told in third person limited, switching from the perspective of one woman to the other, revealing the process by which each woman 'muses' the other: "So these two ladies visualized each other, each through the wrong end of her little telescope."[51]

In part, these switches both mute and codify Wharton's early formal tendency toward multivocality ("American and English reviewers of fiction are so disinclined to recognize that novels may be written from a dozen different standpoints," she wrote disgustedly to Sara Norton in 1906).[52] The codification of point-of-view switches that took place over her career suggests a codification of the division of sympathy, and of mediation. More important, it also suggests a powerful illustration of Wharton's idea that the subject must be seen from many angles to be understood. The angle, in this case, is the perspective of an individual character upon the subject itself, which is invariably some shared social condition: "'I was just thinking,'" one character says to the other during a quiet moment, "'what different things Rome stands for to each generation.'"[53] Separately, neither character's perspective can adequately tell the tale: During one passage in the middle of the story, in fact, the "two ladies" reflect *simultaneously* on "how little they knew each other."[54] And yet, when the two perspectives mesh, the story coheres: The two women share small confidences that, when joined together, accidentally reveal that they also share complicity in an earlier sexual scandal, and even share family trees. In this manner, Wharton resolves her earlier irresolution toward the division between muse and poet by creating a formal pattern within "Roman Fever" in which multivocality is a necessary component of narrative resolution, rather than an expression of authorial ambivalence.

Each character in "Roman Fever" conceals a secret, muselike, and each character tells a story inspired by the other. Wharton barely even seems to intercede.

Social Manifestations

For Edith Wharton the short story was the equivalent of a room designed by an architect who did not particularly care how attractive the room would be to its occupants. The short story writer's task was to adopt the role of decorator; given a set of abstract formal and cultural rules for what makes a salable short story (the literary equivalent of the abstract rules that the architect used to construct the outlines of the room), the writer's goal was to fill the story-room with decoration and furniture, hiding its deficiencies, emphasizing its strengths. This formulation, in turn, implied an utter identification between the author and the subject ("Nothing but deep familiarity with his subject will protect the short-story writer" [TSS, xxxviii]); Wharton applied a personal standard to the writing of fiction that entailed identifying herself with the subject-character who was written about, the decorator-writer who mediated between the Architect's rules and the pursuit of personal satisfaction, but not the Architect – or, at best, an idealized but embattled Architect represented by a submerged classical tradition.

If nothing else, Wharton's reconstruction of the phrase "economy of materials," and the concept of economy in general, brilliantly exemplify exactly what she means by restoring an old room (in this case, Poe's review) rather than destroying it. The difference between Wharton's approach to the short story and Poe's is that Poe believed he could clear the ground, and Wharton believed that the house was already built. Institutionally speaking, this is the exact equivalent of the difference between Poe's belief that he could found his own magazine, and Wharton's acceptance of the idea that she had to deal with the magazines, and the editors, and the audiences, that were already in existence.[55] In contemporary discussions of the short story, of course, Wharton's vision – if not her name – has considerably more popularity. Her use of multivocality, however muted, predated the current era where multivocality is virtually institutional; her construction of authorship as a mediating craft is unquestionably more attuned to contemporary critical trends than Poe's; her de-emphasis of the idea that the development of the protagonist is all that matters in any prose form is central to virtually any contemporary attempt to remove the short story from the shadow of the novel. It is also central to contemporary discussions of the purpose of short storytelling in general. As Frank O'Connor wrote of "The Overcoat," the short story was more fit for the modern era than the novel because it dealt with human types, not individuals – it acknowledged dehumanization, and used pathos to force people to recognize and empathize with their 'type.'[56]

In fact, Wharton's gestures of comparing the short story to architecture and to drama, and her concomitant emphasis on situation, subject, and enclosure, have become (with or without her direct influence) among the most popular strategies for modern critics attempting to bring prestige to the contemporary short story. As Thomas Gullason writes in "The Short Story: An Underrated Art," the mainstream aesthetic of American fiction exalts the ability of narrative to represent a series of changes, character development, or complex movements; by these standards, the novel is the narrative form, because it can more plausibly reproduce a larger amount of activity than a shorter fiction.[57] The classic gesture of short story defense has been to respond to this aesthetic, to unearth somehow the genre from an American affinity for bulk and breadth and scope – and the concomitant impression of authorial (and individual) freedom created by those standards.

Poe's review of Hawthorne became the anthem of the counter-aesthetic of American fiction: If personal freedom was the implicit virtue of the novel as a narrative form, then the explicit virtue of the short story was the repudiation of waste. Wharton, not unexpectedly, developed a theory of the short story that mediated between these two standards: Her emphasis on waste does not so much supplant personal freedom as a literary value, as respond to it, seeking a balance that is neither wasteful nor overly restrictive. More significantly, her use of spatial metaphors attempted to unearth the short story from the model of linear narrative, and from the idea that the genre should, like the novel, be expected to focus on character explication. No compliment pleased Wharton more than when a critic or reader told her that she had succeeded in writing a good narrative with sketchy characters:

> I am particularly and inordinately pleased with what you say of my having – to your mind – been able to maintain my reader's interest in a group of persons so intrinsically uninteresting, except as a social manifestation . . .[58]

Working in a genre in which depersonalization was virtually inevitable (or the writer's greatest hurdle), Edith Wharton's pessimism toward the idea of individuality would prove to be a tremendous source of insight.

It need only be added that Wharton would dislike enormously these attempts to place her at the cutting edge. And when reading "Telling a Short Story," it is still difficult to tell whether she believed that enclosure was superior to open freedom because it was a more realistic statement of cultural realities, or whether she had surrendered early. And "Telling a Short Story," despite its spatial metaphors, is also laden with linear models for narrative, and with similarly conservative utterances. It is as though Wharton, even within a mythical cultural marketplace of her own construction, couldn't resist the mediate, multivocal position: a position that almost inevitably left her glancing backward while moving forward, safely away from the Cutting Edge as she knew it – perhaps the only short story writer of the early century who could please both Sinclair Lewis and *Scribner's,* and who could successfully raise the ante on Poe's (also mediating) vision of popularity for the American auteur.[59]

4

HANDBOOKS AND WORKSHOPS

A BRIEF HISTORY OF THE CREATIVE
WRITING 'REVOLUTION'

When some man of a different race than ours, living in a more congenial civilization, whose training from his youth up has been adopted to a future artistic profession, succeeds in painting the great picture, composing the great prelude, writing the great novel, don't say he was born a "genius," but rather admit that he was made "to order" by a system whose promoters knew how to wait.

Frank Norris, "Novelists to Order – While You Wait," syndicated 23 Feb. 1903, reprinted in Pizer, ed., *Literary Criticism* (1964) 17.

For the serious writers of the early twentieth century, the how-to-write-a-short-story handbook constituted a literary movement of enormous and ominous potential. Sherwood Anderson complained of the "tremendous standardization of life" exemplified in the handbook literature, and offered the "Modern Movement" as "an effort to re-open the channels of individual expression." James T. Farrell wrote of a "cabalistic lore" that "explicitly affirms and enforces an acceptance of the aims and ideals that are part of the ideological structure of capitalism." Cleanth Brooks and Robert Penn Warren devoted their *Understanding Fiction* (1943) to the premise that "if one learns anything about fiction . . . it is that there is no single, special technique or formula for writing good fiction." Edward J. O'Brien, first editor of the *Best American Short Stories,* stated that "you cannot turn out short stories by mass production like Ford cars." And Douglas Bement, a handbook author himself, wrote in 1931 of "the twentieth-century writing hysteria," a phenomenon he believed would attract the attention of "scholars of the twenty-first century."[1]

If the scholars of the late twentieth century have not remembered Bement's "writing hysteria," the reasons are readily evident. As the above quotes suggest, the handbook literature attracted the displeasure of authors and critics devoted to Modernism, Marxism, New Criticism, and the academic preservation of the short story – a fair if incomplete compendium of early twentieth-century literary movements that have endured in the second half of the century. In comparison to the writings of these authors, the short story handbooks appear dry, naive, and almost unreadable. Most significantly, however, Bement's "writing hysteria" has not been remembered because what looked like an aberration in 1931 has become the status quo sixty years later. As Roger Angell has observed recently, "if you open the windows, you can hear the sound of typewriters driven by people writing stories all over the country"; if the handbooks themselves have been forgotten, the "downpour of literary republicanism" (to borrow Joe David Bellamy's phrase) that they in part catalyzed has become a hard fact of the genre.[2]

In this context, the short story handbook tradition seems worthy of reevaluation, both as a cultural phenomenon and as a significant chapter in the history of American fiction. Created by a community of freelance writers, magazine editors, and scholars (many of whom considered themselves peripheral and oppressed representatives of academia), circulated within a polymorphous network of magazine advertisements, correspondence schools, and prestigious universities, and designed to appeal to a broad section of the American public, the short story handbooks were perhaps the only commercially motivated, populistically modeled critical movement in the history of American letters. Within the history of the short story, the handbooks possess seminal significance. If the critics and scholars of the late nineteenth century labored to construct the "short story" as a genre, the handbook writers of the early twentieth century worked with doubled ardor to lay down the rules for what constituted a short story, and what did not. They were, in the most liberal terms possible, building a consensus: on the short story, and on what constituted the rules for a national form of literary expression.

And on the teaching of creative writing. Despite the haphazard, correspondence-school quality of many of their efforts, the handbook writers were members of the first generation of scholars to embrace creative writing as an academic discipline. If the analytical fervor with which they approached the discipline seems quaint to modern observers, it is worth noting that many of the basic elements of that approach have been adopted by later generations of creative writing teachers and students. During our own era, in which the creative writing graduate program is enjoying unprecedented growth and "short-story publication appears to have become one of the missions of American higher education,"[3] the short story handbooks provide a vital link in understanding how the symbiotic relationship between academia and the short story evolved, and how the pedagogy of the short story became intertwined with the practice.

THE AUTHORS' HAND-BOOK SERIES

THE PLOT OF THE SHORT STORY

AN EXHAUSTIVE STUDY, BOTH SYNTHETICAL AND
ANALYTICAL, WITH COPIOUS EXAMPLES,
MAKING THE WORK

A PRACTICAL TREATISE

BY

HENRY ALBERT PHILLIPS

FORMERLY ASSOCIATE EDITOR OF THE METROPOLITAN MAGAZINE

INTRODUCTION BY
MATTHEW WHITE, Jr.
EDITOR OF THE ARGOSY

THE STANHOPE-DODGE PUBLISHING COMPANY
LARCHMONT, NEW YORK

Title page from H. A. Phillips, *Plot of the Short Story* (Larchmont, NY: Stanhope-Dodge, 1912).

The Secrets of Successful Writers

The history of the short story handbook may be divided into several phases, and several subgenres. The first phase began in the 1890s and continued until approximately 1920: During this period, short story pedagogy evolved from fragmentary essays in periodicals into bound volumes, multiple editions, and ever-increasing levels of analytical and definitional density. In the second phase, which continued until the beginning of World War II, a critical and institutional counterresponse occurred. Modernist, regionalist, and Marxist critics all constructed biting responses to the handbook's staunchly formalist and nationalist vision. Authors such as

Cleanth Brooks and Robert Penn Warren composed the short story anthologies that would be associated with the New Critical movement, and that would allow collegiate instructors to dissociate themselves – and the short story – from the overwrought and commercial aura of the early strivings of the creative writing profession.[4] Concomitant with these developments, the creative writing program became nationally accepted as an alternative to the generally perceived seediness of the handbook-driven network: The first program was founded at the University of Iowa (Edward J. O'Brien called Iowa City "the Athens Of America" in 1936) in steps between 1922 and 1939.[5]

During the postwar period, the handbook tradition frayed somewhat. The handbook itself faded from vogue in the 1950s, as the commercial opportunities for short story writers also faded. Although a trickle of new handbooks continued to appear (i.e., Writer's Digest's *Handbook of Short Story Writing* [1970], Rust Hills's *Writing in General and the Short Story in Particular* [1977], Hallie Burnett's *On Writing the Short Story* [1983]),[6] the market for how-to-do-it short story books had all but disappeared by 1960, limited primarily to a few reissues of popular late forties and early fifties editions. In these handbooks, the analytical tone and ideological ambition that had marked the earlier tradition was replaced by an almost fearful conservatism ("Don't Stray from the Norm," one 1953 handbook warns its reader).[7] While the early handbook authors believed that an Ideal Short Story existed, these later authors responded to the constraints of a debilitated short story market that was split between literary and pulp magazines, and academic and commercial formulas; they simply told their readers how to write marketable stuff, and abandoned (or were deprived of) the naive grandeur of their predecessor's ambitions. Those ambitions, rather, were inherited during the postwar period by the work of the New Critics, who (like Poe) recognized that the short story made both a powerful illustration of and justification for literary theories emphasizing close reading, intensity, authorial control, and unity.

The short story handbooks of the late nineteenth and early twentieth centuries were mongrel textbooks, born of numerous influences. It is tempting, first of all, to seek an academic tradition of rhetoric and composition within which to situate these books. If anything, however, the lack of a consensus on these subjects was a major issue for late nineteenth-century humanities professors. As Laurence Veysey has observed in "The Plural Organized Worlds Of The Humanities," the late nineteenth century was a flux period for the standard college curriculum marked by the spread of the elective system, the professionalization of scholarship, and the rapid growth of new disciplines. Within the humanities department, these changes were enacted in a debate between old-line defenders of "culture" and the Greek Classics, and a cache of younger professors who thought of the English literary tradition – what we now know as the "canon" of Shakespeare, Chaucer, et al. – as "a giant only lately liberated from chains."[8] No event codified this split more completely than the formation of the Modern Language Association in 1884 as a professional organization within academia that forcefully advocated the study of English and other modern languages. The earliest volumes of the *Publication of the MLA* (*PMLA*) devoted a significant number of pages to essays and round-table discussions decrying the lack of secondary and collegiate courses and textbooks on English subjects, while professors nationwide sought respect for the English and American literary traditions. James Garnett of the University of Virginia wrote in the second *PMLA* that "every college teacher has been struck, I doubt not, with the lack of preparation in English on the part of his students," and asked for "'a fair field and no favor'" from fellow academics and college administrators.[9] T. W. Hunt of Princeton spoke of the "persistent opposition of those from whom better things were expected," and wrote anthemically of "the rightful place of English (in the Curriculum.)"[10]

Although these scholars foremost desired greater respect for the study of modern literature, they also insisted that primary schools place greater emphasis on the basics of grammar, so that composition instructors on the college level could introduce more sophisticated issues of style into their curriculum. Charles Thwing, for instance, produced an oft-quoted study of twenty American colleges that tabulated that university students received ten hours of study in foreign tongues for every one in English. John McElroy and A. S. Hill argued at the first MLA convention that Ivy League schools were "graduating every year men of high scholarship in other things, yet 'whose manuscripts would disgrace a boy of twelve.'" Although McElroy observed in 1884 that "textbooks have been multiplied . . . in the last dozen or twenty years," scholars clearly remained dissatisfied with the quality of those books that were available: "There is a tendency to abandon the study of the development of our style, possibly from lack of text-books," T. Whiting Bancroft noted at the MLA proceedings in 1886, "we hope books on the subject will be furnished."[11]

These professional developments in academia possessed profound significance for the evolution of the short story, both during this period and the period that followed. As discussed in Chapter 2, the growth of the American magazine establishment, spurred by nationalist adjustments in the international copyright agreements during the last two decades of the nineteenth century, created a domestic situation in which commercial magazine fiction became enormously profitable, and was more-or-less "rehabilitated" by American scholars as a genre of high literature labeled the "short story." If these economic and ideological developments explain much of the reason why the short story was embraced with such definitional and nationalist fervor, then it is equally significant that the modern English department as an institution was also forming during this period.

At the very least, there are suggestive links between the development of the English department, and the genrefication of the short story. In a sense, the two endeavors shared a similar *parvenu* aura, a yearning for a "rightful place," and an anxiety about establishing tradition. It is difficult to imagine Brander Matthews creating his post facto tradition of American short story writing in "The Philosophy of the Short Story,"[12] for instance, without being immersed in an academic climate equally eager to establish pedagogical and historical guidelines. In particular, however, it is most significant that the teaching of writing *as a discipline* was being organized during this period. In competition with the classics and the sciences for professional respectability, late nineteenth-century scholars devoted themselves to two strategies. The first was to establish that the American and English canon was as literarily valuable as the classical canon. As Veysey has written, however, the new breed of literary scholars of the late nineteenth century was distinguished from the old breed by its willingness to adopt scientific paradigms for literary activity.[13] Accordingly, that new breed was adamant in its belief that the technical aspects of English composition could be taught with the same rigor and discipline as chemistry or mathematics: "The teaching of language," Garnett insisted, "is as strictly *scientific* as that of any one of the natural sciences."[14]

In pursuing this second strategy, late nineteenth-century scholars encouraged the scientific, or pseudo-scientific, explication of writing as a preferred method of gaining respectability for the English department with the academic marketplace. Frank Norris, surveying "The 'English Courses' of the University of California" in 1896, was dismayed to find that each Berkeley student was

> set to work counting the "metaphors" in a given passage. This is actually true – tabulating them, separating them from the "similes," comparing the results. He is told to study sentence structure. He classifies certain types of sentences in DeQuincey and compares them with certain other types of sentences in Carlyle.

The popularity of Freytag's famous triangle similarly illustrated the readiness with which teachers and students alike were willing to accept mathematic descriptions of the forms of narrative.[15] Thus, the definitional energy of literary scholars anxious to quantify the act of composition was introduced into domestic culture at almost the same time as when short story writing suddenly became a profitable enterprise, and a source of national pride. It is likely that the short story handbooks would have been produced with or without the existence of these professional developments; it is similarly likely that the evolution of a consensus on the teaching of writing would have occurred without the historical developments that catalyzed the "creation" of the short story. The growth of interest in English as a discipline, however, clearly established an academic mandate for writing textbooks that, when combined with the commercial demand for short stories, made the explosion of interest in short story handbooks a virtual inevitability – and also made inevitable the anxious scientific tone of those endeavors.

Beyond academia, however, another mandate was forming. As Edward Shils has noted, the almost exponential growth of scholarly disciplines and specialties during the turn-of-the-century period was driven by a diffusely American belief that "systematically acquired knowledge was . . . a step toward redemption" that offered "the prospect of the transfiguration of life by improving man's control over the resources of nature." In fact, recent historians and critics of the 1880–1920 period have created a vivid portrait of a culture both divided and empowered by a romance with its dominant technology – what Cecelia Tichi calls the "gear-and-girder" world. David Noble, for instance, identifies the late nineteenth century as the period in which "modern science-based industry" first developed, and "industrial enterprise in which ongoing scientific investigation and the systematic application of scientific knowledge to the process of commodity production" became standard corporate practices. Peter Conn describes as paradigmatic Frank Lloyd Wright's attempts to "dissolve . . . the tension between art and machinery," and to create an architectural philosophy that would illustrate his stated belief that "we may find (machines) to be the regenerator of the creative conscience in our America." Most recently, Tichi in *Shifting Gears: Technology, Literature, Culture in Modernist America* used sources ranging from magazine advertisements to major Modernist figures to illustrate how machine aesthetics – in particular, the emphasis on "maximal efficiency and minimal waste" – first became pervasive American values during the early part of the twentieth century.[16]

In one sense, the handbook writers were simply part of what

Shils calls the "national mission" of American education during the turn-of-the-century period;[17] but they were also engaged in designing a national art form during a period in which individuals throughout the range of American life were evaluating the regenerative possibilities of the "mechanization" of human nature. More specifically, they were also engaged in designing a national art form during a period in which artists, writers, and architects throughout the country were considering, or condemning, the transformative power of the machine in the fine arts. The short story handbook – the short story itself, in fact – was an icon of the same period that produced the first IQ tests, the Efficiency Movement, the engineer as silent movie hero, and the assembly line.[18] If skeptics doubted the ability of the handbook to transform (through scientific principles) its reader into a professional writer, proponents needed only to point to the latest issue of *Scribner's* or *Harper's,* where invariably some ex-handbook-student's well-honed story threaded its way among advertisements attesting to the transfiguring power of the washing machine, the automobile, and the college education.

As Bliss Perry observed in his *Study of Prose Fiction* (1902), American magazines throughout the last two decades of the nineteenth century had been providing would-be short story writers with a considerable body of free advice on how to compose in the form. In the *North American Review* in 1894, for instance, George Cable anticipated one hundred years of creative writing workshops by telling his readers that "short stories were a good stepping stone" to writing longer and better fiction. Frederick Bird, who understood Poe more directly than most of his contemporaries, advised in *Lippincott's* in the same year that magazine fiction had its "own clientele, its own rules, its own tone and tradition," and "character." F. Hopkinson Smith observed in an interview in the *Boston Herald* that the short story should have a "bit of life, an incident such as you would find in a brief newspaper paragraph."[19] Similar advice could be found in *Bookman, Scribner's, Cornhill Magazine,* the *Atlantic,* many newspapers, and virtually every magazine that published either fiction or criticism.[20]

For the most part, these articles constituted the working body of knowledge and advice to which handbook writers turned: C. R. Barrett noted in *Short Story Writing* (1898) that "I am considerably indebted" to "the frequent fragmentary articles on the short story, many of them by successful short story writers, published in current periodicals."[21] Concomitant with the publication of these fragmentary articles, short story courses began appearing on college curricula. One source claims that the first course in short story writing ("The Art of the Story") was offered at the University of Chicago in 1896 by E. H. Lewis; Bliss Perry, according to his own statement, was teaching a course in fiction writing at Princeton at the same time.[22] Similarly, Sam Sloan at the University of Iowa offered "The Short Story" in the course catalog for 1900: one semester of "studies in descriptive and narrative prose," emphasizing "Poe, Hawthorne, and Their Successors," and one semester of "Practice in descriptive and narrative writing, the short story being the form selected."[23]

The introduction of these courses into the English curriculums of American colleges was only a small portion of the development of short story pedagogy, however. One of the most fascinating aspects of the early development of the creative writing system is the extent to which the demand for short stories spawned a pseudo-collegiate network of extension and correspondence courses, which supplemented and even overwhelmed the efforts of more "serious" scholars to bring respectability to the new discipline. Precisely because of the commercial success of the short story during this period, and the apparent ease with which a short story could be written, the appeal of a course in short story writing reached far beyond that small subset of American culture then attending college, or having access to higher education. Thus, while Perry and Matthews taught at Ivy League colleges, Blanche Colton Williams, author of the best-selling *Handbook on Short Story Writing* (1917), labored at extension and summer courses at New York City area colleges, and Maren Elwood claimed that she taught 1,500 students yearly at the Extension Division of the University of California.[24] Similarly, many more authors were simply nonacademic freelance writers (i.e., H. Bedford-Jones, William Byron Mowery, Richard Summers), who recognized the economic potential in sharing (or appearing to share) their trade secrets, and offered those secrets part-time in classrooms as well as in textbooks of their own design.[25] One handbook author even noted – with mixed pride – that several of his students had produced "How to Write" books before they had published fiction.[26]

Further, although every major publishing house issued at least one short story handbook (and often more: MacMillan, Dodd, Mead, Heath, Reeves et al. all offered at least two handbooks or associated texts in their catalogues during the 1910s and 1920s), the largest handbook publisher was the Home Correspondence School, which offered at least nine different books on short story writing between 1912 and 1918.[27] Frequently, individual authors organized their own correspondence schools: In the early thirties Laurence D'Orsay advertised his Professional Collaboration Ser-

vice, in which he promised to cowrite a professional-level story for a
fee.[28] The same periodicals that published editorials and advice for
short story writers also printed advertisements for these correspondence schools, which promised to sell "the secrets of successful
writers" at affordable prices.[29] These correspondence schools pro-
liferated throughout the early part of this century and quickly
developed a shadowy reputation among literary critics – Kobold
Knight wrote in 1940 that correspondence schools were being routinely organized by "illiterate railway clerks, hospital-inmates . . .
in fact, by anyone who could scrape together the money for advertisement."[30]

For these reasons, it is difficult to estimate exactly how many
handbooks were published, or how well they sold. Nevertheless, J.
Berg Esenwein in *Writing the Short Story* was able to collect a (recom-
mended only) list of over seventy titles published between 1898 and
1928 that dealt exclusively or primarily with short story composition; when supplemented by a routine computer search to gather
texts from 1928 until World War II, this catalogue swells to over
one hundred.[31] Similarly, the more successful books typically went
through multiple editions, often in the same year – a publishing
benchmark for a best-seller. Esenwein's book (one of at least three
handbooks he wrote) went through sixteen editions in fifteen
years, between 1908 and 1923; Pitkin's *Art and Business of Story
Writing* was issued in ten different editions between 1912 and 1923;
Williams's *Handbook* required steady reissues from 1917 until 1944.
As Eugene Current-Garcia has written, the short story handbook
of the early twentieth century, in terms of popularity, seemed to be
outstripping the short story itself.[32]

In fact, the handbook and the story were working in cultural
concert. Although the American magazine has lost some of its prestige since the advent of radio, motion pictures, and television, it
had until 1920 owned a virtual monopoly on the American mass
marketplace, and until the postwar era had continued to exert
enormous economic and cultural power. Magazines were to 1920
audiences what television is to contemporary audiences: "the best
media in the world for selling tooth-brushes, automobiles, and
canned soup," in Bement's words. In attempting to explain the
appeal of the handbooks, it is only a partial response (though a
necessary one) to say that the short story was offering substantial
financial rewards to those individuals who could reach publication
in the more popular magazines. In addition, short story writing
itself simply possessed enormous cultural cachet. Stewart Beach
wrote in *Short Story Technique* (1929) that short story writing was "a
thrilling profession, sometimes an adventurous profession . . ."

Jean Wick told her students that "success in short story writing means both fame and pecuniary reward." The profession appealed to the would-be writer or student of 1920 in the way that popular musicianship (or, more cogently, movie direction), and not authorship, would appeal to the contemporary student. The short story writer of the early twentieth century was a muted version of the present-day pop star, producing with seemingly little effort 2,000-word masterpieces that reached the largest possible audiences, who then blessed the writer with celebrity, four-figure fees, and leisure time.[33]

In exchange for the right to sell such a large dream, however, the handbook writer also had to embrace the kind of mass consensus that makes pop dreams possible. Until 1930 (and to an extent afterward), the handbooks presented a broad and remarkably homogeneous vision of the short story. Unafraid of diminishing the cultural power of authorship (or confident of the depth of the dream's seduction), the handbook authors outlined formal guidelines, preferred definitions, described what values the individual short story should and should not propound, and discussed magazine policy (at length), mass psychology, American politics, advertising, and typesetting. In an effort to identify every variable that would make a story publishable and then popular, they created an idealized image of The American Short Story, the American Author and, by implication, America itself. At their most earnest, the books were almost social histories of the fiction market, eager attempts to identify some mythical American consensus. At their most opportunistic, they were exquisite examples of the packaging of that consensus. Most often, they were both the victims and the proponents of what N. Bryllion Fagin described in 1923 as "a peculiar psychology" composed partly of the "cheapest form of advertising" and partly of "erudite and conscientious" scholarship.[34]

Breaking into Fiction

The short story handbook could justifiably be described as a literary form, where the author was expected to employ or respond to certain rhetorical and structural strategies. Most followed the example of Aristotle's *Poetics*, and contained a brief introductory section describing the history of the genre, followed by a larger body where the act of writing was divided into elements – plot, character, style, diction, and titles, endings, et al.[35] These books either invoked an academic pose (Esenwein's *Writing the Short-Story* [1908]) or were designed to appeal to businesspeople, advertising personnel, and psychologists (Pitkin's *The Art and the Business of*

Story Writing [1912]). Many handbook authors sought a casual tone that was intended to debunk the academic tenor of most efforts: "Somebody," David J. Gammon told the reader of his *Breaking into Fiction* (1940), "has been throwing a few good curves." Other books were pseudo-anthologies that offered a number of representative short stories followed (or preceded) by text that explained what made the stories publishable (Wick's *The Stories Editors Buy and Why* [1921], D'Orsay's *Stories You Can Sell* [1933]). After 1920, there was also a considerable market for "counter-handbooks," self-abnegating writing textbooks that attacked the idea that writing could be taught (Bement's *Weaving the Short Story* [1931]). Lastly, authors such as Wilbur Schramm (*The Short Story Workshop* [1938]) and Brooks and Warren (the famous *Understanding Fiction* [1943]) composed anthology-textbooks that are generally classified within the New Critical movement, but with their emphasis on unity, suggestion, 'elements,' and the after-the-fact analysis of the author's creative processes that Farrell called an "*a priori* proposition in problem solving," simply bear too many resemblances to the handbook tradition to be labeled a truly autonomous departure from that tradition.[36]

The classic handbook usually began with a preface that established the writer's credibility as an expert on fiction, and established the authority of the idea of a creative writing course. Gammon wrote that "this author believes that almost any person of average intelligence may be taught to write fiction good enough to sell." Blanche Colton Williams claimed that "I not only believe that one can 'learn to write'; I know, because more than once I have watched growth and tended effort from failure to success." In a gesture that prefaces many handbooks, Williams then recites a list of her students' appearances in major magazines:

> Harriet Welles is an example of this sort. Her stories have been running in *Scribner's* for some months . . . I refer, for illustration, to another student, Elizabeth Stead Taber . . . Marjorie Lewis Prentiss comes to mind. . . . I need not refer to Frederick S. Greene – now in France . . .

Pitkin writes similarly that his students "are writing for practically every magazine of consequence in the United States, Canada, and England." Elwood's biography notes that of her 1,500 yearly students, "many have achieved success with leading publishing houses and magazines."[37]

This belief was soundly attacked in the subgenre of the counter-handbooks. Fagin apologized for his participation in the creative writing system by observing that

The share of injury I may have contributed has simply been the unavoidable accompaniment of being engaged in a profession grounded upon the popular belief that literature is a trade, like plumbing, or tailoring . . . That it is in the interests of the profession to foster and perpetuate this popular belief needs no elaborate substantiation . . .[38]

In the introduction to Bement's *Weaving the Short Story*, Edward J. O'Brien congratulated the author for a similar act of professional and ideological self-abnegation: "He violates the most important rule of their (the teachers') trade union. He makes it abundantly plain at once to every honest student that short story writers are born, not made. He sends three-fourths of his class home."[39]

In general, however, the counterhandbooks occupied a curious position in short story pedagogy. They were, after all, short story handbooks that offered writing advice while claiming that writing could not be taught. Rather, the difference between these texts and short story handbooks that catered openly to democratic visions of classfuls of great writers was one of emphasis, and not open contradiction. If one part of the seduction of the short story was the seeming ease with which it was composed (Perry wrote that "here is a form of literature easy to write and easy to read"),[40] a corollary effort was exerted to preserve the glamour of the profession. For the most part, this effort was devoted to elevating the short story into a national form of expression; but attention was also paid to the idea that creative writing could not be taught, and that it remained the province of a natural aristocracy. The majority of short story handbooks – the most artistic, it could be argued – intermixed the two strategies in a manner designed to maximize the appeal of short story writing, while preserving the authority of creative writing as a discipline.

Even the most radical handbooks contained apologia for the democratizing promises they offered. Barry Pain wrote that "if the whole art of writing could be learned . . . from a little handbook, two results would follow – anybody who wished could be a successful writer, and neither from the artistic nor the commercial point of view would the success be worth having." Esenwein, whose handbooks obeyed the scientific method with sincere ardor, cautioned his reader several times that there was no such thing as "recipes for 'how to write a story.'" But the author who was most capable of manipulating the twin conventions of accessibility and aristocracy was undoubtedly Pitkin. While claiming that

the short story is the highest form of American art. As to this there is not the slightest dispute he also encouraged his reader that "you can go pretty far in this art with only moderate application." Similarly, although observing that the "intense interest" of Americans in the short story had made "the American product superior to the stories from any other part of the earth," he also assured his reader that "the average story of the average magazine can be written with a year's training." In this manner, the American average is exalted to the level of universal excellence, making excellence (in the fine arts, at least) something every American can possess with a little effort.[41]

Introductory chapters then attempted to define the short story, and present a brief history of the form. The histories usually divided the genre's history between a 4,000-year-old tradition of storytelling (with the books of the Bible, Chaucer, Boccaccio, and the French *fabliaux* receiving prominent mention), and a more recent tradition beginning with Poe, Irving, Hawthorne, and often Maupassant. This history was then followed by a chapter entitled "Definition," which varied little from handbook to handbook. Like Esenwein, who composed a chapter entitled "What a Short Story Is Not," many handbook authors found it easier to define what a short story was not, rather than what it was: Barrett apologized that his "book may seem to be merely a catalogue of 'Don'ts.'"[42]

Nevertheless, the short story was defined with near-uniformity of opinion. The handbook writers accepted Poe's description of the short story as producing "a certain unique or single effect" (as well as his vocabulary of "effect," "impression," and "suggestion") with fidelity made more remarkable by the fact that Poe was rarely given direct credit.[43] For Carl Grabo, for instance, "the short story aims at a single effect." Pitkin wrote that the "American ideal" was "a single effect." E. A. Cross insisted upon "the necessity of producing a single effect." Notestein and Dunn observed that "the short story is a narrative producing a single emotional impression . . . in a single climactic incident." Mary Orvis called it "Poe's rule," and wrote that "the principle of unity is an artistic ideal that cannot under any circumstances be violated. It is absolute . . ."[44]

In many handbooks, a chapter on "gathering material" followed the introduction. This chapter advised the student to collect newspaper clippings in carefully organized files, or to experience 'life': "Mix with all types, not as a self-conscious observer . . . but as a friend."[45] In extreme cases, the reader was advised to keep files on neighbors and friends, or to "make a study of race characteristics by comparison of the various nationalities whose representatives you meet."[46] The remaining chapters of the handbook were then devoted to the individual elements of the story. The chapter on plot usually received considerable attention, as did setting, character,

PRODUCING YOUR EFFECTS 111

LAW OF INTENSIFICATION

When you have made the above analysis, you will be ready to understand the following law of intensification without further explanation.

1. Intensity is the amount of a given quality per impression.
2. The more the suggestions and associations of a given "Flavor" presented to your reader in a single sentence or passage, the stronger his emotional reaction and the weaker his tendency to think of irrelevant and conflicting matters at the time.
3. Hence the rule of technique:
   Having chosen the emotional effect you are to aim at, select and report only those features of setting, character, and complication which produce that effect. If some features needed for the plot do not produce that effect (which often happens) you are to report them as colorlessly as possible so that they set up no antagonistic impression.

THE TWO LAWS OF STORY TELLING

TO CONVEY YOUR MEANING, BE CONCISE AND PRECISE!

TO CONVEY YOUR EFFECT, REPEAT AND REPEAT!

"Saying a Thing Three Times Makes It True"

You have doubtless heard this cynical remark. It sums up a great psychological truth which underlies most of the

Sample page from Walter Pitkin's *How to Write Stories* (1923), 111.

dialogue, beginnings, endings, and titles: "The purpose of a title is the same as that of a label on a package of merchandise offered for sale."[47] Frequently, the handbook presented a chapter on the different kinds of short stories, providing extra advice about mystery stories, love stories, and so forth. Similarly, the chapter on theme often disseminated advice about what kinds of topics to avoid, with magazine rejection threatened as the punishment for disobedience. Sex and religion were clearly taboo, and polemical, pessimistic, or reflective subject matter was also clearly rejected ("Action must dominate").[48] Authors were steered away from "hackneyed" ideas but were also steered away from original themes, and were advised instead to seek "vivifying elements" to freshen up old ideas.[49]

In the more academic handbooks, every chapter concluded with a set of exercises. Often, the questions inspected the student's comprehension of the chapter's major points:

1. Should an editor decline to publish a brief story solely because
    it does not conform to the standards of short-story form as set
    forth in such a treatise as this? Give reasons supporting your
    answer. . . .
3. Does a knowledge of rules help or hinder a genius? Show
    how . . .[50]

More often, they asked the student to execute a number of research or narrative projects:

114. Carefully attend on chance conversations within your hearing; then endeavor to reproduce them verbatim. . . .
120. Study ten persons. Adequately picture each in a compact
      descriptive characterization of from ten to thirty words. . . .
131. Put before us Christmas day in a Jewish family; in a New
      England or other native American family.[51]

The last section of the handbook discussed manuscript preparation and marketing. Manuscript advice was clinical: margin size, placement of address, and how to avoid offending an editor ("Don't argue with editors, it is bad salesmanship").[52] Marketing advice, however, was more elaborate. The handbooks consistently urged their readers to "study the fiction market as closely and as persistently as a Wall Street broker studies the stock market."[53] Some authors, such as William Byron Mowery (*Professional Short Story Writing* [1953]), devoted several chapters to the description of the different magazine groups, with information on editorial preferences, payment, and response time.[54] Other authors drew broad sociological sketches of the American reading public, blandly noting that "it will shock you to discover what a horde of child minds inhabit the bodies of grown men and women."[55] Overall, the handbook authors openly recognized that "the field of the short story is first of all the field of the magazine"; and they correspondingly made known to their readers that "to be a successful story writer requires a comprehensive knowledge of the policies and preferences of the various periodicals that buy stories."[56]

Within the body of the handbook, the author usually insisted on scientific rigor in the student's approach to short story composition. Pitkin asked his readers not to dismiss his lessons as "quack theory" because they had "been worked out by many different observers and scientists and editors and authors. Some of them were reached two thousand years ago and have not been shaken by centuries of criticism. Some of them are very recent discoveries of psychologists and have been tested in many ways known to scientific method."[57] Esenwein spoke proudly that his "inspirational method and logical order are based upon the best pedagogical approach," and guided teachers toward his supplementary "Laboratory Method for the Study of the Short-Story," another best-selling manual.[58]

In particular, Esenwein's books, which were widely sold and widely quoted, provide a powerful example of the handbook writer's science-oriented ethos. In his chapter "The Opening of the Story," for instance, Esenwein notes that he has "examined and broadly classified the openings of six hundred short-stories, including tales and sketches." The remainder of the chapter describes the results of that research: "Of the six hundred stories examined, only fifty-one – less than ten per cent – were found to begin with conversation, and these were rarely stories of great merit . . . Twenty-six use the opening dialogue to give the setting . . ."[59] In the chapter on dialogue, he presented a graph listing the percentage of words in ten 'great' short stories that were rendered in dialogue:

STORY AND AUTHOR.

	CONVERSATION
" The Outcasts of Poker Flat," Bret Harte	11 per cent
" The Diamond Lens," Fitz-James O'Brien	13 " "
" The Ambitious Guest," Nathaniel Hawthorne	30 " "
" Mrs. Protheroe," Booth Tarkington	38 " "
" A Lodging for the Night," Robert Louis Stevenson	39 " "
" Many Waters," Margaret Deland	43 " "
" A Venus of the Fields," " Georg Schock "	45 " "
" Without Benefit of Clergy," Rudyard Kipling	54 " "
" La Grande Brétèche," Honoré de Balzac	55 " "
" The Gold Bug," Edgar Allan Poe	64 " "
Average proportion of conversation	39 " "

Dialogue chart, J. Berg Esenwein, *Studying the Short-Story* (1912), 246.

Although few authors employed similarly explicit statistical methods, many used elaborate classification mechanisms. By far the most popular scientific trope was the plot diagram, which became such a frequent feature of the handbooks (and such a frequent object of criticism) that authors often apologized for their appearance. Cross wrote that "I strongly disapprove of . . . showing diagrams of plot analysis," but acknowledged that "I have perhaps contributed something to this practice."[60] The purpose of the plot diagram, ostensibly, was to illustrate "the necessity of an organized structure" to the reader.[61] Cross, for instance, presented a hand-drawn series of ladder steps ascending to the story's culmination:

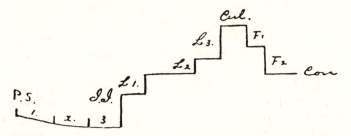

Plot diagram, E. A. Cross, *The Short Story: A Technical and Literary Study* (1928), 41.

Pitkin drew unusual patterns of arrows moving in complex relation to one another, and required his student to do the same for Maupassant's "A Coward," promising that "you will be startled at the result of this exercise":

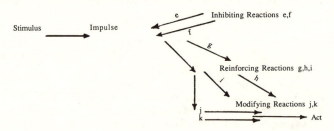

Plot diagram, Walter Pitkin, *How to Write Stories* (1923), 148, 169.

Williams drew structures in which parallel lines represented plots and subplots, and vertical or diagonal lines represented points of contact between subnarratives:

I.   Main line of interest: A father wishes for money, which comes to him, as it happens, through the death of his son. He desires the return of the son, and then negates the wish (A series of three struggles).

II. Second line of interest: A monkey's paw, supernatural agent, causes the fulfilment of three wishes.

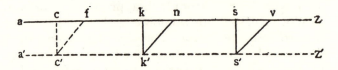

Plot diagram, Blanche Colton Williams, *A Handbook on Short Story Writing* (1920), 73.

With its geometric figures, carefully numbered exercise sequences, and calculatedly outlined chapters, the classic short story handbook resembled a mathematics textbook. In conjunction with this appearance, many handbook authors adopted a psychology that freely mingled organic and mechanistic descriptions of human nature. The handbook writer insistently recognized that "inspiration" and "emotion" were (from a pragmatic viewpoint) as essential to the making of a good short story as was a good plot, or the right size margin. Cecil Hunt, for instance, offered a chapter on "Making the Story Live" preceding a chapter entitled "Recipes For Success," while Foy Evans pointedly told his students that "you can't afford to be stingy with the amount of emotion." Accordingly, the handbook authors labored to quantify the role of emotion in a successful story by embedding their impressionistic scientific vocabulary within an admixture of mass-psychology formulas: Pitkin defined "intensity," for instance, as "the amount of a given quality per impression." Robert Neal, struggling through the same issue, defined the purpose of good fiction as being "to interpret life," then defined "interpret," and then invented something he called "interpretive value" to gauge the quality of a given story. Phillips offered a chapter entitled "Inspiration," and told his reader that "to have a maximum of outpouring" the short story writer "should have a definite inpouring of forces that contribute to the inspiration, association, and suggestion of ideas."[62]

It was a special language – in Farrell's words, a "cabalistic lore" – but it bore the imprint of a particular worldview. In the communal effort to quantify literary value, after all, it would have been far easier for most handbook authors to have said, as did the editor William Clayton, that "the better the story is, the larger is apt to be the check." What they sought, rather, was the point where that claim was justified by human nature, where money making and literary quality met. In the most explicit sense, the handbook authors insisted the short story writer accept that creative activity was a marketable service, and even a trade. Williams, for instance, wrote that "every short-story writer must be both an artist and a man of business . . . only one evidence is admissible: the product." Pitkin defended his lessons by observing that "the final test of every technique is its usefulness in practice." This emphasis on "use" and "practice," however, required an external litmus against which to measure the "success" of the short story product. Accordingly, the handbook authors largely abandoned any system of intrinsic literary value (or, more relevantly, conflated it with external measurements) and gauged merit in terms of public acceptance: "I rank the ability to sell a story nearly as high as the ability to write one," Leslie Quirk claimed.[63]

In turn, the aesthetics of 'product' were incorporated within definitions of the short story, and descriptions of creative activity.
Efficiency was the unquestioned goal: Williams boasted that her
students "learned to direct their energies, with a diminution of dif-
fuseness, to the accomplishment of stronger stories." Hunt wrote
pithily that "as in the expenditure of money, so in words." Emphasis on selectivity (Pain referred to "the art of omission"), rapid pace
("draw a line," Quirk said, "and never deviate"), and lack of waste
("can anything on this page be rewritten in less words?" Evans
asked) predominated: Cross's advice that "the writer of a Short
Story disregards all the experiences except those which pertain to
the plot" was merely typical of a dominant literary philosophy that
insisted upon both economy of effort and efficiency of product.[64]
If the handbook authors followed Poe's lead by insisting that the
short story operate with the greatest possible effect in the smallest
space, they expanded upon his beliefs by insisting that the act of
creative writing could also be streamlined, and made more efficient:

> The artist faces the very same predicament which the physi-
> cian, the manufacturer, the attorney, and the scientist con-
> front. Like them, he can achieve most by attempting least; by
> concentrating upon some one theme, upon some single dra-
> matic pattern, upon some set of characters . . .[65]

It is difficult to underestimate the radical force of this dual emphasis on efficiency. Because the short story was treated as a technological device, rather than an intuitive or unrepeatable act of
creation, the literary philosophy of the handbooks was remarkably
(and even smugly) hostile toward the traditional canon of literature, and toward the idea of canonization itself. Like a machine, the
short story was constantly being improved by the efforts of re-
searchers: The handbook authors almost universally recognized
that the contemporary short story was a more efficient, and therefore superior version of the tales of Hawthorne, Maupassant, and
Chekhov. Pitkin claimed that "there are many who outrank or at
least equal Maupassant," and that "there are many short story writers living who are immeasurably superior to Poe in every respect."
Barrett wrote that "the short story is so popular that we seem to be
in a new literary epoch," and described the "modern tests" for
narrative against which Defoe and Addison would "almost stand."
Williams spoke pithily of "the modern narrative requirement,"
against which all stories could be objectively measured.[66]

In this manner, the handbook authors directed their students
away from classics ("he should forget rhetoric, he should preach no
imitation of masterpieces"), and insisted that they "keep our eye on

the next year's models and markets."[67] They deferred to "modern psychology" ("you can hardly afford to overlook the contributions of the psychologists and the social scientists," Orvis told her readers), but mostly they deferred to an experiential world of knowledge and guidance.[68] The true test of a story was "effect," and effect could be readily measured in the lists of successful students, the approval of editors, and the approbation of fellow scholars with which handbook authors laced their introductions. Even those handbook writers who did not possess faith in the magazine market's ability to judge literary merit found themselves comfortable within the ethos of efficiency, selectivity, and practical use upon which that faith was founded. Phillips claimed that "editors seek to gratify their personal aesthetic desires rather than meet the demands of a universal Art"; and yet, his definition of the "universal Art" of the short story as "that most refined, effective and pleasing product," possessing the "all-important single impression" and "a cunning scheme"[69] was in complete accordance with the definitions of handbook authors who genuinely believed that "an editor . . . keeps his tastes sane and fresh and manly."[70] What prevented the majority of short story handbooks from descending into outright cynicism was this implicit, consensual belief that "universal Art," human nature, and the American magazine editor were all guided by the same mercantile values – that a five-hundred-dollar story truly was literature, and that editors were the protectors of a national treasure:

> To Magazine Editors
> Who
> through constructive helpfulness
> and creative vision
> are helping authors to make
> the American short story
> unique in artistry and literary
> merit.

Jean Wick dedicated her handbook of 1921.[71]

A similar ethic pervaded the handbook authors' attitude toward their students. What the handbook authors preached – and preached most forcefully – was socialization. On a specific level, the pressure to conform was most conspicuous in the language of "Must" and "Don't" that dominates the handbook literature:

> I am confident that the intellectual process similar to that which has been outlined must be followed by every author who seeks to construct stories . . .
>
> Clayton Hamilton

> The present treatise . . . does set up certain standards to which the Short Story as a type must conform . . .
>
> Ethan Allen Cross

> I must ask you at the outset to take every point made in the following lessons with the utmost seriousness . . .
>
> Walter Pitkin

This language of "Must" was then enforced with the inevitable threat of magazine rejection. Esenwein, with enormous delicacy, paraphrases an "experienced literary worker" who "will be seconded by every editor" in believing that "there are many writers throughout the country . . . who are failing merely because they are not familiar with the technique of the short story." Other authors spoke more bluntly. Nancy Moore warned her reader to "go and do likewise, or there's a strike against you before your manuscript comes out of its manila envelope." Hunt prefaced a set of exercises by telling his readers that "now, with a discipline that, believe me, will be nothing like so severe as the discipline of the rejection slip, I'm going to ask you to do something in addition."[72]

Ultimately, however, most handbook authors simply wanted their students to internalize the market – in effect, to become representative men and women – rather than to respond externally to the market's dictates. In this manner, the elimination of individual tastes and writing style would be countermanded by the creation of a mind-set that *spontaneously* wrote the kinds of stories people wanted to read: "It is not the material that one needs to acquire," Pain wrote in 1907, "so much as the right point of view."[73] This assumption was most obvious in the amount of effort the handbook authors devoted to circumscribing their students' artistic choices before composition even began – in the choices of subject matter and formal structure that were simply beyond debate. In one case, for instance, William Byron Mowery rejected the credo that the creative writing teacher "should compel students to write much," and offered instead a set of "story directionals," variables that enabled the student to determine what to write and not to write – before setting a word to paper.[74] For the handbook writers, a student who learned to avoid writing about sex because sex was taboo was a good student – but a student who already refused to write explicitly about sex because explicit sex scenes were personally repugnant was a writer who could serve the nation's magazines, and the nation.

On rare occasions, the ideological underpinnings of this pedagogy emerged in surprisingly plain language. Bliss Perry offered a short section titled the "obliteration of personal traits." Cecil Hunt warned his readers that "I mean this: Personal preferences must be completely suppressed . . ." Cody directs his students to "coin your heart's blood into the universal coin of the realm of heart." Walter Pitkin began the introduction to his *Art and the Business of Story Writing* with a repudiation of the concept of artistic freedom:

> There is no doubt that, in some sense, a story is a free creation and spontaneous; and freedom seems to connote a certain emancipation from law . . . The inference, however, is only plausible. There is no soundness in it . . .

In the careful dance of ideology that would sell the handbooks, the romance of the individual and the vision of a community that required little sacrifice from its members would play vital roles. If the handbook authors sold a vision of relative wealth and celebrity to their students, they were generally careful to let them know that the kind of socially sanctioned celebration of the individual that was being offered could be purchased only with the surrender of personal values that their students would usually not have admitted to possessing in the first place. But the attack on individualism that was mounted in these barer moments could not have sold many books: It reveals a certain straightforwardness, rather, that undermines the confidence game, and suggests other motives – a sense of mission, perhaps, or the desire to play lawmaker (with the magazine editor as the enforcer), or perhaps a final refusal to let the dream that they themselves often pursued be sold for too cheap a price.[75]

The Greatest Genius

The most thorough way of understanding the elaborate psychological and ideological framework of the handbook movement is to examine the role of its central protagonist, Edgar Allan Poe. Besides being called "universally quoted" by Pattee, he was likewise labeled "perpetually quoted" by Bliss Perry, and blamed by Bement for the "two dicta which have hung upon the short story like an incubus."[76] It was not uncommon to find the entire review of Hawthorne (or a large portion thereof) repeated verbatim within the text or the appendix of a short story handbook; similarly, his "Philosophy of Composition" was also widely quoted, and his definition of the form was offered by most handbook writers as the unbreakable aesthetic guideline for the short story.[77]

These paper traces illustrate only partly the force of Poe's example within the history of the short story handbook, however. He was, without question, the first creative writing teacher of the mod-

ern era. The short story handbooks shared, if not outright borrowed, his lexicon, his air of professional mystery, his scientific
invocation of impressionistic literary standards, and several of the
specific rhetorical strategies he used to defend the idea that creative writing was a conscientious craft. Although these pedagogical
gestures were visible throughout the review of Hawthorne, they
were most prominent (and more easily iterable) in "The Philosophy
of Composition," especially in those passages in which Poe attempts
to illustrate how the composition of "The Raven" was conducted
with "the precision and rigid consequence of a mathematical
problem:"[78]

> The question now arose as to the character of the word. That
> such a close, to have force, must be sonorous and susceptible of
> protracted emphasis, admitted no doubt: and these consider-
> ations inevitably led me to the long o as the most sonorous
> vowel, in connection with r as the most producible conso-
> nant . . .
>   The sound of the refrain being thus determined, it became
> necessary to select a word embodying this sound, and at the
> same time in the fullest possible keeping with that melancholy
> which I had predetermined as the tone of the poem. In such a
> search it would have been absolutely impossible to overlook the
> word "Nevermore." In fact, it was the very first which pre-
> sented itself . . .[79]

Poe's seemingly logical cogitations and his use of phrases such as
"admitted no doubt," "inevitably," and "absolutely impossible" all
create an atmosphere of scientific precision and necessity; and yet,
the crucial decision, the choice of the word "Nevermore," is under-
statedly described as an intuitive choice ("it was the very first which
presented itself"). In offering to dispel the air of authorial mystery,
Poe composed a document (and a voice) that appeared to explain
everything according to "ordinary induction,"[80] and that explained
nothing the student could actually submit to reiteration. It was a
triumph of personality.
  Many handbook authors invoked Poe's curtain-raising gesture,
and adopted the pose of the author who would reveal the tricks of
the trade. Erle Stanley Gardner told readers of H. Bedford-Jones
The Graduate Fictioneer (1932) that "I still didn't think a professional
writer would really tell the innermost secrets of the game . . . personally, I wouldn't dare do what H. Bedford-Jones has done . . ."
Foy Evans wrote that "I have tried to remember exactly what my
feelings were at each stage of my progress as a writer and I have
tried to convey to the reader knowledge of how I made my prog-

ress." D'Orsay, plagiarizing "The Philosophy of Composition" with engaging impunity, collected his own stories, composed explanatory afterwords, and boasted in the introduction to *Stories You Can Sell* that "for the first time in professional history, writer-readers are taken into the workshop of a professional author and, so far as possible, into his mind; shown step by step how he plans and writes his stories . . ."[81]

Other authors refused Poe's pose, but adopted his method. Poe's after-the-fact description of the composition of "The Raven" became such a powerful model for the handbook authors that the technique became a central focus of many of the texts. Stories were routinely considered as problem-solving activities, during which the author (having discovered a "plot-germ"[82] through private inspiration, or by scouring the local newspapers and neighborhood gossip) would plug in variables until a plot emerged. Handbook authors freely offered their own private systems for manipulating these elements with the greatest efficiency: Beach promised his readers the "X-Ray Method" of composition, for instance, while Summers spoke with pride of his "Story Plan Method" and William Wallace Cook offered his readers "PLOTTO."[83] Choices concerning number of characters, narrative, voice, and percentage of dialogue were then made (in examples as seemingly lucid as Poe's) according to deductive analysis – before, the handbook authors generally insisted, a single word need be pressed to paper.

Nevertheless, although Poe's pedagogical gestures seemed perfectly attuned to the needs of a developing creative writing discipline, it remains unclear whether these twentieth-century authors recognized the appeal of Poe's critical voice and adopted it for their own uses, or whether they were themselves Poe's students. Perry wrote that "if we assent to Poe's reasoning, we are at once upon firm ground," and quoted the review of Hawthorne in its entirety. Clayton Hamilton, in *The Materials and Methods of Fiction* (1912), noted in reference to "The Philosophy of Composition" that "it is greatly to be regretted that he did not write a similar essay outlining in detail the successive stages in the structure of one of his short stories." Hamilton then provides that essay, using Poe's "Ligeia" instead of "The Raven" and promising (in language strikingly paraphrasing Poe's), to illustrate how, "Step by step," "Granted his preestablished design, the progress of his plan was in every step inevitable." For these handbook writers, Poe was valuable because his critical-authorial pose perfectly fit the purposes of their twentieth-century pedagogy: He was an author who composed stories that were 'universally recognized' (in their age, if not his) as being successful, and who convincingly documented how he retained complete consciousness throughout the act of creation: "The greatest genius of all is the one who has the instinctive power to create, and then becomes conscious of the means which he has used," Cross wrote.[84]

As a model author, however, Poe's real-life legacy placed curious restraints upon the handbook writers. It is tempting to draw parallels between Cross's model of "the greatest genius" and the thematic matter of many of Poe's stories – particularly those (such as "The Pit and the Pendulum," or "A Descent into the Maelstrom") that revolve around the idea of descending into subconscious or death states while maintaining consciousness.[85] As Bement (and Baudelaire before him) observed, however, Poe "was the type of man who preached one thing and practised another."[86] Although the review of Hawthorne and "The Philosophy of Composition" appear to offer a complete and frank cataloging of Poe's descent into the creative maelstrom, for instance, the protagonists of his short stories are often victims of the kind of uncontrollable inner impulses that the handbook authors were required to downplay by the constraints of their pedagogy. This anomaly created a potentially uncomfortable contradiction for those authors, of course, who were compelled to tell their readers not to write stories like Poe's – stories that were morbid, reflective, tragic – while praising his formal vision. It remains to be added that few handbook authors resisted Poe for this reason, or even appeared to mind. Within a literary movement where the phrase 'nobody could be taught to write' frequently preceded elaborate instructions on composition, the bifurcated nature of Poe's public figure was not merely consonant; it was inspirational.

The Inalienable Right to Make Fiction

Assessing the influence of the handbooks on the modern short story is a hazy exercise. As Kelly Cherry has observed, "structure" in the traditional sense (that is, in the handbook sense) is rarely taught to contemporary creative writing students, in either textbooks or workshops.[87] The contemporary creative writing student, rather, acquires information about the short story piecemeal from semiautobiographical writers' advisories such as John Gardner's *The Art of Fiction* or Natalie Goldberg's *Writing Down the Bones*, the resurgent breed of writing guidebooks inspired by the success of the workshop system (i.e., Jerome Stern's *Making Shapely Fiction* or the third edition of Janet Burroway's *Writing Fiction: A Guide to Narrative Craft*), the fragments of short story theory culled in the afterwords of anthologies such as Ann Charters's *Story and Its Writer* or Shapard and Thomas's *Sudden Fiction*, essays and interviews published in literary magazines, but mostly from the oral tradition of writerly guidelines and market wisdom that surrounds the workshop and writers' conferences of most universities.[88]

If the modern reader receives tangible evidence of the effect of the handbooks on the contemporary short story, rather, it usually takes the form of the vestiges of a half-internalized, half-repudiated lexicon, the legacy of Poe's emphasis on "effect," "unity," and "impression" – Mary Rohrberger referring to the short story as being "characterized by 'unity of effect,'" or Charters's observation that "short story writers can impress upon us the unity of their vision of life by focusing on a single effect."[89] But even this lexicon, it could be argued, has been chased into the introductions of anthologies (where they often go unread), while fifty years ago it formed the basis of a massive and labyrinthine pedagogy. Because textbooks are not presently a mainstay of creative writing courses, then, an assessment of the handbooks' influence would require an ethnography of the modern workshop system – interviews with teachers and students, as well as editors and textbook writers. Parts of this ethnography have already been conducted: Nancy Bunge's *Finding the Words*, for instance, contains interviews with sixteen authors who teach creative writing; Stephen Wilbers has written a book and several articles describing the development of the University of Iowa Writers' Workshop; essays discussing the creative writing system appear with sporadic regularity in literary magazines; and a few educators have printed books addressing the issue of creative writing from a strict pedagogical viewpoint.[90]

What such an ethnography would reveal (and what it already reveals, to the extent that it has been conducted) is a tremendous amount of continuity between the handbook era and the current workshop era. It is remarkable how much the debate over the value of the workshop (not only for fiction writers, but for poets as well) bears strong resemblances to the conflict over the worth of the short story handbook. Just as the handbooks were criticized for inciting widespread conformity and a lowering of standards for what constituted "literature," contemporary observers speak of an "MFA style,"[91] emphasizing "technical superiority," "elegantly, awarely foolproof":[92] Maureen Howard writes of "short stories everywhere, technically accomplished, mannerly performances with no social concern and little personal vision."[93] Similarly, just as early handbook detractors believed that the handbooks were disseminating a critical, self-conscious vision of creative activity, modern writers are concerned that "the university's demands" lead to "deflated creative souls,"[94] and that more specifically, as Frederick

Manfred describes, "if you are creative . . . something goes wrong in that critical atmosphere in the classroom."[95]

Further, just as early twentieth-century critics worried that the United States was "very kindly indeed" (to use Fagin's phrase) toward its short story writers, contemporary writer-teachers worry that "writing programs, occasional fellowships and subsidized little magazines" have created a "lamentably supportive world" in which, as Bunge describes, "it's not good for literature to have so many writers sheltered by the academy."[96] Both movements, in fact, are driven by the essentially populist notion – best described by Wallace Stegner – that "talent is more common than we think, that it is all over the place."[97] In turn, just as Edward O'Brien and numerous others criticized the handbook as a fraud that flourished by convincing individuals that they could become "writers" with little effort, Nelson Algren has savaged the modern workshop as a "Famous Writers School" working the same territory: "Are you one of the quiet ones who should be a writer?"[98] Lastly, just as the early handbook writers dangled the threat of magazine rejection to coax their students into full cooperation, many workshop veterans believe that the contemporary creative writing program inspires a similar emphasis on publication and status. As Joe David Bellamy has written:

> It seemed to me that the Workshop is set up like a pressure cooker, with a rigid status system depending on publication, and you step into this system and you find that here is a world where, if you publish, you have status. If you do not publish, you have no status. And those who haven't published usually feel pretty dismal. So in a kind of Pavlovian way, it sets up an intense desire to publish, a hunger for it.[99]

In part, this continuity between past and present is a testament to the resilience of the handbook tradition. The discipline of creative writing, after all, was virtually a blank slate at the turn of the twentieth century. For the modern reader, it is easier to register the obvious differences in tone and formulas between the commercial pedagogy of 1920 and the academic pedagogy of 1990 than to recognize the similarities: The emphasis on suggestion ("show, not tell"), the splitting of the individual story into elements, the workshop format where first drafts are submitted for open discussion and revised afterward, and the belief that the short story is a good practice field for young writers are canons so essential to the teaching of creative writing that it is easy to forget (or never recognize) that less than one hundred years ago they did not exist in any usable form. The short story handbooks codified and popularized the most seminal axioms of creative writing pedagogy; it is because the axioms are so central that the influence of the handbooks remains invisible.

For the most part, however, the continuity between past and present is a testament to the fact that the cultural debate defined by the question "Can writing be taught?" (or, as Howard asks, "Could *Moby Dick* or *The Waste Land* or *Gravity's Rainbow* have been written as homework?") remains an open one, while the short story continues to be treated as the genre for apprenticeship. The creative writing workshop was explicitly devised to provide American writers with a cultural niche where they could compose free from the pressures of commercial demand; Stegner has said that "the writing that goes on in colleges and universities . . . is likely to be as free from commercial pressures as writing anywhere." Ironically, in an era where the short story possesses little commercial power, the place of haven is not perceived as the establishment that enforces conformity: "It is a literature that is safe," Cherry notes of the "MFA style," "not only in terms of not saying anything that will offend anyone in the academy, but also safe formally."[100]

In the context of this cultural transformation, the resilience of the question "Can writing be taught?" remains central. At the heart of the creative writing "revolution" exists a basic tension about where literature comes from, and what forms of behavior should be celebrated by the humanities – and although the institutions of academia, publishing, and the short story have transmuted over the past one hundred years, that basic tension has remained a vital issue and dominates the establishments within which it is active. The question "Can writing be taught?" tests the ability of a community to define teachable, a priori values for creative behavior; but more generally, it tests the value of communal structures *at all* within creative activity. It is a popular question, not just for academics but for nonacademics as well, because it enacts a classically American debate between the romance of rugged individualism and the faith in community, within a field of endeavor that has been reserved by that same community for the "sensitive," alienated individual.

Those authors who are most critical of the idea that writing can be taught describe creative activity as a necessarily solitary endeavor. When N. Scott Momaday observes that writing is "a very isolated business, a personal matter," and that he "never found any benefit in workshops or in communities of writers," he merely joins the "great host" that university-affiliated novelist David Madden claims to hear "singing, 'your writing will become anemic, you'll write mostly about academic life, you'll write in a stilted style.'" Even writer-teachers who favor the workshop system express concern about the pressures that a constructive group of peers might exert on the individual talent: William Stafford notes how "it's almost inevitable that surrounded by successful people you will emulate them, you will choose their topics, you will follow their style, and I think it's dangerous." Madden himself, a workshop proponent, nevertheless describes his own attitude toward academia by quoting Byron's "I stood *amongst* them, but was not *of* them." At the basis of these authors' concerns is a belief that writers make a contribution as long as they refuse to subsume their artistic identities to the rules of any institutional structure, no matter how sympathetic: As Algren writes in his visceral attack on the writing program, "it has been Earth's dispossessed who have given Man his most abiding truths," while the "Iowa Writers Workshop, in its thirty-five years of existence," has not "produced a single novel, poem or short story worth re-reading."[101]

In the opposing vision, the workshop system provides a locale in American culture where the writer's traditional alienation and marginality is lessened – either by creating a community of writers, or by lending middle-class respectability to the profession of writing. Bellamy wrote, for instance, that the workshop was "a place where to be a writer was not considered crazy or stupid"; Theodore Weiss, observing that his early career was "usually a secret and lonely, if not furtive, affair," notes appreciatively the "official status . . . and societal approval" of the workshop. Seymour Epstein has spoken more directly of the financial alienation of the writer by noting that "making a living as a writer is such a serious business that there has to be something to fall back on," and concluding that "your creative writing person finds sanctuary in the university today." Bruce Dobler, an Iowa student, described his fears regarding how working-class relatives and friends would respond to his decision to become a writer, and praised the M.F.A. program because "I can't think of a better way for a person to put a good face on dropping out to just write for a few years."[102]

Most contemporary observers of the workshop system fix their opinions between these two opposing visions, dwelling upon the play between communally acceptable and alienated behavior. Marvin Bell tells of students who reject the workshop community, transforming the workshop itself into the model of an intolerant society they sought to escape, and reconstructing themselves as marginal individuals: "They fight the Workshop all the way. They go home every night saying, 'Those sons of bitches don't understand me and don't appreciate me,' and they grow that way." James Alan McPherson, striking a common stance among workshop teachers and students, saves his highest praise for the student who rejects the workshop community, and its financial sanctuary:

There was a student at Virginia who won a big fellowship, showed up a month, and left. This money kept arriving each month, but there was no student to pick it up. Now that's a writer. We'll hear from him some day. That's a writer.

Most significantly, Wallace Stegner (who functions more or less in modern America as the patron saint of the workshop system) describes his vision of the successful workshop in terms that are wholly resonant of free market ideals of self-interest and public good:

A writing class is inevitably competitive, do you see? Everyone's primary concern is his own success, and that success, when something as personal as literature is involved, is acutely personal . . . the trick is to keep the competitiveness friendly, to see to it that individual success stimulates other members of the group, instead of depressing and discouraging . . .

It is a model for community with which Tocqueville would have been familiar.[103]

Overall, the truest legacy of the handbooks is to be found in these snatches of pedagogical advice – in the catalogue of ideological strategies, teacherly poses, and technical gestures that are seductive, if not necessarily inevitable, outcomes of (and often catalysts for) the belief that creative writing should be a discipline of the humanities. As both modern and early-century observers readily noted, the merger between academia and writers "created alot of jobs."[104] If the creative writing "revolution" is perceived as forming a "safety" zone that is also a "danger" (in Stegner's words) for contemporary writers, it also reflects a cultural transformation where writers have voluntarily chosen to subordinate many of the marginalizing aspects of their profession in exchange for several of the basic, pragmatic trappings of respectability – financial security, advanced degrees, and so on.[105] That exchange (and the conflict it engenders), in turn, is internalized within the vision of literature that is passed between writer-teachers and writer-students. It is visible in the pedagogy that preserves the aura of the unteachability of the subject. It is also prominent in the conflict between after-the-fact critical analyses of creative activity and the continued respect for spontaneity – a conflict that is enacted on an institutional level within the hegemonic conflicts between English departments and creative writing programs regarding the latter's autonomy. But most notably, it dominates the ideological foundation for the teaching of writing, and provokes on a communal level a rich and ongoing negotiation between the individual writer's desire to "celebrate his own existence" (in Epstein's words), and to do so in as painless a manner as possible.[106]

BACK HOME AGAIN

BOBBIE ANN MASON'S "SHILOH"

For American writers simply to avow that they have the education, or
the cultivation, that they very often have, is something that isn't done
– they're like politicians who want to adopt a folksy accent.
Susan Sontag, "The Quote Box," *Philadelphia Inquirer Magazine*,
11 June 1989: 8.

In 1980, Bobbie Ann Mason's first major short story, "Shiloh,"
appeared in the *New Yorker*.[1] The story was an immediate critical
success. It was reprinted in *Best American Short Stories* in 1981, and
became arguably the most heavily anthologized short story of the
last decade; the collection that followed, *Shiloh and Other Stories*
(1982), was nominated for the National Book Critics Circle Award,
the American Book Award, and the PEN/Faulkner Award, and
won the Ernest Hemingway Award for First Fiction.[2] Mason's distinctive style traits – popular culture references, present tense,
blue-collar and rural subject matter – have, with or without her
direct influence, become dominant trends in the contemporary
American short story. She is considered one of the chief representatives of a school of fiction variously named "dirty realism,"
"K-Mart realism," or "minimalism": linguistically spare, thematically populist, and consciously antiliterary.[3] This school developed such vogue during the 1980s that Mason's own work went
from being perceived as a "refreshing" or "improbable" change
from what usually appeared in commercial magazines and literary
journals, to being the exemplar of one of the two kinds of fiction
found in those venues. "If," in the words of Lila Havens, "Ann
Beattie is giving us 'bulletins from the front'" – portrayals of mid-
dle- and upper-class angst – Mason is "telling us what it's like back
home."[4]

Back home, of course, is a place the American short story has
spent a great deal of time. From the 1830s and 1840s, when Eastern magazines and newspapers published anecdotes of frontier life
gathered from papers and readers in the South and Southwest, the

short story has always been a site of discourse in which a comparatively well-educated, middle-class audience could read about the fictionalized lives of the more marginal participants in the American political project. The major trends in short fiction during the nineteenth century – realism, local color, dialect – all told stories about rural residents, the poor, and ethnic minorities, in magazines distributed to audiences that either had no link with those socially disenfranchised groups, or had left them "back home."[5]

In the twentieth century, these trends continued, in new transformations. As described in Chapter 2, regional, ideological, and ethnic literary movements were spearheaded by the evolution of a system of "little" magazines that, with their shoestring budgets, provided for the distribution of editorial power among economically marginal groups.[6] At the same time, numerous authors and critics argued that the short story, for structural reasons, was the art form best suited for the description of a heterogeneous culture of "submerged population groups" – the American melting pot.[7] This vision of the short story was then realized in published form within the modern anthology, with its all-but-invisible editor and seemingly unranked inclusion of a multitude of individual voices, which appeared like an ideal metaphor for a diverse and democratic culture. Institutionally, historically, and structurally, everything about the short story implied heterogeneity – everything, perhaps, except the audience, which at its apex consisted of perhaps the upper one-fifth of the social pyramid, and which now rarely extends beyond the comparatively small and homogeneous readership represented by the circulation lists of the *New Yorker* and the university presses.[8]

Mason's work is infused by many of these same tensions and ambitions. She writes stories of blue-collar Kentuckians for the decidedly nonblue-collar readers of the *New Yorker*, the *Atlantic Monthly*, and the *Paris Review*. Having earned a Ph.D. in literature and composed (and published) a dissertation on Vladimir Nabokov's difficult *Ada*, she nevertheless has crafted an antiliterary narrative style, and authorial persona to match: Laughing at an interviewer's insistence that she "must know some big words," for instance, Mason responded that "I don't say them out loud."[9] In this context, it is worth wondering precisely how much cultural distance separates the *Atlantic* publishing one of Mason's blue-collar tales in the name of "dirty realism" in 1983, and publishing a story composed entirely in a Newfoundland patois and lauding its "realism" in 1862.[10] Although Mason's writing is often represented as somehow radical, it is difficult to resist the observation that her populism, and the populism of other "dirty realists," is almost entirely consistent with the ideological composition of one hundred and fifty years of American short story telling.

In this event, the nature of Mason's innovation might not be her much-lauded populist edge, which is neither particularly populist nor innovative. Rather, Mason represents a significant chapter in the history of the short story because of the extent to which she combines many of the century-old narrative strategies of the American short story with a peculiarly postmodern (and postliterate) self-consciousness. Susan Sontag, in the epigraph that prefaced this chapter, observes that one way an American writer copes with life in an anti-intellectual culture is by playing dumb. If America is anti-intellectual because intellectualism constitutes an ostentatious show of superiority that is anathema to democratic culture, however, then the American writer has a second option: He or she can create fiction that undermines the myth structure from which intellectualism (and authorship) has drawn its power. That writer can attempt to 'democratize' literature by using models of authorship, narrative, and protagonism that suggest authors and heroes work within a community, rather than rise gloriously and rebelliously above it.

In doing so, of course, the author risks undermining his or her own authority. The short story "Shiloh" illustrates how Mason has developed a narrative strategy that combines radically democratic visions of creative activity with a residual faith in what she calls the "alienated, superior sensibility."[11] It is a highly seductive strategy, one in which the author balances the conflict between the desire to celebrate oneself and to celebrate one's community by consciously and conscientiously playing dumb, as though playing dumb was, in itself, another American art form. It is also a strategy in which the traditional energies of the short story have provided an institutional and intellectual framework within which Mason and other "dirty realists" could operate, and thus add another chapter to the long and thriving history of one class of Americans writing about another.

The Good Life

I didn't understand the conflict between the type of mind I had and the type of mind I was trying to be.

Bobbie Ann Mason, "Conversation" 133–4.

In published interviews, Mason has been straightforward about the tension inherent in her fiction between home and away-from-home. When asked in 1984 how the people in her hometown – the kind of "everyday people" that populate her stories – have reacted to her success, she responded that "since I hardly know anybody there, I don't really know." She similarly observed that "lower-middle class people" – again, the residents of her stories – "don't have much access to fiction," and would probably "rather be reading *Princess Daisy*" than her work. Despite these limitations, Mason clearly perceives her fiction as having populist ramifications. Her stated ambition is to include in high-culture discourse the kind of characters and models for narrative that would normally be excluded:

> Throughout American literature, the hero was the alienated superior sensibility, the artist, the sensitive young man. I read so much of that in school that by the time I was ready to write, I was sick of reading about that guy, and I thought, "At least he could be a woman," or maybe someone who was not sensitive and not superior. I think that's how I finally arrived at knowing who I was going to write about . . .

For Mason, the issue is not who reads literature, but what kinds of lives are considered worthy of being literature. She perceives herself as part of a larger populist "cultural shift" where the spread of education and wealth allows the "masses" to get access to the "good life"; and just as the masses get access to the good life, Mason gets them (and herself, the daughter of dairy farmers from western Kentucky) access to the 'good' magazines. The result is that, in theory at least, high-culture discourse is transformed and democratized by this infusion of "popular culture," and that "suddenly," in Mason's phrase, "we're discovering that store clerks and cowboys also have valid lives."[12]

Initially, the critical response to Mason's fiction focused on this aspect of her work, on how she seemed to be crossing demographic barriers by presenting her "farmers, store clerks, and truck drivers" in the elegant typescript of the *Atlantic* or Harper and Row publications.[13] The *New York Times* wrote that "the gap to be bridged empathically between her readership and her characters was formidable." The *Chicago Tribune* wrote that "the details of her characters' lives must seem as remote as Timbuktu to the readers of the *New Yorker* or the *Atlantic*." The temptation to consider her fictions valuable simply because they contained factual data about an "exotic culture" was so strong that the *Village Voice* critic reminded his readers that *Shiloh and Other Stories* "was not anthropology." These critical reactions indicate that what made Mason's work exciting in 1982 was not just what she said, but where she said it. She was genuinely perceived as having infused high- and middle-

culture sites of publication and readership with a realistic, uncondescending dose of low culture – and, more important, as having
somehow bridged an empathetic gap that divided Americans into
those separate classes.[14]

These are, of course, high-culture voices who are deciding what
constitutes a realistic, uncondescending portrait of low culture.
Mason has said that she has heard "rumors" that some residents of
her hometown who have read her fiction dislike it because it makes
them seem "too much like country people."[15] It is, in fact, almost
too easy to deconstruct Mason's populism (and the cheerful response it has received), given that the entire project is virtually
invisible to the classes of people it is supposedly empowering. Her
literary politics are founded upon the troubling and decidedly un-
populist assumption that "store clerks' lives" are valid only to the
extent that they are discussed in the *New Yorker* and taken seriously
by an upper-middle-class audience. Similarly, her critics (if not necessarily her readers) do not question the possibility that her work
might not be a "realistic" vision of lower-class life at all, but an
imaginative reconstruction that appeals to an upper-middle-class
audience for many reasons, some of them potentially antagonistic.
Given her own tension regarding her Kentucky roots – she has
spoken of feeling "threatened" by home, but recently relocated
there from Pennsylvania – the possibility that her fiction contains
ambivalent impulses toward home is rarely considered.[16]

Just as the praise for Mason fails to account for the possibility
that her success might have more to do with the empathy she shares
with her readership than with her characters, however, these criti-
cisms ignore the possibility that Mason herself is both conscious of,
and fascinated with, these very issues. Thus, although Mason has
congratulated herself for 'validating' lower-class lives, she more
often observes that the "strength of my fiction has been the tension
between being from there and not from there."[17] She has similarly
suggested the popularity of her fiction can be attributed to the
large number of people who, like her, have left behind blue-collar
upbringings and joined a rising middle class. For that audience,
reading her stories, like writing them, constitutes an act of reconciliation with the home that is left behind:

> My work seems to have struck a chord with a number of read-
> ers who have left home and maybe who have rejected it, and I
> think it startles them because they thought they were rid of
> it . . .[18]

For Mason, her work appeals to a broader audience because she
brings to a high-culture site of discourse the sort of popular culture

references and concerns that she believes have been repressed from high-culture discourse. The "home" that is left behind is not just rural Kentucky, but the "popular culture" that is repudiated (or diluted) by a rising middle class, or an entrenched upper class. As Mason recognizes, however, the repression of that popular culture is rarely complete: The appearance of her K-Mart brand names and rock music references on the pages of the *New Yorker* represents something like the bubbling up of a political subconscious, intruding itself on high-culture lives in a manageable form.

In many ways, Mason's consciousness of class difference is the key to her fiction. She has said that "it's the most extraordinary thing to move out of your class," and the quote resonates across virtually every aspect of her narrative project.[19] Not only does it describe her own rise from the daughter of dairy farmers to respected writer, but it also seems to describe her stories themselves, which appear like representatives of an entrenched underclass in sites of discourse in which that underclass theoretically rarely finds a voice. As she herself suggests, most of her audience is also displaced out if its class of origin, and finds her stories appealing for the reconciliation they offer. And, unsurprisingly, class and cultural displacement are also the major thematic matter of her stories: The *New York Times,* for instance, wrote that "ominous forces of disorientation are loose in Masonland," and observed that Mason's stories invariably deal with the personal and emotional consequences of sweeping social change.[20]

In this context, whether or not Mason is a working-class heroine is not a relevant issue. If the most significant aspect of her fiction is the manner in which it seems to jump across demographic barriers (while dealing thematically with the consequences of social dislocation), then we should value that jump (and her exploration of the consequences) as the central element of her work, not a tangential one. Caught between her sympathy for the underclass and her desire to run away from it, Mason has constructed a body of fiction and a narratology for the rising middle class, a way of telling stories that tries to balance the dictates of a radical populist program with an affection for the individual that rises above populism. "Shiloh" provides the first, and best, example of that narratology.

Country People

The two protagonists of "Shiloh," Leroy and Norma Jean Moffett, are not in control of their lives. Rather, they appear to be moved by larger external forces which they only dimly recognize and certainly do not understand. The most active force in "Shiloh," for

114   THE AMERICAN SHORT STORY

instance, appears to be the feminist movement, which makes its way to the Kentucky couple through a television set broadcasting "Donahue."[21] The story presents Norma Jean's evolution toward what Donahue himself might call "self-actualization" (she takes college courses, begins working out, gets a job, and eventually tells Leroy that she wants a divorce), and Leroy's lapses toward a childlike confusion. Her movement toward fulfilling some ideal of individuality, however, is mitigated throughout by her confusion over the reasons for her actions. When Leroy asks Norma Jean if her request for a divorce is a "women's lib thing," for instance, she answers, "don't be funny"; later, she adds "I don't know what I'm saying. Forget it."[22]

Similarly, Leroy, who has come to realize that "he never took time to examine anything," nevertheless "forgets where he hears things anymore," and seems lost in nostalgic fantasies of starting over, exemplified by his desire to build a log cabin as their 'new' homestead. Neither he nor Norma Jean seems to recognize the stress that losing their baby several years earlier has had on their marriage, even though Leroy recalls having heard "that for most people losing a child destroys the marriage."[23] Fittingly, Norma Jean's announcement that she wants a divorce takes place in a cemetery, where Leroy seems to sense the link between his failing marriage and death in general, but cannot quite make the more personal connection between his imminent divorce and the loss of their son: "Leroy is trying to comprehend that his marriage is breaking up, but for some reason he is wondering about white slabs in a graveyard."[24]

That final scene is set, appropriately, at a National Historical Site, the Civil War battleground at Shiloh, Tennessee. Leroy, attempting to explain the failure of his marriage, widens his perspective and seeks to locate his and Norma Jean's place within a larger scope of historical change:

> General Grant, drunk and furious, shoved the Southerners back to Corinth, where Mabel and Jet Beasley were married years later, when Mabel was still thin and good looking. The next day, Mabel and Jet visited the battleground, and then Norma Jean was born, and then she married Leroy and had a baby, which they lost, and now Leroy and Norma Jean are here at the same battleground . . .

Leroy's epiphany, however, comes not when he successfully locates his place in history, but when he recognizes his inability to understand the forces of social change that have affected his life, an inability reflected in his rote listing of battleground names and family milestones. In a central line, Mason poetically describes these forces as "the insides of history":

> Leroy knows he is leaving out a lot. He is leaving out the insides of history. And the real inner workings of a marriage, like most of history, have escaped him . . .

At this point, Leroy recognizes his desire to build a log cabin as a refusal to adjust to social change, and dedicates himself to "get moving again." This optimistic moment is undermined by the very conclusion, however: Leroy, with one bad leg and one leg asleep, barely capable of "moving" in any sense, nevertheless strides hopefully toward Norma Jean, who is gesturing in what is either a welcoming wave or a muscle exercise designed to increase her own strength. The story ends at that ambiguous moment: It is as if Leroy's recognition that he has not understood the "inner workings" of past events is no guarantee that he will understand them in the future.[25]

The third-person narrator, interestingly, seems to be in a similar position. The story is told in an artfully awkward prose, on a level of vocabulary equivalent to that of Leroy and Norma Jean (Mason has said, probably exaggerating, that she limits herself to a six-hundred-word lexicon).[26] Just as Norma Jean and Leroy seem confused over the reasons for their own behavior, the narrator seems unwilling or unable to locate, and emphasize, the 'meaningful moments' within the story. "Shiloh," like most of Mason's stories, has a flat texture, seems unplotted, and ends with an ambiguous and elliptical image ("The sky is unusually pale – the color of the dust ruffle Mabel made for their bed") that provides no sense of closure.[27] Superficially at least, Mason refuses to appear any more in control of the narrative than her characters are in control of their lives.

In doing so, she creates an authorial persona that is bound empathetically to the lives of the people she believes to be trapped inside history. She is unafraid of analyzing herself from the same historicist perspective, even though that perspective often undercuts her own authority by implying that she is not in control of the process of composition:

> I can't analyze it in detail and I'm not sure I can say why I choose to write that way, or even if I choose. I think things like that must be determined by larger social forces . . .[28]

Much of what Mason says about her own work is informed by this same self-deprecating, and antiliterary, perspective. Responding to a student's complicated interpretation of the dust-ruffle image that closes "Shiloh," for instance, she denies knowledge of the implications the student found, and instead observes that she writes "innocently."[29] Similarly, she has described her decisions about plot and closure in terms that suggest she dislikes making conscious choices about composition, and prefers instead to do anything she can to "get at that subconscious": "When you're writing a story, there comes a moment when it feels right to quit. Sometimes that just happens . . . It comes out of a feeling . . . It's — I'm not used to being analytical about it."[30] In describing her own work process as a sequence of unplanned choices dictated by subconscious or external forces over which she has little control, Mason creates a vision of her own creative activity that is identical to her vision of the lives of her characters, and that is modeled on a distinctly historicist perspective on behavior. Just as she says that her stories are composed "innocently," and conclude at a moment she has neither planned nor analyzed afterward, her characters "don't think of their lives as a story with coherence: They're just in it, they don't know what's going to happen next or why anything's happening."[31]

This is, as Sontag notes, an old game; but Mason practices it with unusually intricate self-consciousness. Unlike her characters, who appear both trapped within history and unable to recognize its influence on their lives, Mason's knowing "innocence" is coordinated with a deliberate effort on her part to control the effect of external conditions on her creative output. Her acceptance of these effects, in turn, places her in a position of both superiority over and sympathy with her characters: sympathy, because she accepts her own helplessness as well as theirs; superiority, because she recognizes and identifies them, and makes them major elements in her empowerment as a writer. In an interview with Lila Havens, for instance, Mason echoes Norma Jean's comments on the feminist movement, but with a telling difference: Where Norma Jean denies that feminism is a factor in her behavior, Mason notes that she "internalized" feminism, and then "moved on" — that is, she consciously accepted an external social movement into her subconscious, so that it would become an element in her "innocent," socially unaware poetic.[32] It is the precise difference enacted in her demographic relationship to her characters: Norma Jean and Leroy Moffett and Mason were all born and raised in lower-middle-class rural Kentucky, but while the Moffetts labor at rising above or repudiating the conditions of their lives, Mason has "moved on," acquired a Ph.D., and gained control of those same conditions (and the Moffetts themselves) as the resources of her fiction.

In a like manner, she denies being explicitly "political," but her thoughts on the purpose of her writing are laced with phrases such as "class struggle," suggesting that she has also, to some extent, internalized Marxism, and then moved on. This internalization of Marxist ideology is perhaps the most crucial aspect of her fiction. Throughout interviews, she has used the term "superior sensibility" (or variants thereof) to describe the model for fiction she believes has been unnecessarily dominant in the past.[33] In its place, Mason substitutes a model for the behavior of characters in fiction in which they move in coordination with communal values, or are moved (hesitatingly or not) by the force of those communal values. Similarly, her model of authorship appears to disdain the notion that the serious writer is a superior sensibility by presenting narrators and implied authors that seem neither more alienated nor more sensitive than their characters: "I don't feel superior to these people," Mason notes of her subjects, "I feel I'm luckier."[34]

The Insides of History

As mentioned earlier, "Shiloh" has been one of the most anthologized stories of the 1980s; along with selections from Jayne Anne Phillips, Louise Erdrich, Raymond Carver, Anne Beattie, and a handful of other authors, Mason's story has been consistently selected by textbook and commercial anthology editors as a representative of the best the 1980s short story had to offer.[35] In a significant sense, the popularity of "Shiloh" provides a further illustration of the most radical implications of Mason's narratology, and the kinds of publishing patterns that would be produced by the institutionalization of that narratology. The inference of Mason's poetic is that worthy fiction is not produced by individuals who control the resources of their fiction and the circumstances of its reception, but by individuals who respond "innocently" to a mixture of external and subconscious forces. In the past, it has been a commonplace of literature that special individuals might possess this special innocence – they might, for instance, be the Aeolian Harps through which God chose to communicate to Man. But the peculiar nature of Mason's repudiation of the alien, superior sensibility is that it widens the franchise of "innocence" to people who lack any special spiritual insights or charismatic gifts of artistic ability, as well as to those who have no knowledge of tradition or craft. She widens the franchise of potential artists to those who are truly "innocent," and respond "innocently" to external social forces – which is to say, virtually everybody. This model of creative activity, carried to its institutional fulfillment, would justify a system of publication and canonization where multivocal sites of discourse such as anthologies or magazines dominate, and where conservative assumptions about the consistent quality of an author's oeuvre are replaced by greater accessibility to the processes of publication and canonization.

Mason's own descriptions of the composition of "Shiloh" and her other early stories vividly illustrate the degree of her commitment to this model. Rather than describing the act of writing (about which she is almost consistently unforthcoming), Mason focuses on the correspondence between herself and Roger Angell of the *New Yorker,* who rejected nineteen of her stories before accepting one:

> We developed a correspondence and he really encouraged me a great deal, and I got very excited about what I was doing and worked very hard. Usually what he told me were not bits of advice on revising but just sort of subjective responses about the central reasons he didn't think they could publish the story, and he would offer a general criticism . . . it was fairly general, but usually he would make one or two comments that would hit right at the problem with the story, and it would give me something to think about. . . .[36]

As Mason describes it, "Shiloh" and her personal writing style were the product of a lengthy, impressionistic dialogue between herself and Angell who, as fiction editor of the *New Yorker,* might reasonably be called a living metonymy for the short-story publishing establishment. That her personal style could be perceived as the product of an engagement between herself and an external representative of the publishing community, rather than the product of some isolated, alien poesis, is a possibility that Mason characteristically does not seem to mind.

In fact, "Shiloh" itself, with its reliance on historicizable forces and the present tense, seems to invite the interpretation that it was generated by a moment of interaction between editor, author, genre, and culture, rather than by an isolated author. Mason relentlessly uses brand names, and references to songs that are popular at a given point in time, to historicize her stories to points in history (responding to a question about why she refers to songs and cultural figures by name in *In Country,* for instance, Mason says that "*In Country* was in the summer of '84. There are only a few years in which that story could take place").[37] In effect, this use of popular culture references creates a special language that not only dates the story to a specific moment in time but also makes it less readable as the years pass after its publication. These are all factors that justify "Shiloh"'s presence in current anthologies as a representative of the kind of short stories contemporary culture has to offer to the tradition. These factors also moderate the criticism Mason so often receives for writing "*New Yorker*-type stories" – a contemporary subgenre (to be distinguished from the "New Yorker" stories of previous generations) that she, in fact, did much to help create. As a study of her poetic clearly indicates, composing a story that contained within itself the unconscious traces that define a community was the entire point of her creative efforts, not an awkward aftereffect.

These factors also suggest that "Shiloh" will not be so heavily anthologized in the future, unless contemporary culture remains static enough so the special language of popular culture references means as much in 2002 as it did in 1982. To a certain extent, Bobbie Ann Mason is writing a kind of disposable *literature:* serious fiction that addresses specific moments in time, which could be written only in specific moments in time, and that is initially published in sites of discourse (magazines) that are themselves more disposable than the bound volumes within which serious writing is usually enveloped. Friction occurs when this ideology clashes against more conservative assumptions about authorship: When, for instance, Mason herself keeps writing and publishing, she is implying that she can continue deliberately to produce those extraordinary moments when a community interacts with an individual (or an individual interacts with her subconscious) to produce a memorable story, a notion that contains within itself the main elements of the alien, superior sensibility with a uniquely Marxist twist.

Of course, Mason has continued writing and publishing her stories in bound volumes. The irony of Mason's philosophical flexibility concerning external social forces is that it accommodates the kind of self-deprecation that might be expected from a beginning, but not an established, author. That flexibility is part of a narratology for a rising class of people with divided sympathies; but not for an entrenched one. And a survey of the interviews Mason has granted in the seven years since her initial success suggests that as she has grown more confident with her own authorship, she has also repudiated the self-deprecating models of behavior that formed the philosophical underpinning for her rejection of the alien, superior sensibility, and – to some extent – for her preference for the short story.

In an early interview, for instance, she dwells on her relationship with Roger Angell and the *New Yorker,* and speaks in modest terms about her own critical success: "I'm still really quite surprised that my work has made the impression it has."[38] More recently, however, she dwells on the fact that she now composes alone, and shows her work to no one prior to sending it to her publishers. In a similar manner, her stance toward the alien, superior sensibility has altered considerably. In an interview conducted in 1989, Mason describes her evolution as an artist, and describes her repudiation of that sensibility using the same anecdote found in earlier interviews, but with a crucial twist at the conclusion:

> I thought, "Well, I'll write a kind of *Huckleberry Finn* novel about a *girl*. I won't write about the sensitive young man, won't write about the artist, the sensitive youth coming of age. I'll write about somebody who is insensitive, and who doesn't wear glasses." And I found out that you couldn't do that! There's no story there . . .[39]

Interestingly, though, there is no conspicuous way to tell from Mason's fiction exactly when she made this discovery; her subject matter and her major themes have remained comparatively unchanged, and it could be easily argued that her most recent novel, *In Country,* is very much a kind of *Huckleberry Finn* about a girl. All Mason seems to have discovered, rather, is the point where her life has finally diverged completely from those of her characters — where her private story cannot be told without a sensitive artist figure performing at the center, and possibly wearing glasses.

"Write What Pleases You"

Mason's ethos of fiction represents a forceful embodiment of the major ideological concerns that have surrounded the development of short fiction in this country. It is impossible to miss the resemblance between William Carlos Williams's paradigmatic claim that the brevity of the short story matched the "heterogeneity" and "brokenness" of lower-class lives, for instance, and Mason's own belief that the lives of the underclass do not follow structured plot lines, and require a new kind of 'story' (or, for that matter, Raymond Carver's observation that writing a novel was impossible while he had to think about paying the rent).[40] It is equally difficult to ignore the echoes of Poe's affinity for disposable literature in Mason's celebration of the present tense. Bret Harte's conscious regionalism, James Farrell's Marxist exasperation with traditional short story forms, and Edward O'Brien's over-the-top exclamations about ethnic inclusion all resonate in Mason's faith in the populist possibilities of her fiction. In general, the two most widely circulated canons of the late nineteenth and twentieth centuries regarding short fiction are that the genre is easy to read and to write, and that it therefore represents a significant alternative to older modes of determining literary value; Mason's self-deprecating efforts to restructure the form somehow capture both the abnegating and

ambitious aspects of these two canons, and with the kind of atten-
tiveness to communal voices that seems entirely typical of Mason's
work.[41]

In particular, however, one aspect of Mason's fiction – what she
calls the tension between "from there" and "not from there" – is
especially central to attempts to understand the historical development of the American short story, as well as its current state. To the
extent that the short story had radically democratic implications,
those implications have been played out within high- and middle-
culture spheres. For this reason, it is significant that the short story
was accepted, however tentatively, as a genre of high literature, as
opposed to being identified as a genre of popular culture. Within
the field of popular culture, the short story would be considered
the *least* democratic of art forms; but among a play of literary
genres consisting of novels, poetry, and drama, the short story as it
developed in the late nineteenth century clearly represented the
most accessible, most easily written, and most widely dispersed
form of high literature. This distinction, in turn, illustrates how the
short story was never a democratizing project in the purest sense,
but part of an attempt to infiltrate high-culture discourse with
middle- and low-culture influences – while leaving the aristocratic
underpinning of high literature intact. Throughout its existence,
the short story project has been an attempt to wrest "literature"
from genres (i.e., the novel, lyric poetry) and sites of publication
(i.e., bound volumes) that were associated with a European (and
upper-class American) form of cultural capital that even a newly
moneyed bourgeois aristocracy could not buy itself into. It was the
literary icon of the rising middle class.

All of these factors clearly resonate within Mason's fiction. Just as
her creative activity mediates between genuinely populist impulses
and faith in the ideology of individualism, the development of the
short story in America has been marked by the tension between
these two conflicting beliefs. Specifically, because the short story
project never completely questioned the aristocratic underpinning
of literature – the faith that certain texts and certain individuals
were intrinsically better than others – it was placed at a natural
disadvantage within a purely literary discourse among genres that
did not have to bear the burden of being associated with attempts
to level definitions of excellence. The consequence is that even
contemporary critics and students of the short story often perceive
it as a site of discourse where the community, in the form of mercantile considerations or academic guidelines, exercises a restrictive amount of control over the individual artist. For many, this
belief is corroborated by the brevity of the short story itself, which

seems somehow to restrain the writer, in contrast to the freedom he or she might practice within the wide open spaces of the novel. Mason, for instance, has described the short story as a "constrained" form, and has spoken of the things that an author cannot do within those limitations.[42]

This was, however, a natural consequence of the manner in which the American short story had been sold to the American reading and writing public. The immense, almost universal popularity of Edgar Allan Poe and his review of Hawthorne's *Twice-Told Tales* (1842) within discussions of the American short story illustrates the extent to which future short story practitioners and proponents had accepted that their genre would be associated with Poe's hyperconscious (and possibly hoaxing) insistence that the composition of high literature was a quantifiable process within which intuition played no part whatsoever.[43] This insistence that the short story could be defined scientifically by someone other than the author dovetailed smoothly with ideological arguments that claimed that the short story was America's art form, and could therefore be defined not according to practice, but according to what the individual observer believed America's art form should represent.[44] It similarly addressed the desires of both the magazine and academic establishments, which could profit substantially by claiming that the individual short story had to respond to a set of predetermined rules. The result of this conflation of institutional desires and ideological arguments was that by 1930, the short story had been subjected to a veritable avalanche of definitions, theoretical treatises, and best-selling how-to handbooks.

And even after the death of the short story as a commercial genre, this definitional energy remained a fact of the genre. The entire system of graduate programs and creative writing courses that has developed in the last forty years would have been an impossibility without a founding ideology that claimed that the composition of high literature was a craft that could be quantified and taught.[45] This same ideology, with a slight twist, also empowered the New Critics, who made the short story a staple in high school and college English courses by recognizing that the relative length of a short story implied that it had been better crafted than a novel, and would better reward close reading (and would also make it more easily taught, a nontrivial pragmatic issue).[46] If, in other words, the short story has been consistently attacked as a site of formulaic writing, it has been for reasons that are grounded in the most forceful celebrations of the genre – that it is a site of discourse where the community has a say in the composition process.

And so, despite the fact that the short story was the literary icon of a rising and entrepreneurial middle class, rhetoric about the short story could subvert in remarkable ways the ideology of individualism upon which that rise was based. Walter Pitkin, for instance, one of the leading writers of how-to short story handbooks during the period of their great popularity, dispensed advice that derided even the most innocuous defense of individualism:

> What you should do is to get interested in the same subject matter and in the same problems of modern life which the successful writers are dealing with. And then form your own impressions and opinions about these and write what pleases you in the popular language of the day. One of the most pernicious pieces of advice ever given to young writers was that famous utterance of O. Henry: "There is only one rule to success in literature. Write what pleases you."[47]

Pitkin's advice is especially striking because it was directed toward a generation of young middle-class Americans who saw the short story as an opportunity to make money and be artists at the same time — an idyllic conflation of bourgeois and aristocratic ideals founded specifically on the desire to do exactly what "pleased you." But what is also striking about Pitkin's advice is that, with his recommendations to internalize external social movements and write in "the popular language of the day," it greatly resembles Bobbie Ann Mason's own approach to writing fiction.

This statement is not made even remotely to suggest that Mason was influenced in any way by Pitkin, any other short story handbook writer, or any explicit knowledge of the development of the short story in this country. The resemblance between her approach and Pitkin's is cited here because it illustrates how the decision to write short stories, then as well as now, constitutes an archetypal response to the conditions of American culture. Just as Pitkin wrote explicitly for an audience of would-be artists that chose the short story over other genres because it conferred a degree of bourgeois respectability, Mason developed a literary politics that balanced an immense sympathy toward popular culture (she has joked in interviews that she is a writer because she is too shy to be a rock star) with an almost equal empathy for those who repudiated popular culture for something presumably better.[48] In this respect, it is significant that Bobbie Ann Mason jokes about wanting to be a rock star; but it is equally significant that she persistently tried to publish in the *New Yorker*, rather than publishing in the smaller literary magazines in which beginning short story writers often find their first audience. To publish in the little magazines would constitute an act of wholehearted sympathy (which she clearly doesn't feel) with high culture literariness, just as the desire to be a rock star is an acknowledgment of the continuing pull of popular culture in her ambitions. Only the *New Yorker* – the short story writer's Mecca – could offer a reconciliation of these mixed desires, by giving Mason critical vogue with the upper class, enough readers to be considered popular, and the kind of middle-class respectability that can come only to the writer who is well paid for her efforts.

Mason's success, and her influence, also illustrate the degree to which modern trends in the short story have a historical precedent. The state of the contemporary American short story, with its populist orientation ("experiment is out, concern is in," Elizabeth Spencer wrote in 1983)[49] and its academic institutions, represents a rebirth of the strong nationalist expectations and the emphasis on technique that have been its major tenets since the nineteenth century. A school of fiction such as "minimalism," which promotes literary values such as economy and sparseness and encourages the individual writer to concentrate on each individual sentence, is certainly a logical development in an academic climate where there are currently two hundred graduate writing programs yearly conferring close to a thousand degrees on would-be short story writers – many of whom will become writing teachers and find that it is both easy and profitable to insist on teachable values such as economy of composition. This academic climate, however, was predated by the interest of the New Critics in the short story in the 1940s, which evolved from the explosion of short story handbooks and courses in the 1920s, which in turn was authorized by the immense influence of Brander Matthews's "Philosophy of the Short Story" (1885) – a treatise that, borrowing from Poe, insisted the short story was a superior art form precisely because it abided by the kind of rules that could be taught in school.[50]

These pedagogical developments, in turn, would have been unlikely without the existence of a demand somewhere within the American political unconscious for an art form that acted like a mercantile object, and that somehow combined the best elements of being an aristocrat with being a good populist. It was this idyllic unification of classes that Poe promised American artists in "The Philosophy of Composition," when he claimed that he would show how it was possible *deliberately* to compose a piece of writing that would "suit at once the popular and critical taste."[51] Bobbie Ann Mason is Poe turned inside out: Playing dumb where Poe played smart, shrinking her vocabulary and pointing her pen down the social ladder instead of up, she has nevertheless founded her project upon the same uneasy but radical rejection of the romance of the artist, and has weaved similarly slippery constructions of class and democracy into an ambitious, partially hoaxing, and easily imitable literary politics. Her work suggests that the distance between Poe's imperial pedagogical pose, and the deliberately self-deprecating and rustic Americana of one hundred years of local color, dialect, regionalism, and minimalism, is slim when measured in terms of class, writerly aspiration, or audience.

POSTSCRIPT
IOWA CITY

The summer week I received my doctorate, I visited a friend in Iowa City for four days. Iowa City is a singular community in American life, perhaps the only place in the country where the literary and social promises described in the previous pages have taken root in the soil, the only place where literary ambition and the cult of authorial personality can be palpably viewed in the casual daily workings of urban life. It is, as a waiter in Chicago described to me, "the most literary little town" he had ever visited: "a community of the imagination," as Paul Engle called it in 1964.[1]

Iowa City is, of course, home of the Iowa Writers' Workshop, the first and most prestigious graduate creative writing program. Since its founding between 1922 and 1939, the Workshop has grown rapidly into an American literary and publishing institution.[2] *Esquire* has regularly listed Iowa as a "hot center" (or at least a significant planet) in its periodic maps of the "American literary universe" (itself another institution, and some future cultural historian's gold mine).[3] The list of ex-students and teachers who have paused in Iowa is formidable: Ex-students include Flannery O'Connor, Raymond Carver, Jayne Anne Phillips, Norman Dubie, Andre Dubus, Tracy Kidder, John Gardner, Wallace Stegner, Mona Van Duyn, Gail Godwin, James Tate, Robert Bly, W. D. Snodgrass, William Stafford, Mark Strand, W. D. Kinsella, Laura Jensen, T. C. Boyle, and Philip Levine; teachers have included John Irving, Donald Justice, Philip Roth, John Crowe Ransom, R. V. Cassill, Norman Mailer (who "invaded," according to one then-student), William Kennedy, Anne Tyler, John Cheever, Robert Stone, Anthony Burgess, Leonard Michaels, Grace Paley, and numerous others.[4] Robert Dana remembers in a 1981 reminiscence that his workshop teachers in 1952 were "Karl Shapiro, Robert Lowell, and John Berryman," while another ex-student recalls that the 1966 fiction staff consisted of Vance Bourjaily, Kurt Vonnegut, Nelson Algren, William Murray, and Jose Donoso.[5] The number of ex-Iowans who currently publish or teach in other venues is, arguably, dominant: Estimates (also courtesy of *Esquire,* and Iowa's own brochures) sug-

126

gest that as many as one-quarter to one-third of those American writers whom publishers and critics consider "distinguished" have passed through Iowa City at some early point in their careers.[6] During the last thirty years, when the creative writing workshop and the academically supported author have become basic facts of literary life, Iowa's pioneering status, isolated locale, and lofty alumni roll have all become the stuff of literary folklore.

Iowa City is sufficiently small, and sufficiently focused, that even a visitor who had no interest in the Workshop (who perhaps had business instead with the cement concerns on the edge of town, the feed-corn farmers, or the Quaker Oats plant in Cedar Rapids that fills the air around that city with the smell of Captain Crunch breakfast cereal) would nevertheless be impressed by the literariness of the city. The book stores, of course, are excellent, and (in the Midwest at least) somewhat legendary: The Prairie Lights store has appeared in a nationally syndicated comic strip, and people in St. Louis could tell me the names of the women who worked at the Haunted-By-The-Creek. What makes Iowa City literary, however, is the aura of the Workshop itself, and the manner in which it transforms the normally aliterary (and even anti-intellectual) aspects of small town life into writerly milestones. During my one evening at the Fox Head bar (students call it the Fox Head, town regulars call it Dave's; either way, it is a Workshop staple), for instance, an angry drunk accosted our table and demanded that we tell him certain basic facts about the narrative of Chekhov's "Lady and the Pet Dog" about which he had grown foggy. Another drunk is famous for challenging Workshop students to fist fights in order to humble them (like the Dave's–Fox Head name bifurcation, a suggestive indication of tension between town and Workshop that seems mostly absent); more pathetically, he is also known for losing these fights.

The city is meant to be toured. *Let's Go: The Budget Guide to the USA 1992*, tells its reader that "Iowa City is the setting of over fifty contemporary novels."[7] Every house potentially bears the status of having sheltered a famous author, and most current Workshop students can tell you where Frank Conroy lives, where Marilynne Robinson or Kurt Vonnegut stayed during their briefer tenures, or where John Irving placed his real *and* his fictive families. Similarly, the same apartments are cycled through passing generations of Workshop students, and are informally commemorated across time and distance: Students can tell you the ancestral lines of their homes, who published where and when, while professors of creative writing across the country all share the same *spiritus mundi* of street names, bars, and restaurants. Even non-Workshop denizens tell the (almost certainly fictitious) story that places Raymond Carver and John Cheever outside John's Grocery every morning at seven, waiting impatiently for the store to open so they could be first on line to buy liquor. Iowa City loves to tell stories about authors.

If part of the appeal of Iowa City is the reflected glamour of famous writers, however, another equally important part lies in the promise of future authorship that the program seems to offer in large quantity. Nor is this promise exclusively the birthright of the graduate students. During my brief visit, dozens (if not hundreds) of Elderhostel visitors roamed the city, where they were receiving a three-week course in writing literature: They spoke informally but excitedly of the stories they would write now that they were retired, doted on their student-teachers with grandparently pride, and even paid some of them to edit the memoirs and novels they had already composed (the students, in turn, spoke enthusiastically of the financial possibilities presented by an ever-increasing geriatric population). Other courses are offered to non-Elderhostel non-Workshop customers, and attract an eclectic, international student body of serious would-be authors: I met, for instance, a man from Salvador, Brazil who came to Iowa City to take a course in memoir writing so he could return to Brazil and write a biography of his there-famous grandfather – an indication of the long reach of Iowa's reputation, and its promise.

The closer one approaches the Workshop itself – its offices, its students – the more concentrated this sense of a truly literary *community* becomes. The administrator sits beside a bulletin board filled with photographs of the writers who have taught at the Workshop, and their children (whom she calls "Workshop babies"; she clearly distinguishes between the children who were born or conceived in Iowa City, and those who were not). A random hour in her office in the summertime consists of two or three calls from well-known authors, and hearing the names of Nobel Prize-winning writers dropped in conversation, not as reference points for intellectual banter, but as possible dinner guests. The wall above the photocopier is covered with bulletins for public readings by famous authors, and crayon renditions of that wall by Workshop babies. The wall next to the secretary's desk has been devoted to bookshelves containing publications by Iowa graduates or teachers; after eighteen months of collecting, two ceiling-high bookshelves are already overcrowded.

The sense of a literary community, and the effect of living among these icons of literary celebrity is strongest among the graduate students enrolled in the program. Any creative writing workshop is, in general, an insular grouping; in a city as small as Iowa City, and with the concentrated prestige focused upon the program there, it is doubly so. Much has been made of the camaraderie among creative writing students, and much has also been made of the competition. But when creative writing graduate students gather to talk, they generally do not talk about literature. They talk about each other: about their apartments, their teachers, their sex lives, their successes (or, rather, other people's successes – nobody talks about their own). They gossip, create subgroups with shifting loyalties, and create and spread personal myths of self. The workshops themselves are treated delicately, because they are often traumatic experiences: One student I spoke to observed that if he wanted constructive and caring criticism of his work, the last place he would go to would be a community of recent college graduates all wanting to be writers, all competing for the same slender perks.

But he is there, of course. The description of Iowa City that I have just provided is necessarily sketchy and impressionistic, as befits an informal four-day visit. But every conversation that I had with the students there suggested that they are fully aware of how complicated a cultural gesture the idea of a creative writing workshop has become. My sense of Iowa City is that the "community of the imagination" that the writers there have constructed is an urban planner's equivalent of the ambivalent rejection of the romance of the artist, and the uneasy embrace of literary professionalism, which this book has traced throughout the history of the short story. Iowa City provides further evidence that the dream of authorship is so strong that it moves the landscape, and leaves magazines, schools, alternate subeconomies, and genres in its wake. It provides a concentrated illustration of how important it can be to Americans to tell their stories, and tell them right; and in doing so, it provides an indication of the deeper cultural reasons why the short story and the workshop remain in the "hot center" of any map of American cultural life.

The workshop is a kind of classic American social form: the community bound (and hierarchical structure built) by storytelling and autobiography. Support for this generalization can be found in traces throughout American literary and cultural history: I am thinking, for instance, of Ben Franklin's *Junto*, his "club of mutual improvement" where each member was required to "produce and read an essay of his own writing" every three months; or Frederick Douglass's *Heroic Slave,* where (as described by Robert Stepto) the abolition movement is portrayed as groups of good storytellers and good listeners, who then retell the stories they have heard until the entire nation is bound by autobiographical storytelling; or, more directly, of the fraternitylike writers' clubs formed in college towns in the nineteenth and early twentieth centuries, who bore club colors, banners, and fight songs into battle with other clubs; or, most simply, the Quaker tradition of testimony. Most specifically, I am thinking of the Puritan conversion narrative, the description of personal religious transformation that each would-be visible saint was required to deliver in the churches of seventeenth-century New England. The listening congregation then decided whether that individual should join the Elect (and share the considerable secular privileges of that distinction), based upon the conviction and apparent authenticity (and attention to certain doctrinal and social guidelines) of that telling.[8]

The workshop resembles all these institutions, without bearing precise relation to any. In the workshop community, individuals are required to help one another, according to the social contract among them; simultaneously, they vie for the right to be labeled the voice of the community, a title that can be awarded only with the cooperation of a community of individuals competing for the same honor. Success is awarded not (or not necessarily) to the individual whose voice is most discordantly powerful; but rather, it is awarded to the voice that is resonantly typical, the voice that speaks for the community (if the community chooses to canonize the voice for less evident reasons, of course, they will seek out these resonances; this is one of the functions of criticism). Election is, of course, publication: One student commented that publication in the *New Yorker* conferred upon the writer the kind of privileges within the community that he could equate only with sudden status changes in primitive tribes and medieval churches.

Overall, the entire workshop experience bears the legacy of a roughly democratic and congregational ancestry. A traditional workshop in the fine arts features a master and students, who are tutored individually or collectively according to the master's inclination – most workshops in the visual arts still maintain this format. The creative writing workshop leader might choose to be authoritarian, but the nature of the institution requires a building of consensus, a chiming of voices. It is for these reasons that I remained attentive to the conversations that workshop students hold outside their classroom. Their gossip and competition is sometimes cruel, sometimes tender, but it seems to me to be the heart of the workshop, and it is almost certainly where the most intense storytelling occurs. If the approval of the workshop group (in tandem with publication) represents the validation of self and of experience, the gossiping is the weighing of self: It represents the workshop students' eagerness to share and judge the quality and charisma of their subjective perspectives (which is what, after all, they have brought to market), to tell and retell the story of the immediate experience, and to register its importance. It is as though the Puritan conversion narrative, which standard intellectual history portrays to us as a test, was in fact a compulsion: as though the individual's faith in the basic value of his or her life story was so unshakable, or the self-conscious desire to tell it was so fierce, that the risks of failing were beyond regard.[9]

Then, of course, there are students who take no chances with the congregation. During my visit, I stayed in the apartment of a student who was out of town, riding in the annual cross-Iowa bicycle race. He was one of the two or three students that particular year who was elected: He had won the Nelson Algren short story contest and a Stegner fellowship from Stanford in short order, and his stories had already showed up in several of the journals that graced Prairie Lights' magazine stand. In absentia, he seemed to me to be the model (though not typical) Iowa student. His apartment was a true garret, ideal for the serious, semi-impoverished writer: two small rooms over the garage of a ranch house, low ceilings, poor ventilation. But it was the contents of his apartment that seemed most relevant. Manuscripts were strewn everywhere, of course. But so were magazines: There were roughly fifty magazines in the apartment (I took the liberty of counting only those that were visible without opening shelves or drawers). All but one was the *New Yorker,* and the exception was *Esquire.* He had perhaps seventy-five books; and although it would be inaccurate to say his tastes ran wholly to modern fiction, it was clear that the most visible, most dog-eared books were recent American models, especially Vintage contemporaries, their brethren, and fiction from recent Iowa graduates or teachers. Otherwise, his apartment was almost bare: piles of clothes, and a few posters and tapes.

I admired his purpose. His apartment looked as though he had had no life worth recording prior to his rooting at Iowa (a gross and unfair mistake, as it turns out), or that he chose to remake himself as the archetypal young American writer upon his matriculation there. His taste in writing was entirely preprofessional: He read work that was published only where he wanted to publish, or was published by people he already knew. If his tastes seemed narrow, they were directed; and although few of the other students I met shared his focus (i.e., they read books that were written before 1980), most envied his success. He was the pure product of Iowa, and his taste in literature paid homage to the other pure product of Iowa: It is simply not possible that the *New Yorker* means

Advertisement, Philadelphia *City Paper,* week of 26 July–2 August 1991: 48.

as much to people in New York as it does to people in Iowa City. It sits in piles in most apartments, sometimes studied closely, sometimes derided bitterly (there is an anti-*New Yorker* camp among the students, who refuse to read it, or 'submit' to it), but everywhere charged with meaning. Considering founder Harold Ross's famous statement that the magazine would not be written for the little old lady from Dubuque, this is more than ironic.[10] Ninety miles down the road from that old lady, his mid-America-spurning magazine is totem.

NOTES

Introduction

1 Quoted in Jessica Benson, "Short On Paper, Long On Popularity," *Philadelphia Inquirer* 19 Nov. 1989: 2-J.
2 Rogers Worthington, "Writer's Camp," *Chicago Tribune Magazine* 5 Feb. 1989: 12.
3 Eugene Current-Garcia and Bert Hitchcock, "Contemporary Flowering," introduction to section five of *American Short Stories* (Glenview, IL: Scott, Foresman, 1990) 658.
4 Benson 2-J.
5 Ruth Suckow, "The Short Story," *Saturday Review of Literature* 4 (19 Nov. 1927) 317.
6 Peter Prescott, introduction, *Norton Book of American Short Stories* (New York: W. W. Norton, 1988) 14.
7 Ralph Waldo Emerson, "The Poet," *The Collected Works of Ralph Waldo Emerson,* intro. Joseph Slater, vol. 3 (Cambridge, MA: Belknap Press of Harvard University Press, 1983) 3–24.
8 Edgar Allan Poe, *"Twice-Told Tales,"* review of *Twice-Told Tales,* by Nathaniel Hawthorne, *Graham's Magazine* May 1842: 298–300. Reprinted in Edgar Allan Poe, *Essays and Reviews,* ed. G. R. Thompson (New York: Library of America, 1984) 569–77.
9 Joyce Carol Oates, "Speaking About Short Fiction: An Interview with Joyce Carol Oates," with Sanford Pinsker, *Studies in Short Fiction* 18 (1981): 240.
10 This paragraph was written in summer 1991. Since that date, the friend who "fluffed away" to Idaho has removed even further, and now lives on a farm in inland Brazil; the friend who remained within the publishing establishment continues to publish short stories, and is marketing a novel.
    A third member of that workshop has described her experiences in print. See Julie Fishbein, "The Poetry of Medicine," *JAMA* 264 (19 Dec. 1990): 2999. "In 1985 I went to graduate school to become a writer. It was a fascinating time for me, surrounded by famous poets, and everyone involved in the act of making art. In fact, everyone was writing about the process of art, writing poetry about writing poetry. But I soon felt something was missing in the poems, something vital and vibrant, which I couldn't quite pinpoint."
11 See Ed Dinger, ed., *Seems Like Old Times* (Iowa City, IA: 1986) 83–8, for anecdotal information about Flannery O'Connor's stay at the University of Iowa placed in context. Maureen Howard also tells an "apocryphal" O'Connor story in "Can Writing Be Taught at Iowa?" *New York Times Magazine* 25 May 1986: 45. For more detailed information,

see Jean Wylder, "Flannery O'Connor: A Reminiscence and Some Letters," *North American Review* Spring 1970: 58–65. This information, although subjective (one person's reminiscence in an in-house book dedicated to the Iowa Writer's Workshop Golden Jubilee), both supports and illuminates the anecdote I have described: O'Connor avoided the classroom discussions, and isolated herself from the other students (58). Wylder also describes one O'Connor in-workshop reading that was so powerful the class was silenced in response: "That we had nothing to say about Flannery's story was a tribute to her genius" (62). Myth-making or not, this is a suggestive story.

In workshop programs in general, some of the most repeated anecdotes concern famous writers who were not received well during their workshop days: In Iowa, for instance (see Postscript), several students told me that Raymond Carver was denied aid for his second year, and dropped out of the program in response. There is no reliable way to verify this anecdote, but its repeatability is, again, suggestive.

12   Marjorie Perloff, "Homeward Ho! Silicon Valley Pushkin," *American Poetry Review* Nov./Dec. 1986: 45. Wallace Stegner, *On the Teaching of Creative Writing*, ed. Edward Connery Lathem (Hanover, NH: University Press of New England, 1988) 51–2.

13   Frederick Lewis Pattee, "The Present Stage of the Short Story," *English Journal* 12 (1923): 443–9.

14   Quoted in Thomas A. Kennedy, review of *The American Short Story: 1945–1980* by Gordon Weaver, *Midwest Quarterly* 30 (1988): 281.

15   See back cover of *Sudden Fiction: American Short-Short Stories*, ed. Robert Shapard and James Thomas (Salt Lake City: Peregrine Smith Books, 1986). Foy Evans, *Let's Write Short-Shorts* (Athens, GA: Bulldog Publishers, 1946). See also *Writing the Short Short Story*, ed. Sylvia Kamerman, 1946.

16   Brander Matthews, *The Philosophy of the Short Story* (New York: Longmans, Green and Company, 1901; New York: Peter Smith, 1931). Matthews's treatise had a variegated publication history. Excerpts first appeared anonymously in the *Saturday Review* (London) in 1884. Matthews then published "The Philosophy of the Short Story," *Lippincott's* 36 (Oct. 1885) 366–74. This essay was then included in Matthews, *Pen and Ink: Essays on Subjects of More or Less Importance* (New York: Longmans, Green and Company, 1888). The 1901 edition was the most complete, including an appendix and preface.

1. Poe's Magazine

1   Frederick Lewis Pattee, *The Development of the American Short Story* (1925; New York: Biblo and Tannen, 1975) 134. Henry S. Canby, "Free Fiction," *Atlantic Monthly* July 1915: 61.

2   Ruth Suckow, "The Short Story," *Saturday Review of Literature* 4 (19 Nov. 1927): 317. Charles E. May, "The Unique Effect of the Short Story," *Studies in Short Fiction* 13 (Summer 1976): 289.

3   William Charvat, "Poe: Journalism and the Theory of Poetry," *The Profession of Authorship in America, 1800–1870* (Columbus: Ohio State University Press, 1968), 86. For Charvat, Poe had two "obsessions" during his late career: his magazine and "the idea of" his poem *Eureka*, which he also hoped would gain both commercial and critical success. Still, Charvat notes that the magazine was the "more impor-

tant," and finds evidence within Poe's essays and letters to support this
claim (85).

4 See Edgar Allan Poe, *Complete Stories and Poems* (Garden City, NY: Doubleday and Company, 1966). "William Wilson": 156–70. "The Tell-Tale Heart": 121–4. "The Imp of the Perverse": 271–5. "The Black Cat": 63–9.

5 Edgar Allan Poe, *"Twice-Told Tales,"* review of *Twice-Told Tales*, by Nathaniel Hawthorne, *Graham's Magazine* May 1842: 298–300. Reprinted in Edgar Allan Poe, *Essays and Reviews*, ed. G. R. Thompson (New York: Library of America, 1984) 569–77. Poe also wrote about *Twice-Told Tales* in the April 1842 issue of *Graham's Magazine:* see 254. This review is reprinted in Poe, *Essays* 568–9. See also Edgar Allan Poe, *"Tale-Writing – Nathaniel Hawthorne,"* review of *Mosses from an Old Manse*, by Nathaniel Hawthorne, *Godey's Magazine and Lady's Book* Nov. 1847: 252–6. Reprinted in Poe, *Essays* 577–88.

6 Pattee 134.

7 Poe, *"Twice-Told Tales"* 571.

8 Poe, *"Twice-Told Tales"* 571–2.

9 Poe, *"Twice-Told Tales"* 572.

10 Edgar Allan Poe, "The Philosophy of Composition," *Graham's Magazine* April 1846: 163–7. Reprinted in Poe, *Essays* 14–15.

11 Poe, "Composition" 13–14.

12 William Carlos Williams, *In the American Grain,* introduction, Horace Gregory (New York: New Directions, 1956) 216.

13 Edgar Allan Poe, "Penn Magazine Prospectus," *Philadelphia Saturday Courier* 13 June 1840: 2. Reprinted in Arthur Hobson Quinn, *Edgar Allan Poe: A Critical Biography* (New York: Cooper Square Publishers, 1969) 307.

14 Edgar Allan Poe, "To Charles Anthon," Oct. 1844, letter 186 of *Letters of Edgar Allan Poe*, ed. John Ward Ostrom, vol. 1 (New York: Gordian Press, 1966) 270.

15 Charvat observes that Poe's claim that he was "essentially" a "magazinist" to be "an extraordinary statement," "since by that date he had published three collections of verse, a two-volume collection of tales, a romance, and a textbook" (Charvat, "Poe," *Profession* 87).

16 Edgar Allan Poe, "To John P. Kennedy," 21 June 1841, letter 114 of *Letters* 1: 164. Edgar Allan Poe, "Stylus Prospectus," *Saturday Museum* 4 March 1843: 3. Reprinted in Quinn 376. Poe, "Penn" 2. Reprinted in Quinn 307–8.

17 See, for instance, Poe, "Stylus" 3, reprinted in Quinn 376; Poe, "Penn" 2, reprinted in Quinn 308; or Poe, "To James R. Lowell," 4 Feb. 1843, letter 151 of *Letters* 1: 221.

18 See Poe, "To James R. Lowell," 30 March 1844, letter 173 of *Letters* 1: 247; Poe, "To Dr. Thomas Chivers," 27 Sept. 1842, letter 145 of *Letters* 1: 215; Poe, "To Frederick W. Thomas," 27 Oct. 1841, letter 127 of *Letters* 1: 185; Poe, "To Frederick W. Thomas," 1 Sept. 1841, letter 124 of *Letters* 1: 180.

19 Poe, "To Robert T. Conrad," 22 Jan. 1841, letter 108 of *Letters* 1: 154.

20 Poe, "To Charles Anthon," *Letters* 1: 268.

21 Michael Allen, *Poe and the British Magazine Tradition* (New York: Oxford University Press, 1969) 196–7.

22 Drew Faust, *A Sacred Circle* (Philadelphia: University of Pennsylvania Press, 1986) 94.

23 Hammond quoted in Faust 95. Ruffin quoted in Faust 92.

24 Faust 90–1.
25 It would be more accurate to say that the people who were running magazines were also poets and authors, not vice versa. Although individuals such as George Graham ran magazines without ever contributing to them, authors such as James Russell Lowell also performed editorial functions, and many editors simply published their own work.
26 Poe, "To Charles Anthon," *Letters* 1: 268.
27 Quinn 422–3.   .
28 Poe, "To Charles Anthon," *Letters* 1: 268.
29 Poe, "To Charles Anthon," *Letters* 1: 269.
30 Poe, "To Evert A. Duyckinck," Nov. 1845, letter 215 of *Letters* 1: 301.
31 Poe, "To Charles Anthon," *Letters* 1: 270. Ralph Waldo Emerson, "The Poet," *The Collected Works of Ralph Waldo Emerson*, introduction by Joseph Slater, vol. 3 (Cambridge, MA: Belknap Press of Harvard University Press, 1983) 24.
32 Quinn 436.
33 Poe, "To James R. Lowell," Letters 1: 247.
34 Poe, "Penn" 2. Reprinted in Quinn 309.
35 Poe, "To F. W. Thomas," 25 Feb. 1843, *Letters* 1: 224. Williams 219.
36 Poe, "Penn" 2. Reprinted in Quinn 306.
37 Poe, "To Charles Anthon," *Letters* 1: 268.
38 Quinn, for instance, writes that "the general conditions which operated against the success of the *Pioneer* were those which defeated Poe" (336), although it is not clear what "general conditions" he believes are pertinent: Within one week of the *Pioneer*'s first appearance, for instance, Lowell contracted an eye ailment, trekked to Staten Island for a special treatment that likely included opium and cocaine, and remained in New York until after the *Pioneer*'s demise (C. David Heymann, *American Aristocracy: The Lives and Times of James Russell, Amy, and Robert Lowell* [New York: Dodd, Mead and Company, 1980] 66–9.) Still, the resemblances between Lowell's *Pioneer* effort and Poe's would-be journal are significant, as are the differences. Poe, in a letter to Lowell on 4 Feb. 1843 ("To James Russell Lowell," *Letters* 2: 221–2) wrote that he was "gratified" by "a certain coincidence of opinion and of taste . . . in the minor arrangements, as well as in the more important details of the journal." Lowell's prospectus (excerpted in Ferris Greenslet, *James Russell Lowell: His Life and Work* [Boston: Houghton, Mifflin and Company, 1905; Detroit: Gale Research Company, 1969]: 56–7) and introductory editorial (Lowell, "Introduction," *Pioneer*, Jan. 1843: 1–3) speak of providing a "healthy and manly Periodical Literature" as an alternative to the "namby-pamby love tales and sketches" of the popular journals (*Lowell* 56). Like Poe, Lowell sought to use high-quality paper, high-quality engravings, and wanted to pay authors substantially more than any other magazine; like Poe, he tried to create a "critical department" that would be impartial in its reviews of current literature (*Lowell* 56).
    Unlike Poe, however, Lowell resisted the inclination to claim anthemic status for his journal. He denied, for instance, that "the restless spirit of the age" added greater significance to the periodical literature than to novels, writing instead that "they who have not, struggle to get, and they who have gotten, clench their fingers to keep," and adding that "is there any more danger to be looked for in

the radicalism of youth than in the conservatism of age?" ("Introduction" 2). While Poe spoke that he needed "caste," Lowell wrote that the quest for a "*National* literature" should be avoided precisely because it produced "caste," and "widen[ed] the boundary between races" ("Introduction" 1). In fact, Lowell's *Pioneer* provides a valuable contrast to Poe's efforts: Although both men appear to agree on several minor (but resonant) details of journal operation, Poe avoids gender politics but insists on class politics; Lowell, with his emphasis on "manly" literature, does the exact opposite. Similarly, although both men sought to found a literary magazine that would achieve both commercial and critical success, Lowell treats that goal as an end in itself; Poe insists on the anthemic example such a magazine might present.

See also Frederick Mott, *A History of American Magazines*, vol. 1 (1930; Cambridge, MA: Harvard University Press, 1966) 735–6.

39   Allen, 191–4. Allen uses J. B. Hubbell, *The South in American Literature 1607–1900* (Durham, N.C.: 1954). See also Faust 94.

40   Poe, "To F. W. Thomas," *Letters* 1: 224.

41   Allen 157; Quinn 330–45; Poe, "To Charles Anthon," *Letters* 1: 269; Poe, "To Daniel Bryan," 6 July 1842, letter 139 of *Letters* 1: 205. Charvat 86.

42   Alexis de Tocqueville, *Democracy in America*, ed. Phillips Bradley, trans. Henry Reeve (New York: Vintage, 1945). See Volume II, Second Book, Chapter 13: "Why The Americans Are So Restless In The Midst Of Their Prosperity": 144–7.

43   Theodore Peterson, *Magazines in the Twentieth Century* (Urbana: University of Illinois Press, 1964) 291–2.

44   "Unity" is an extremely flexible value. If Poe chose, he could have used "unity" to argue *against* the short story: A single volume of a journal that ran only short stories, for instance, would contain many voices, while a single-volume novel would be "unified." Poe's use is selective, and it is probably wrong to assume that his preference for short stories and magazines flowed from a disinterested interest in the concept of "unity" in any form, except to the extent that "unity" represented the kinds of homogeneous audience and homogeneous culture that Poe relied upon throughout his attempts to found his magazine.

45   The distinction between the novel as an "old form" and the short story as a "new form" is, at best, conditional. Circa 1840, the novel was still a comparatively new, flexible form; more significantly, as Charvat describes (Charvat, "Poe: Journalism and the Theory Of Poetry," *Profession* 87), novels were published in serialization, or appeared periodically in paperbound sections, further diminishing the distinction that would associate the short story with the magazine, and the novel with the bound volume. What is significant about Poe's vision, perhaps, is the extent to which he forces these distinctions. His emphasis on unity, for instance, downgrades the association between the serialized novel and the magazine, and enforces the link between the short story and the magazine. Moreover, that association serves as a subtle act of literary independence: The serial novels were often pirated British imports. For Poe to undermine their status on the American market would conceivably create demand for his "new" form: It would certainly free American magazine pages for American authors.

It is possible at least to tentatively claim that Poe's strategy became industry practice by 1900. Throughout the nineteenth century, two trends could be observed among American and British periodicals: first, late-century (approximately 1885–1900) periodicals in both countries were publishing more short stories and fewer serial novels than their mid-century (1850–85) equivalents ("In the country papers the short story takes the place of the chapters of a serial which used to be given," Howells wrote in his "Editor's Study," *Harper's Monthly* Feb. 1887: 483), which in turn were publishing *more* serials than their 1830s and 1840s predecessors (see Charvat, "The People's Patronage," *Profession* 309). And second, American periodicals were publishing more short stories, and were devoting a higher percentage of their pages to short stories, than were similar British journals (see Howells 484). These trends were far from overwhelming, however. The following per-issue statistics, which are intended to be anecdotal and not comprehensive, illustrate:

British
Longman's (1887–9): 2 serials, 1 short story.
Cornhill (1871): 2 serials, 0 short stories.
(1890): 2 serials, 1 short story.
Blackwood's (1843): 2 serials, 0 short stories.
(1892): 2 serials, 1 short story.
Fraser's (1839): 1 serial, 1 short story.
(1867): 1 serial, 1 short story.
New Monthly Magazine (1846): 3 serials, 0 short stories.
New Review (1890): 1 serial, 0 short stories.
Pall Mall (1895): 4 short stories, 1 serial.
MacMillan's (1888): 2 serials, 0 short stories.

American
Ladies' Repository (1846–7); no fiction.
(1876): 4 short stories, 1 unserialized novel chapter.
Lippincott's (1869): 2 short stories, 1 unserialized novel chapter.
(1893): 2 short stories, 1 unserialized novel chapter.
Knickerbocker (1844): 3 short stories, 0 serials.
Graham's (1843): 4 short stories, 1 serial, 1 two-part serial.
Harper's (1850–1): 2 short stories, 2 serials.
(1891): 2 short stories, 2 serials.
Century (1893–4): 4 short stories, 1 serial.
McClure's (1893): 3 short stories, 0 serials.
Munsey's (1895–6): 3–4 short stories, 3 serials.
Atlantic (1859): 1 short story, 2 serials.
(1890): 2 short stories, 1 serial (serial discontinued in 1915–16).
Scribner's (1871): 2 short stories, 1 serial.

The distinction between a short story and a novel or novelette was far from codified during this period, however. Certain short stories (for instance, one of the three that appeared in each issue of *Lippincott's*), contained three "chapters," and might justifiably be called novelettes rather than short stories. Similarly, many American and British journals carried serial nonfiction, or published sketches, playlets, sermons, or short stories printed within travel essays as examples of local humor. See Alvin Sullivan, ed., *British Literary Magazines, the Victorian and Edwardian Age: 1837–1913* (Westport, CT: Greenwood Press, 1984).

46 Donald Pease, *Visionary Compacts* (Madison: University of Wisconsin Press, 1987) 164.

47 See Katherine Dieckman, "Lish Fulfillment," *Village Voice,* 2 June 1987: 46. She compliments *The Quarterly,* a new journal, for its "book-like dimensions," and "because it neither looks nor acts like most literary magazines."

48 Poe, *"Twice-Told Tales"* 571.

49 Poe, *"Twice-Told Tales"* 572.

50 Poe, "Composition" 16.

51 The Norton Critical Edition of *The Confidence Man* provides several newspaper excerpts and essays discussing the "confidence man" as a cultural icon of the 1840s and 1850s. See Melville 227–9. See also Tom Quirk, *Melville's Confidence Man: From Knave to Knight* (Columbia: University of Missouri Press, 1982). Karen Halttunen, *Confidence Men and Painted Women: A Study of Middle-Class Culture in America, 1830–1870* (New Haven: Yale University Press, 1982).

52 Edgar Allan Poe, "The Black Cat," *Complete Stories and Poems* 65.

53 Nina Baym, *Novels, Readers and Reviewers: Responses to Fiction in Antebellum America* (Ithaca, NY: Cornell University Press, 1984) 44.

54 Marc Chenetier, "Living on/off the 'Reserve': Performance, Interrogation, and Negativity in the Works of Raymond Carver," *Critical Angles: European Views of Contemporary American Literature,* ed. Marc Chenetier (Carbondale: Southern Illinois University Press, 1986) 173. Raymond Carver, "Fires," in *Fires* (Santa Barbara, CA: Capra Press, 1983) 25, 27, 26.

2. The Land of Definition

1 Peter Prescott, introduction, *The Norton Book of American Short Stories* (New York: W. W. Norton, 1988): 14. A. Walton Litz, prefatory note to the revised edition, *Major American Short Stories* (New York: Oxford University Press, 1980). Heather McClave, introduction, *Women Writers of the Short Story: A Collection of Critical Essays* (Englewood Cliffs, NJ: Prentice-Hall, 1980) 1. A. Robert Lee, introduction, *The Nineteenth-Century Short Story* (Totowa, NJ: Barnes and Noble, 1985) 7.

2 William Dean Howells, "Some Anomalies of the Short Story," *North American Review* 173 (Sept. 1901): 424. William Peden, *The American Short Story: Front Line in the National Defense of Literature* (Boston: Houghton Mifflin Company, 1964) 1. Archibald L. Bouton, foreword, *The American Short Story: A Study of the Influence of Locality in its Development,* by Elias Lieberman (Ridgewood, 1912) viii. Walter B. Pitkin, *How to Write Stories* (New York: Harcourt, Brace and Company, 1923) viii. Boris Eichenbaum, "O. Henry and the Theory of the Short Story," *Readings in Russian Poetics: Formalist and Structuralist Poetics,* eds. Ladislav Matejka and Krystyna Pomoroska (Cambridge, MA: MIT Press, 1971) 229.

3 Ruth Suckow, "The Short Story," *Saturday Review of Literature* 4 (19 Nov. 1927): 318.

4 James T. Farrell, "Nonsense and the Short Story," *The League of Frightened Philistines and Other Papers* (New York: Vanguard Press, 1945) 72.

5   Johan J. Smertenko, "The American Short Story," *Bookman* 56 (January 1923): 584.

6   Fredric Jameson, *The Political Unconscious: Narrative as a Socially Symbolic Act* (Ithaca, NY: Cornell University Press, 1981) 106.

7   Brander Matthews, *The Philosophy of the Short Story* (New York: Longmans, Green and Company, 1901; New York: Peter Smith, 1931) 49. See also Matthews, "The Philosophy of the Short Story," *Lippincott's* 36 (Oct. 1885) 371, for the version without the footnote.

8   Walter A. Dyer, "A Short Story Orgy," *Bookman* 51 (April 1920): 218.

9   *Short Stories for Spare Moments* was a popular collection gathered from *Lippincott's Magazine* in 1869–70. Frederick Lewis Pattee, *The Development of the Short Story* (1925; New York: Biblo and Tannen, 1975) 249.

10 Review of Brander Matthews's *Philosophy of the Short Story, London Academy,* 30 March 1901. Reprinted in Eugene Current-Garcia and Walton R. Patrick, eds., *What is the Short Story?* (Glenview, IL: Scott, Foresman and Company, 1974) 49. See also Matthews 61.

11 Howells, "Editor's Study" 483.

12 Frederick Mott, *A History of American Magazines, 1865–1905,* vol. 3 (1938; Cambridge, MA: Harvard University Press, 1967) 4–5.

13 Mott 4.

14 *The Nation* (14 Nov. 1895): 342. Quoted in Mott 11.

15 Mott 11, 15–17.

16 Mott 9, 12, 14, 110.

17 William Archer, "The American Cheap Magazine," *Fortnightly Review* 93 (May 1910): 922. Interestingly, Archer, unlike most of the commentators quoted in this chapter, was indifferent to the rise of the American short story, writing in this article that the British and American short stories were roughly equivalent in quality, but that he read neither.

18 "Cheap Magazines," *The Independent* 47 (27 June 1895): 867. This writer, it should be noted, is not pleased with the "revolution" in publishing economics: Rather, his article is a defense of the magazines that were threatened by the changes in engraving costs.

19 For Poe, see Chapter 1. For Irving, see Stanley T. Williams, *The Life of Washington Irving* (New York: Oxford University Press, 1935) 424. For general background, see William Charvat, "Literary Economics and Literary History," *The Profession of Authorship in America, 1800–1870* (Columbus: Ohio University Press, 1968) 285–6. See also Charvat, "The Conditions of Authorship in 1820," *Profession* 30–2.

20 Matthews 62.

21 Howells, "Editor's Study" 484. Charvat, "The People's Patronage," *Profession* 308.

22 *Ladies' Home Companion* 29 (Nov. 1882): 1. Mott 113. Mott quotes several other useful sources describing the rise of the short story during this period.

23 Pattee 311.

24 "The Lounger," *The Critic* Aug. 1890: 84.

25 Arthur Reed Kimball, *Atlantic Monthly* 86 (July 1900): 124.

26 See, for instance: "the genuine short-story abhors the idea of the novel" (Matthews 30). See also Matthews 15, 35, 73.

27 As Laurence Veysey has written, the last ten years of the nineteenth century were a period when "most academics professors of history ... were glad to celebrate the nation's past," and when many amateur historical organizations (i.e., the Daughters of the American Rev-

olution) were founded to exalt American history as well. Laurence Veysey, "The Plural Organized World of the Humanities," *The Organization of Knowledge in Modern America*, eds. Alexandra Oleson and John Voss (Baltimore: Johns Hopkins University Press, 1979) 69–70.

28 Matthews 77. Lieberman 14. Pattee 141. Eichenbaum 235.

29 Mary Rohrberger, introduction, *Story to Anti-Story* (Boston: Houghton Mifflin Company, 1979) 2–3. Ann Charters, introduction, *The Story and Its Writer* (New York: St. Martin's Press, 1987) 3. McClave 1–2. Lee.

30 Charles Johnson, excerpted in "The Tradition," *Sudden Fiction: American Short-Short Stories*, eds. Robert Shapard and James Thomas (Salt Lake City: Peregrine Smith Books, 1986) 232.

31 See the back cover of Shapard and Thomas.

32 See Edward J. O'Brien, ed., *Best Short Stories of 1928 and the Yearbook of the American Short Story* (New York: Dodd, Mead and Company, 1928), though any year during the period will do. The yearbook included biographical data, a bibliography of every short story published in America (each one rated on a three-asterisk system), a bibliography of every article written on the short story, ratings of the performances of individual magazines, and other information. See also *The Dance of the Machines: The American Short Story* (New York: MacCaulay Co., 1929). For parodies, see John Riddell, "Short Best Stories," *Dance* 259–68. The *New York Times* quote can be found in its review of Edward O'Brien, ed., *Best Short Stories of 1927*, *New York Times Book Review* (11 Dec. 1927): 2.

33 Edward J. O'Brien, *The Advance of the American Short Story*, 2nd ed. (New York: Dodd, Mead and Company, 1931; St. Clair Shores, MI: Scholarly Press, 1972) 18–19.

34 O'Brien, *Advance* 15–17.

35 Suckow 318.

36 Bret Harte, "The Rise of the 'Short Story,'" *Cornhill Magazine* July 1899: 8. V. S. Pritchett, "Short Stories," *Harper's Bazaar* July 1953: 31.

37 Quoted in Pattee 317.

38 Quoted in Jessica Benson, "Short on Paper, Long on Popularity," *Philadelphia Inquirer* 19 Nov. 1989: 2-J.

39 Theodore Peterson, *Magazines in the Twentieth Century* (Urbana: University of Illinois Press, 1964) 61.

40 *The Guild Pioneer*, Jan. 1923. Quoted in Hoffman 269. *Outsiders*, May 1928. Quoted in Hoffman 289. Norman MacLeod, *Jackass*, Jan. 1928. Quoted in Hoffman 288. Charles Allen, "The Advance Guard," *Sewanee Review* 51 (July/Sept. 1943): 425–9. Stephen Vincent Benet to Charles Allen, Sept. 1939. Quoted in Allen 15. This analysis is also a major thesis in Theodore Peterson and Frederick J. Hoffman, Charles Allen, and Carolyn Ulrich, *The Little Magazine: A History and a Bibliography* (Princeton: Princeton University Press, 1946). See especially: Peterson 49, 61, 64, 77; Hoffman, preface. See also Mott, Chapter 1.

41 Matthews 57.

42 Eugene Current-Garcia, *The American Short Story before 1850: A Critical History* (Boston: Twayne, 1985) 98–101.

43 Quoted in Pattee 280.

44 Eugene Current-Garcia and Bert Hitchcock, eds., *American Short Stories* (Glenview, IL: Scott, Foresman/Little Brown, 1990) 659.

45 Mark Twain, *Complete Humorous Sketches and Tales*, ed. Charles Neider

(Garden City, NY: Doubleday, 1961). Thomas Bangs Thorpe, *A New Collection of Thomas Bangs Thorpe's Sketches of the Old Southwest,* ed. David C. Estes (Baton Rouge: Louisiana State University Press, 1989). Augustus Baldwin Longstreet, *Georgia Scenes* (Harper Brothers, 2nd edition, 1847; Atlanta: Cherokee Publishing, 1971).

46   William Carlos Williams, "A Beginning on the Short Story" (Yonkers, NY: Alicat Press, 1950) 11. Frank O'Connor, introduction, *The Lonely Voice: A Study of the Short Story* (New York: World, 1963) 20, 40–1. Suckow 318. Yoli Tannen, "Is a Puzzlement," *Masses and Mainstream* 10 (Jan. 1957): 17. John Updike, introduction, *Best American Short Stories 1984,* eds. John Updike and Shannon Ravenel (Boston: Houghton Mifflin, 1984) xii–xiii.

47   O'Connor 39. Tannen 17.

48   Nina Baym, *Novels, Readers, and Reviewers: Responses to Fiction in Antebellum America* (Ithaca, NY: Cornell University Press, 1984) 36.

49   F. O. Matthiessen, *American Renaissance* (New York: Oxford University Press, 1941) ix, xii.

50   *Harper's New Monthly Magazine,* mid-1850s editorial. Quoted in James D. Hart, *The Popular Book: A History of America's Literary Taste* (New York: Oxford University Press, 1946) 86.

51   Hart 286.

52   Harold G. Merriam, "Expressions of Northwest Life," *The New Mexico Quarterly* (May 1934): 128–9.

53   O'Brien, *Advance* 16.

54   Laurie G. Kirszner and Stephen R. Mandell, eds., *Literature: Reading, Writing, Reacting* (Fort Worth: Holt, Rinehart and Winston, 1991). The second edition of this anthology will be issued by Harcourt, Brace, Jovanovich. Kirszner quoted in interview with author, April 5, 1991.

The comments in the paragraph in the text specifically address those anthologies that attempt a comprehensive representation of the different ethnic groups contained within American culture. Anthologies also exist (i.e., *The Way We Live Now: American Plays and the AIDS Crisis* [ed. M. Elizabeth Osborn], *New Worlds of Literature* [ed. Jerome Beaty and J. Paul Hunter], or the *Before Columbus* Foundation collections) that either present minorities exclusively, or use issues of cross-culturalism or ideology as organizing principles. At present, these anthologies represent within the textbook market what short stories or poems by minority authors have generally represented within any individual traditional anthology: the "nuggets on the outside" of a core of standard texts, and textbook strategies.

55   Peterson 124, 128.

56   Peterson 77.

57   Edmund Wilson, "The Literary Worker's Polonius," *The Shores of Light* (New York: Farrar Straus and Young, 1952) 593.

58   Marianne Moore to Charles Allen, 2 July 1941 (unpublished). Quoted in Hoffman 205. *Janus* (Nov. 1929). Quoted in Hoffman 291.

59   Katharine Fuller Gerould, "The American Short Story," *Yale Review* 13 (July 1924): 650. Gerould quotes Bliss Perry (see Chapter 4), and describes his criticism as typical of the "high brow distrust" of the short story that was prevalent in the late nineteenth century.

60   Thomas Gullason, "The Short Story: An Underrated Art," *Studies in Short Fiction* 2 (Fall 1964): 21–2. Pattee 272. Rudolph quoted in Benson 2-J.

61 Jameson 105.
62 Howells, "Editor's Study" 483.
63 John Cheever, in "Is the Short Story Necessary," roundtable discussion with Elizabeth Janeway, Shirley Hazzard, and Harry Mark Petrakis, *The Writer's World,* Elizabeth Janeway, ed. (New York: McGraw-Hill, 1969) 256.
     During a visit to Iowa City, Iowa (14–18 July 1991), I spoke with four Workshop students (who requested anonymity) who described an unspoken understanding among the fictioneers there that they were expected to write about poor and otherwise marginalized characters, whether or not their backgrounds were poor, middle-class, or upper-class.
64 Peterson 129.
65 Rogers Worthington, "Writer's Camp," *Chicago Tribune Magazine* (5 Feb. 1989): 12.
66 O'Brien, *Best 1928* 336–7 lists thirty-four articles on the subject of the "American Short Story." O'Brien published a "Yearbook of the American Short Story" appendix to his *Best* anthology every year from 1915 until his death in 1941. In 1918 he began including a section titled "Articles on the Short Story." This section provides an excellent gauge for evaluating the extent to which the "American Short Story" became an item of debate. In the 1918 yearbook, for instance, O'Brien listed one article on the "American Short Story"; in 1921, 1; in 1922, 3; in 1924, 21; in 1926, 28; in 1928, 34; in 1932, 14; in 1934, 32; in 1936, 28; in 1940, 16. For most of those years, the "American Short Story" subject listing contained more entries than any other subject heading, including "The Short Story." Prominent magazines and newspapers listed included *American Mercury,* the *New York Times,* the *Saturday Review of Literature, Books,* and the *New Republic;* prominent authors (with repeat entries) included H. L. Mencken, Frances Newman, and Clifton Fadiman. Edith Mirrielees, Canby, Suckow, Smertenko, Brickell, Cory, and other authors quoted at length in this chapter are also prominent.
     O'Brien's citations are not completely dependable, however. Many of these articles are reviews, and often very short reviews. In addition, many of these reviews rarely mention (if they mention at all) the state of the American short story. It appears that O'Brien used "American Short Story" as his "Miscellaneous" category as well: Carl Van Doren's 1927 *Nation* review of a *Smart Set* anthology is listed under the "American Short Story" in O'Brien's 1928 *Yearbook,* for instance, although the 'American Short Story' is not mentioned once.
     In 1941, Martha Foley became editor of the *Best* annual; its name was changed to *Best American Short Stories,* and the long form of the yearbook was discontinued.
67 Canby, *Free* 65–6.
68 Herbert Ellsworth Cory, "The Senility of the Short Story," *Dial* 65 (3 May 1917): 379.
69 Cory 380.
70 See Dyer, note 18. Helen R. Hull, "The Literary Drug Traffic," *Dial* 67 (6 Sept. 1919): 190–2.
71 Dyer 217.
72 Cory 380. See also Baym 36–43. Baym documents how similar metaphorical patterns were used to describe the novel during the first half

of the nineteenth century: Novels could make "the mind ungovernable and thus jeopardize the agencies of social and psychological control" (39). This approach arose in response to the novel's popularity, and makes a worthwhile comparison to the treatment of the short story in the same terms a century later, a period in which the novel was treated as the form for cool reflection.

73   Smertenko 585. O'Brien, *Dance* 145–6. Hull 190.

74   Hull 190.

75   A few other major magazines also segregate advertising from text, most notably *National Geographic;* many magazines, however, place much of their advertising in the back pages – i.e., the *New York Times Magazine.*

76   Howells, "Anomalies" 422–3.

77   Peden 3.

78   Howells, "Anomalies" 423–4.

79   Edith R. Mirrielees, *"The American Short Story," Atlantic Monthly* 167 (June 1941): 714.

80   Mirrielees 714.

81   Truman Capote, "The Art of Fiction XVII," interview with Pati Hill, *Paris Review,* Spring–Summer 1957: 37. See also William Faulkner, 1957, quoted in Philip Stevick, *The American Short Story 1900–1945: A Critical History* (Boston: Twayne, 1984) 129. In response to the question "Do you think it's easier to write a novel than a short story?" Faulkner replies, "Yes sir. You can be more careless, you can put more trash in it and be excused for it."

82   O'Brien, *Dance* 148. O'Brien, *Advance* 5.

83   Frank Norris, "The Decline of the Magazine Story," *Wave* (30 Jan. 1897) 3.

84   Suckow 318.

85   The *New York Times* review of Edward O'Brien, ed., *Best Short Stories of 1927* (11 Dec. 1927): 2.

86   Isaac Rosenfeld, "Great American Desert," *New Republic* 109 (Oct. 1943): 461.

87   Canby, *Free* 68. Farrell 76. Suckow 318.

88   Suckow 317.

89   Charles E. May, "The Unique Effect of the Short Story," *Studies in Short Fiction* 13 (Summer 1976): 289.

90   Peden 3.

91   Gerould 650. See also Frederick Bird, "Magazine Fiction and How Not to Write It," *Lippincott's,* Nov. 1894: 651, 653. Bird observes that magazine fiction has "its own clientele, its own rules, its own tone and tradition." He notes that "a book bears a certain halo of dignity, though almost wholly traditional and suppositious," while magazines and the stories contained within them "are supposed to be ephemeral," "moral and inoffensive as well as entertaining." He concludes that the difference between writing a novel and writing a magazine fiction is "a question of conformity or dissent."

92   Nadine Gordimer, "South Africa," in the "International Symposium on the Short Story," *Kenyon Review* 30 (1968): 457. See also Charles E. May, *Short Story Theories* (Athens: Ohio University Press, 1976). This volume contains a number of essays devoted to understanding why the short story has received "healthy neglect" or outright denigration from literary critics. See also Peden, the first chapter especially.

93 Smertenko 587. Hershel Brickell, "What Happened to the Short Story?" *Atlantic Monthly*, Sept. 1951: 75–76. Falcon O. Baker, "Short Stories for the Millions," *Saturday Review* (19 Dec. 1953): 48. Current-Garcia and Hitchcock 658.
94 Smertenko 587. Rosenfeld 461. Hull 190.

3. Edith Wharton

1 Frederick Lewis Pattee, *The Development of the Short Story* (1925; New York: Biblo and Tannen, 1975) 134.
2 Edith Wharton, "Telling a Short Story," *The Writing of Fiction* (New York: Charles Scribner's Sons, 1925) 33–58. Reprinted in Edith Wharton, *The Collected Short Stories of Edith Wharton,* ed. R. W. B. Lewis, vol. 1 (New York: Charles Scribner's Sons, 1968) xxxi. All quotes are from this edition.
3 Edgar Allan Poe, "The Philosophy of Composition," *Graham's Magazine* April 1846: 163–7. Reprinted in Edgar Allan Poe, *Essays and Reviews,* ed. G. R. Thompson (New York: Library of America, 1984) 13–25.
4 For sample references to Wharton's fascination with enclosure, see R. W. B. Lewis, *Edith Wharton: A Biography* (New York: Harper and Row, 1975) 121, 206, 207, 221, 231; Elizabeth Ammons, *Edith Wharton's Argument with America* (Athens: University of Georgia Press, 1980) 48–9, 88, 116.
5 See Judith Fryer, *Felicitous Space: The Imaginative Structures of Edith Wharton and Willa Cather* (Chapel Hill: University of North Carolina Press, 1986), which was consulted after this chapter was written. Fryer also focuses upon *The Decoration of Houses,* and explores the political implications of Wharton's architectural aesthetic throughout her fiction. In addition, she provides background on American suburban architecture during the period, and places Wharton's work within the context of other turn-of-the-century public architectural and civic projects.
6 Gregg Camfield, University of Pennsylvania, October 23, 1990.
7 Frank Lentricchia, "Foucault's Legacy: A New Historicism," *The New Historicism,* ed. H. Aram Veeser (New York: Routledge, 1989) 231–2.
8 Ammons 28–9.
9 R. W. B. Lewis, introduction, *The Letters of Edith Wharton,* R. W. B. Lewis and Nancy Lewis, eds. (New York: Scribner's, 1988) 9.
10 Wharton, "To Rutger B. Jewett," 10 Aug. 1928, *Letters* 515.
11 Ammons 28–9.
12 Edith Wharton, *The Custom of the Country* (New York: Charles Scribner's Sons, 1913). See also Ammons 97–123.
13 Examples of her literary business astuteness can be found throughout R. W. B. Lewis's *Edith Wharton: A Biography.* A few instances: She complained to her publisher of 'underadvertising' for *The Greater Inclination* in 1899 (88); sent an aggrieved request for the royalties for *The Decoration of Houses* in 1899 (93); offered to do an additional story to complete the volume *Crucial Instances* in 1900 (98); requested changes in the cover, size, and price of *The Valley of Decision* in 1901 (104); demanded changes in the cover of *The House of Mirth* in 1904 (151); responded affirmatively to Charles Scribner's request that she include a 'strong man' in her next book in 1905 (151); and so on. In

1904, Scribner's assigned a new editor, William Crary Brownell, to Wharton. Lewis notes the tone of "amiable joking" Brownell struck in answering Wharton's grievances: "When his own book on the Victorians came out in the fall of that year, he told Mrs. Wharton: 'I am now writing my publishers that friends inform me they have seen no announcement, are unable to etc. etc.'" (133).

14   Ammons 19.
15   Lewis, *Biography* 3.
16   Wharton, "To Sara Norton," 30 Sept. 1902, *Letters* 72. Lewis, *Biography* 111, 149.
17   Lewis, *Biography* 59.
18   Edith Wharton, *French Ways and Their Meaning* (London: Macmillan and Company, 1919) 107.
19   Ammons 3.
20   Lewis, *Biography* 110–11, 119.
21   Lewis, *Biography* 151.
22   Lewis, *Biography* 152.
23   Edith Wharton, *A Backward Glance* (New York: D. Appleton-Century and Company, 1934) 5.
24   Wharton, *Glance* ii.
25   Wharton, "To Barrett Wendell," 15 May 1899, *Letters* 39.
26   Wharton, "To F. Scott Fitzgerald," 8 June 1925, *Letters* 482.
27   Irving Howe, "The Culture of Modernism," *The Decline of the New* (New York: Harcourt, Brace and World, 1970) 7.
28   Wharton, "To Robert Grant," 26 Feb. 1906, *Letters* 103.
29   Howe 15.
30   Andrew Ross, *The Failure of Modernism: Symptoms of American Poetry* (New York: Columbia University Press, 1986) 5, 6.
31   Edith Wharton and Ogden Codman, Jr., *The Decoration of Houses*, introduction, John Barrington Bayley and William A. Coles (1897; New York: W. W. Norton and Company, 1979). All quotes from this edition.
32   Edith Wharton, "The Fulness of Life," *The Collected Stories*, ed. and intro. R. W. B. Lewis, vol. 1 (New York: Charles Scribner's Sons, 1968) 14.
33   See Edgar de N. Mayhew and Minor Myers, Jr., *A Documentary History of American Interiors from the Colonial Era to 1915* (New York: Charles Scribner's Sons, 1980) 193–310. For practitioners of the art of home design, the late nineteenth century was a period of unprecedented respectability, opportunity, and excess. As Mayhew and Myers describe, the rapid proliferation of Gothic, Elizabethan, and rococo architectural fads at mid-century, coupled with the popularization of mass production techniques for home furnishings, created a glut of styles and furniture on the American home decor market. Simultaneously, the same revolution in magazine publishing that was creating a vogue for the short story was also catalyzing the creation of a market for home decor periodicals, which in turn declared and propounded new design schemes with almost dizzying speed. During the final thirty years of the nineteenth century, there were Renaissance revivals (both German and Italian), French revivals (Francis I, Henry II, Henry IV, Louis XIII, Louis XIV, Louis XV, Louis XVI, and Empire), English revivals (Elizabethan, Jacobean, Queen Anne, Chippendale, Sheraton, Adam, and Heppelwhite), as well as Japanese,

Chinese, Turkish, Moorish, and Persian fads. American decorator-writers suggested designs for the "Wigwam style," the "Frontier style," and even the "Aztec style." Even movements that were self-enclosed and founded upon homogeneous æsthetic principles, such as William Morris's Aesthetic Movement, became subsumed within a stylistic ethos in which, according to Mayhew and Myers, "many guidebooks stressed that a rich assortment of diverse objects was not only educational but also revealing of the culture and taste of those who dwelt within" (197). The fashionable Victorian drawing room of the turn of the century was littered with indiscriminately authentic and ersatz fragments of five hundred years of world history and culture; it was Modern, *nouveau riche* middlebrow, and virtually unlivable all at the same time.

See Fryer 30–1 for an overview of the state of American suburban architecture during this period.

34 Eugene Current-Garcia, *O. Henry (William Sydney Porter)* (New York: Twayne, 1965) 38, 41. O. Henry, "A Dinner At ———," *The Complete Works of O. Henry*, fore. William Lyon Phelps (Garden City, NY: Garden City Publishing, 1937) 983.

35 James D. Hart, *The Popular Book: A History of America's Literary Taste* (New York: Oxford University Press) 208. See also 86, 91.

36 William Dean Howells, "Editor's Study," *Harper's New Monthly* 74 (Feb. 1887): 483.

37 Howells, "Editor's Study," 483.

38 Frank Norris, "Why Women Should Write the Best Novels: And Why They Don't," *Boston Evening Transcript*, 13 Nov. 1901: 20. Reprinted in Donald Pizer, ed., *The Literary Criticism of Frank Norris* (Austin: University of Texas Press, 1964) 36. The second quote from Norris can be found in "The Decline of the Magazine Short Story," *Wave* 15 (26 Dec. 1896): 3. Pizer 49.

39 See Bret Harte, "The Rise of the 'Short Story,'" *Cornhill Magazine*, July 1899: 1–8.

40 Wharton, "To Robert Grant," 19 Nov. 1907, *Letters* 124.

41 See Chapter 4.

42 In fact, Poe does warn his readers in the review of Hawthorne not to overvalue narrative thrift; what is most striking is that he does so only once, in one short phrase, and that phrase was rarely cited by his twentieth-century proponents. It would be incorrect to claim that Wharton effects a complete alteration of Poe's model; but she does clearly insist with self-conscious and intense emphasis that narrative frugality is not, in itself, a virtue.

43 Edith Wharton, *Italian Villas and Their Gardens* (New York: The Century Company, 1904) 250.

44 Edith Wharton, "The Muse's Tragedy," *Stories* 1: 76.

45 Wharton, "To Sara Norton," 30 Sept. 1902, *Letters* 72.

46 Wharton, "To Edward L. Burlingame," 10 July 1898, *Letters* 36.

47 Wharton, "Roman Fever," *Stories* 2: 833.

48 Wharton, "Fever," *Stories* 837.

49 Wharton, "Fever," *Stories* 834–5.

50 Wharton, "Fever," *Stories* 833.

51 Wharton, "Fever," *Stories* 836.

52 Wharton, "To Sara Norton," 24 Feb. 1902, *Letters* 59.

53 Wharton, "Fever," *Stories* 837.

54 Wharton, "Fever," *Stories* 835.
55 Wharton once wrote that Poe, Whitman, and Emerson "are the best we have – in fact, the all we have." She also included Poe as a character in her novella, *False Dawn*. See Lewis, *Biography* 236–7.
56 Frank O'Connor, *The Lonely Voice: A Study of the Short Story* (New York: World, 1963) 13–45.
57 Thomas Gullason, "The Short Story: An Underrated Art," *Studies in Short Fiction* 2 (Fall 1964): 13–31.
58 Wharton, "To William Roscoe Thayer," 11 Nov. 1905, *Letters* 96. See also Wharton, "To Sara Norton," 24 Feb. 1902, *Letters* 59: She writes that her work could be "regarded as the picture of a period, not of . . . persons."
59 Wharton, "To Sinclair Lewis," 28 Nov. 1921, *Letters* 448–9. Lewis dedicated *Babbitt* to Wharton.

4. Handbooks and Workshops

1 Sherwood Anderson, "New Orleans, *The Double Dealer,* and the Modern Movement in America," *Double Dealer* 3 (March 1922): 119–21. James T. Farrell, "Nonsense and the Short Story," *The League of Frightened Philistines and Other Papers* (New York: Vanguard Press, 1945) 75, 77. Cleanth Brooks and Robert Penn Warren, *Understanding Fiction* (New York: Appleton-Century-Crofts, 1943) 569. Edward O'Brien, *The Dance of the Machines: The American Short Story and the Industrial Age* (New York: MacCaulay Company, 1929). Douglas Bement, *Weaving the Short Story,* introduction by Edward J. O'Brien (New York: Ray Long and Richard R. Smith, 1932) xi.
2 Angell quoted in Herbert Mitgang, "A New Life for the Short Story," the *New York Times,* 20 Mar. 1985: C17. J. D. Bellamy, "A Downpour of Literary Republicanism," *Mississippi Review* 40/41 (Winter 1985): 31–9.
3 Eugene Current-Garcia and Bert Hitchcock, "New Academic Influences," introduction to Section 5 of *American Short Stories* (Glenview, IL: Scott, Foresman/Little Brown, 1990) 658.
4 See note 2. See also Wilbur Schramm, *The Story Workshop* (Boston: Little, Brown, 1938). Schramm was a major figure in the development of the Iowa writing program.
5 Stephen Wilbers, *The Iowa Writers' Workshop* (Iowa City: University of Iowa Press, 1980). See Chapter 2 especially. See Susan Lohafer, introduction, *Short Story Theory at a Crossroads,* eds. Lohafer and Jo Ellyn Clarey (Baton Rouge: Louisiana State University Press, 1989) 4–5.
6 Frank A. Dickson and Sandra Smythe, eds., *Handbook of Short Story Writing* (Cincinnati: Writer's Digest, 1970). Unlike most earlier handbooks, this text is an anthology of shorter pieces. Rust Hills, *Writing in General and the Short Story in Particular* (Boston: Houghton Mifflin, 1977; revised in 1987). Hallie Burnett, *On Writing the Short Story* (New York: Harper and Row, 1983). See also Damon Knight, *Creating Short Fiction* (Cincinnati: Writer's Digest, 1981).
7 William Byron Mowery, *Professional Short-Story Writing* (New York: Crowell, 1953) 256.
8 Laurence Veysey, "The Plural Organized Worlds of the Humanities," *The Organization of Knowledge in Modern America, 1860–1920,* eds. Alexandra Oleson and John Voss (Baltimore: Johns Hopkins University

Press, 1979) 52–6. Edward S. Joynes, "Readings in Modern Language Study," *PMLA* 5 (1890): 45.

9   James Garnett, "The Course in English and Its Value as a Discipline," *PMLA* 2 (1886): 61, 73. See Veysey 74. Forty young professors, mostly from Johns Hopkins and Harvard, and cliquish, founded the MLA in 1884. The organization had a heavy pedagogical emphasis until the twentieth century.

10 T. W. Hunt, "The Place of English in the College Curriculum," *PMLA* 1 (1884–5): 120–1.

11 Charles Franklin Thwing, *American Colleges: Their Students and Work* (New York: Putnam, 1878). Quoted in Hunt 121. John G. R. McElroy, "The Requirements in English for Admission to College," *PMLA* 1 (1884–5): 195, 197. McElroy quotes Hill, 195. T. Whiting Bancroft, "Proceedings of the MLA at Baltimore, December, 1886," *PMLA* 2 (1886): vii.

12 Brander Matthews, *The Philosophy of the Short Story* (New York: Longmans, Green and Company, 1901; New York: Peter Smith, 1931).

13 Veysey 53: Young academics "accepted a scientific vocabulary and model for intellectual endeavor."

14 Garnett 68.

15 Norris, "The 'English Courses' of the University of California," *Wave* 15 (28 Nov. 1896): 2. On page 3, Norris defends the English courses at Harvard. Freytag, *Technique of the Drama* (S. C. Griggs and Company, 1898).

16 Edward Shils, "The Order of Learning in the United States: the Ascendancy of the University," Oleson and Voss, *The Organization of Knowledge in Modern America, 1860–1920* 46. Cecilia Tichi, *Shifting Gears: Technology, Literature, and Culture in Modernist America* (Chapel Hill: University of North Carolina Press, 1987) xii. David Noble, *America by Design: Science, Technology, and the Rise of Corporate Capitalism* (New York: Knopf, 1977) 5. Peter Conn, *The Divided Mind: Ideology and Imagination in America, 1898–1917* (New York: Cambridge University Press, 1983) 221. Conn quotes Frank Lloyd Wright, *Modern Architecture: Being the Kahn Lectures for 1930*, preface by E. Baldwin Smith (Princeton: Princeton University Press, 1931) 16.

17 Shils 46.

18 For a brief description of the Efficiency Movement, see Tichi 76–87. Also, Tichi 98: Over one hundred silent movies featured 'the engineer' as the hero. In general, *Shifting Gears* provides a strong background for a discussion of the short story handbook. Tichi illustrates how "the perceptual boundary between what is considered to be natural, and what technological" (33–4) disappeared during this period. Many authors, such as Wharton, London, Herrick, et al., combined organic and mechanical paradigms of behavior in metaphorical clusters throughout their fiction; other authors, such as Ezra Pound and William Carlos Williams, consciously adopted the "energy transforming machine" as the "central conception" (xii) for a new poetics. When Tichi speaks of "words or sentences" that "were viewed as component parts by authors self-identified as designers" (35), or describes Ezra Pound's attempt to use "Efficiency" as a literary value that would allow the artist to "escape from the human passivity inevitable in an unstable world" (93), her observations clearly correlate with this chapter.

19 Bliss Perry, *A Study of Prose Fiction* (Boston: Houghton, Mifflin and

Company, 1902) 364–71. George W. Cable, "Afterthoughts of a Storyteller," *North American Review* 158 (Jan. 1894): 18. Frederick M. Bird, "Magazine Fiction and How Not to Write It," *Lippincott's,* Nov. 1894: 651. F. Hopkinson Smith, "How to Write Short Stories," *Boston Herald.* Quoted in Esenwein, *Studing the Short-Story,* 60.

20   As C. R. Barrett's quote (see following note) indicates, the most convenient method of approaching this source material is to refer to the appendixes or introductory chapters of the handbooks, which are stocked with references from the period. See Bliss Perry's appendix (see note 19); or 41–71 of Esenwein.

21   Charles Raymond Barrett, *Short Story Writing: A Practical Treatise on the Art of the Short Story* (New York: Baker and Taylor Company, 1898) 9.

22   Perry v. Barrett 9.

23   Wilbers 36.

24   Blanche Colton Williams, *A Handbook on Short Story Writing* (New York: Dodd, Mead and Company, 1920). Sylvia Kamerman, biographical note to Maren Elwood, "Characterization in the Short Short Story," *Writing the Short Short Story,* ed. Sylvia Kamerman (Boston: The Writer, 1946) 86.

25   H. Bedford Jones, *The Graduate Fictioneer,* introduction by Erle Stanley Gardner (Denver: Author and Journalist Publishing Co., 1932). Richard Summers, *The Craft of the Short Story* (New York: Rinehart and Company, 1948). William Byron Mowery, *Professional Short-Story Writing* (New York: Crowell, 1953).

26   Kobold Knight, *A Guide to Fiction Writing* (London: Blackie and Son Limited, 1940) 11.

27   See Esenwein 426–38. This is the most thorough catalogue of short story handbooks available from the period.

28   See Laurence D'Orsay, *Stories You Can Sell* (Parker, Stone and Baird, 1933) viii. D'Orsay also wrote *Landing the Editor's Checks,* and *Writing Novels to Sell.*

29   Advertisement, *Bookman* (Nov. 1919): 86.

30   Knight 153.

31   See note 27.

32   See also J. Berg Esenwein, *Studying the Short-Story* (New York: Noble and Noble, 1912); J. Berg Esenwein and Mary D. Chambers, *The Art of Story Writing* (Home Correspondence School, 1913). Walter B. Pitkin, *The Art and the Business of Story Writing* (New York: Macmillan Company, 1912). See also Pitkin, *How to Write Stories* (New York: Harcourt, Brace and Company, 1923). See also the *National Union Catalog: Pre-1956 Imprints* (Chicago: Mansell Information, 1968) for lists of different editions. Eugene Current-Garcia and Walton Patrick, eds., *What is the Short Story?* (New York: Scott, Foresman and Co., 1974) 46.

33   Bement xi. Stewart Beach, *Short-Story Technique* (1929) 171. Jean Wick, *The Stories Editors Buy and Why* (Boston: Small, Maynard and Company, 1921) ix.

34   N. Bryllion Fagin, *Short Story-Writing: An Art or a Trade?* (New York: Thomas Seltzer, 1923) 126.

35   Aristotle, *Aristotle: Poetics,* translation and introduction by Gerald F. Else (Ann Arbor: University of Michigan Press, 1970).

36   David J. Gammon, *Breaking into Fiction* (St. Ives: Matson's Publications, 1940) 11. Farrell 77.

37 Gammon 7. Blanche Colton Williams, *How to Study "The Best Short Stories"* (Boston: Small, Maynard and Company, 1919) vii–viii. Pitkin, *How to Write* 2. Kamerman 86.

38 Fagin 2.

39 O'Brien, introduction to Bement vii.

40 Perry 329.

41 Barry Pain, *First Lessons in Story-Writing* (London: Literary Correspondence College, 1907) 69. Esenwein xii. Pitkin, *How to Write* viii, 3.

42 Esenwein 17–29. Barrett 8.

43 Poe, "*Twice-Told Tales*," review of *Twice-Told Tales*, by Nathaniel Hawthorne, *Graham's Magazine* May 1842: 298–300. Reprinted in Edgar Allan Poe, *Essays and Reviews*, ed. G. R. Thompson (New York: Library of America, 1984): 569–77.

44 Grabo quoted in Williams, *Handbook* 6. Pitkin, *How to Write* 101. Ethan Allen Cross, *The Short Story: A Technical and Literary Study* (Chicago: A. C. McClurg and Company, 1928) 13. Notestein and Dunn quoted in Williams, *Handbook* 6–7. Mary Burchard Orvis, *Short Story Writing* (New York: Ronald Press, 1928) 11.

45 Cecil Hunt, *Short Stories: How to Write Them* (London: Herbert Jenkins, 1950): 99.

46 Williams, *Handbook* 188.

47 Cross 82.

48 Fagin 12.

49 Barrett 57.

50 Esenwein 32.

51 Robert Wilson Neal, *Short Stories in the Making* (New York: Oxford University Press, 1914) 24, 25, 28, 29 (supplemental exercises).

52 Hunt 166.

53 Pitkin, *How to Write* 289.

54 Mowery, chapters 4, 5, 6: "Magazine Groups I," "Magazine Groups II," "Story Types."

55 Pitkin, *How to Write* 271.

56 Fagin 67.

57 Pitkin, *How to Write* 1.

58 Esenwein xiii–xiv.

59 Esenwein 126–7.

60 Cross xi.

61 Cross 40.

62 Hunt, see Chapters 8 and 9. Foy Evans, *Let's Write Short-Shorts* (Athens, GA: Bulldog Publishers, 1946) 78. Pitkin, *How to Write* 111. Neal 1. Phillips 103.

63 For Farrell, see note 1. Clayton was the editor of *Telling Tales* magazine. Quoted in Wick 355. Williams, "*Best*" viii. Pitkin, *Art* x. Leslie W. Quirk, *How to Write a Short Story* (Ridgewood, NJ: The Editor Company, 1911) 71.

64 Williams, *Handbook* v. Hunt 68. Pain 29. Quirk 45. Evans 59. Cross 63.

65 Pitkin, *Art* 242.

66 Pitkin, *How to Write* ix. Barrett 11. Williams, *Handbook* v.

67 Pitkin, *Art* ix. Bedford-Jones 93.

68 Orvis 102.

69 Phillips xiii, 13, 15, 63.

70 Esenwein 369.

71 Wick. See dedication.

72   Hamilton 196. Cross 15. Pitkin, *How to Write* 1. Esenwein. Nancy Moore, "Short Short Formula," Kamerman 29. Hunt 37.
73   Pain 23.
74   See Mowery, Part I: "Directionals."
75   Perry 312. Hunt 126. Cody 142. Pitkin, *Art* v.
76   Perry 304. Bement 7. Frederick Lewis Pattee, *The Development of the American Short Story* (1925; New York: Biblo and Tannen, 1975) 134.
77   Edgar Allan Poe, "The Philosophy of Composition," *Graham's Magazine* April 1846: 163–7. Reprinted in Edgar Allan Poe, *Essays and Reviews:* 13–25.
78   Poe, "Philosophy" 15.
79   Poe, "Philosophy" 18.
80   Poe, "Philosophy" 17.
81   Gardner 13. Evans xiii. D'Orsay vii.
82   Barrett 49. See also Esenwein 43; Evelyn May Albright, *The Short Story: Its Principles and Structure* (New York: Macmillan, 1907) 28.
83   Beach. See Chapter 1, "The X-Ray Method." Summers 51–72. For Cook, see Bedford-Jones 117.
84   Perry 306. Clayton Hamilton, *The Materials and Methods of Fiction* (Garden City, NY: Doubleday, Page and Company, 1912) 189–96. Cross 12–13.
85   Edgar Allan Poe, "The Pit and the Pendulum," *Complete Stories and Poems* (Garden City, NY: Doubleday and Company, 1966) 196–207. Poe, "A Descent into the Maelstrom," *Complete Stories* 108–20.
86   Bement 8. Charles Baudelaire, "New Notes on Edgar Poe," preface to *Nouvelles histoires extraordinaires par Edgar Poe* (1857). Reprinted in English in Eric Carlson, ed., *The Recognition of Edgar Allan Poe: Selected Criticism since 1829* (Ann Arbor: University of Michigan Press, 1966) 53–8.
87   Kelly Cherry, in Nancy L. Bunge, *Finding the Words: Conversations with Writers Who Teach* (Athens, OH: Ohio University Press, 1985) 21. See also Wallace Stegner, *On the Teaching of Creative Writing*, ed. Edward Connery Lathem (Hanover, NH: University Press of New England, 1988).
88   John Gardner, *The Art of Fiction: Notes on Craft for Young Writers* (New York: Knopf, 1984). See also Gardner, *On Becoming a Novelist* (New York: Harper and Row, 1983). Natalie Goldberg, *Writing Down the Bones: Freeing the Writer Within* (Boston: Shambhala, 1986). See also Goldberg, *Wild Mind: Living the Writer's Life* (New York: Bantam, 1990). Jerome Stern, *Making Shapely Fiction* (New York: Norton, 1911). Janet Burroway, *Writing Fiction: A Guide to Narrative Craft*, 3rd ed. (Boston: Little, Brown, 1991).
       The Story and Its Writer, ed. Ann Charters (New York: St. Martin's Press, 1987). *Sudden Fiction: American Short-Short Stories*, eds. Robert Shapard and James Thomas (Salt Lake City: Peregrine Smith Books, 1986).
       See also: Sharon Sorenson, *How to Write Short Stories* (New York: Prentice Hall, 1991). Jean M. Fredette, ed., *Handbook Of Short Story Writing, Volume II* (Cincinnati: Writer's Digest, 1988). Ray Bradbury, *Zen in the Art of Writing: Essays on Creativity* (Santa Barbara, CA: Capra Press, 1990). Christi Killien and Sheila Bender, *Writing in a Convertible with the Top Down: A Unique Guide for Writers* (New York: Warner,

1992). Barnaby Conrad, ed., *The Complete Guide to Writing Fiction* (Cincinnati: Writer's Digest, 1990). Several publishers have recently reissued classics of the how-to-be-a-writer genre: Brenda Ueland, *If You Want to Write* (1938; St. Paul: Graywolf, 1987); Willa Cather, *Willa Cather on Writing*, foreword by Stephen Tennant (Lincoln, NE: University of Nebraska Press, 1988); Lajos Egri, *The Art of Creative Writing* (1965; New York: Citadel Press, 1990). Although publishers were slow to recognize the rise of the creative writing workshop during the 1980s, since 1987 they have acknowledged the market for a new selection of short story handbooks.

89   Charters 3. Mary Rohrberger, introduction, *Story to Anti-Story* (Boston: Houghton Mifflin Company, 1979) 3.

90   For Bunge, see note 87. For Wilbers, see note 5. See also: Wilbers, "Looking Back on the Iowa Pressure Cooker," *Iowa Alumni Review* 30 (Feb./March 1977); "Inside the Iowa Writers' Workshop: Interviews with Donald Justice, Marvin Bell, and Vance Bourjaily," *North American Review* 262 (Summer 1977); "Interview with Jack Leggett," *prairie grass* 1 (1 Apr. 1977); "Robert Bly Returns," *prairie grass* 3 (1 Feb. 1978).

See also: Louis Filler, ed., *A Question of Quality: Popularity and Value in Modern Creative Writing* (Bowling Green, OH: Bowling Green University Popular Press, 1976). Ben Siegel, ed., *The American Writer and the University* (Newark, DE: University of Delaware Press, 1989). Bill Corcoran and Emrys Evans, eds., *Readers, Texts, Teachers* (Upper Montclair, NJ: Boynton/Cook Publishers, 1987). Sheila B. Nickerson, *Writers in the Public Library* (Hamden, CT: Library Professional Publications, 1984).

The following articles can also be consulted. Maureen Howard, "Can Writing be Taught at Iowa?" *New York Times Magazine*, 25 May 1986: 34–48. Marjorie Perloff, "Homeward Ho! Silicon Valley Pushkin," *American Poetry Review* (Nov./Dec. 1986): 37–46. Donald Morton and Mas'ud Zauarzadeh, "The Cultural Politics of the Fiction Workshop," *Cultural Critique* 11 (Winter 1988–9): 155–73. Peter Stitt, "Writers, Theorists, and the Department of English," *American Writing Programs Newsletter* 19, 3 (Sept./Oct. 1987): 1–3. Katherine Dieckman, "Lish Fulfillment," *Village Voice* 2 June 1987: 46. See also John W. Aldridge, Jason Mitchell, Russell Banks, letters, *Atlantic* (July 1992): 13–15.

91   Cherry, quoted in Bunge 30.

92   Phil Hey, quoted in Wilbers, *Workshop* 130–1.

93   Howard 47.

94   Ben Siegel, "Introduction: Poets, Novelists, and Professors – A Bittersweet Mix," *The American Writer and the University* 11.

95   Frederick Manfred, quoted in Bunge 79.

96   Fagin 8. "Lamentably supportive world" is from Richard Wilbur, quoted in Bunge 180. Bunge 99.

97   Stegner 12.

98   Nelson Algren, "Hand in Hand through the Greenery with the Grabstand Clowns of Arts and Letters," *The Last Carousel* (New York: G. P. Putnam's Sons, 1973) 76.

99   Wilbers, "Looking Back" 6.

100   Howard 34. Stegner 54. Cherry, quoted in Bunge 29.

101   N. Scott Momaday, quoted in Bunge 89. David Madden, "The Real-Life Fallacy," *The American Writer and the University"* 185. Stafford quoted in Wilbers 131. Algren 80.

102   Bellamy quoted in Wilbers, "Looking Back" 7. Theodore Weiss, "Poetry, Pedagogy, Per-versities," *The American Writer and the University* 154. Seymour Epstein, quoted in Bunge 36. Dobler quoted in Wilbers, *Workshop* 129.

103   Bell quoted in Wilbers, "Justice" 11. James Alan MacPherson quoted in Bunge 85. Stegner 65–7. Alexis de Tocqueville, *Democracy in America,* translation by Henry Reeve, ed. Phillips Bradley (New York: Vintage, 1945). See, for instance, Volume II, Second Book, Chapters 2 and 4: "Of Individualism in Democratic Countries," and "That the Americans Combat the Effects of Individualism by Free Institutions." See also Volume II, Second Book, Chapter 13, "Why the Americans are so Restless in the Midst of their Prosperity."

104   Stegner 50.

105   Stegner 50, 54.

106   Epstein, quoted in Bunge 37.

5. Back Home Again

1   Bobbie Ann Mason, "Shiloh," *New Yorker* (20 Oct. 1980): 50–7. Mason's "Offerings" was published in the *New Yorker* earlier that year.

2   *Best American Short Stories 1981,* eds. Hortense Calisher and Shannon Ravenel (Boston: Houghton Mifflin Company, 1981) 171–84. Bobbie Ann Mason, "Residents and Transients: An Interview with Bobbie Ann Mason," *Crazy Horse* (Feb. 1984): 87. Bobbie Ann Mason, *Shiloh and Other Stories* (New York: Harper and Row, 1982).

3   Mason, "Residents" 95. See, for instance, Nancy Pate, "The Real Small-Town South," review of *Me and My Baby View the Eclipse,* by Lee Smith, *Philadelphia Inquirer* 12 Mar. 1990: 2-E. Kim Herzinger, "Introduction: On the New Fiction," *Mississippi Review* 40/41 (Winter 1985): 8. Joe David Bellamy, "A Downpour of Literary Republicanism," *Mississippi Review* 40/41 (Winter 1985): 31–9.

4   Mason, "Residents" 87.

5   See Chapter 2. For a discussion of the development of the short story of the 1830s, see Eugene Current-Garcia, *The American Short Story before 1850: A Critical History* (Boston: Twayne, 1985) 91–9.

6   Frederick J. Hoffman, Charles Allen, and Carolyn Ulrich, *The Little Magazine: A History and a Bibliography* (Princeton: Princeton University Press, 1946) v–vi, 1–6.

7   Frank O'Connor, *The Lonely Voice: A Study of the Short Story* (New York: World, 1963) 20, 40–1.

8   See Chapter 2. James Hart, *The Popular Book: A History of America's Literary Taste* (New York: Oxford University Press, 1950) 286. Theodore Peterson, *Magazines in the Twentieth Century* (Urbana: University of Illinois Press, 1964), and F. L. Mott, *A History of American Magazines, 1865–1905* (1938; Cambridge, MA: Harvard University Press, 1967), both discuss magazine circulation rolls in detail.
     For a discussion of anthology selection processes, see Chapter 2. See also Peter S. Prescott, introduction, *The Norton Book of American Short Stories* (New York: W. W. Norton, 1988) 14. "I decided to resist

the temptation to define, to any strict degree what a short story is. To define is to exclude, and there's something in the American character that resists exclusion; for a collection of American stories I needed a vulgar comprehensiveness."

9   Bobbie Ann Mason, "A Conversation with Bobbie Ann Mason," ed. David Y. Todd, *Boulevard* 4-5.3-1 (Spring 1990): 135.

10 F. L. Pattee, *The Development of the American Short Story* (1925; New York: Biblo and Tannen, 1975) 170.

11 Mason, "Residents" 95. In Bobbie Ann Mason, "An Interview with Bobbie Ann Mason," ed. Enid Shomer, *Black Warrior Review* 12.2 (1986): 98, she refers to the "alienated hero," and the "superior sensibility." In Mason, "Conversation" 134, she speaks of the "sensitive young man," in the same context.

12 Mason, "Residents" 89, 90, 95, 96.

13 Suzanne Freeman, "Where the Old South Meets the New," review of *Shiloh and Other Stories*, by Bobbie Ann Mason, *Chicago Tribune Book World*, 31 Oct. 1982: 3.

14 David Quammen, "Plain Folk and Puzzling Changes," review of *Shiloh and Other Stories*, by Bobbie Ann Mason, *New York Times Book Review*, 21 Nov. 1982: 7. Freeman 8. Geoffrey Stokes, review of *Shiloh and Other Stories*, by Bobbie Ann Mason, *Village Voice Literary Supplement*, 9 Nov. 1982: 7.

15 Mason, "Residents" 90.

16 Mason, "Conversation" 135.

17 Mason, "Conversation" 135.

18 Mason, "Residents" 88.

19 Mason, "Residents" 102.

20 Quammen 7.

21 Mason, "Shiloh" 50.

22 Mason, "Shiloh" 57.

23 Mason, "Shiloh" 50.

24 Mason, "Shiloh" 57.

25 Mason, "Shiloh" 57.

26 Mason, Shomer "Interview" 96.

27 Mason, "Shiloh" 57.

28 Mason, "Residents" 101.

29 Mason, "Residents" 97.

30 Mason, "Conversation" 138–9.

31 Mason, "Residents" 101.

32 Mason, "Residents" 94.

33 Mason, "Residents" 95.

34 Mason, "Residents" 88.

35 Eugene Current-Garcia and Bert Hitchcock, eds., *American Short Stories* (Glenview, IL: Scott, Foresman/Little, Brown, 1990), for instance, includes Ursula LeGuin, Raymond Carver, Bobbie Ann Mason, Alice Walker, Joy Williams, Tobias Wolff, Tim O'Brien, David Michael Kaplan, Jayne Anne Phillips, Louise Erdrich, and Michael Martone in the "Contemporary Flowering" section. Ann Charters, ed., *The Story and its Writer* (New York: St. Martin's Press, 1987) includes Ann Beattie, Raymond Carver, Alice Adams, Louise Erdrich, Mark Helprin, Jamaica Kincaid, David Leavitt, Ursula LeGuin, Bobbie Ann Mason, Alice Munro, Cynthia Ozick, Grace Paley, Jayne Anne Phillips, and Alice Walker. Michael Meyer, *Bedford Introduction to Literature* (New York: St.

Martin's Press, 1987) uses Carver, Erdrich, Mason, Phillips, and Mark Strand for the "Album of Contemporary Stories." Laurie G. Kirszner and Stephen R. Mandell, eds., *Literature: Reading, Reacting, Writing* (Fort Worth, TX: Holt, Rinehart, and Winston, 1991) includes Amy Tan, Anne Tyler, Alice Walker, Alice Munro, Mason, Madison Smartt Bell, Lorrie Moore, Charles Baxter, and Louise Erdrich.

36 Mason, "Residents" 98.
37 Mason, "Conversation" 141.
38 Mason, "Residents" 104.
39 Mason, "Conversation" 134.
40 William Carlos Williams, "A Beginning on the Short Story" (Yonkers, NY: Alicat Press, 1950) 11. Raymond Carver, "Fires," in *Fires* (Santa Barbara, CA: Capra Press, 1983) 26.
41 For discussions of O'Brien, Farrell, Harte, et al., see Chapter 2. For bibliographical information, See Chapter 2, notes 10, 48, 52.

An interesting distinction can be made between "insider" local colorists, and "outsider" local colorists. "Insiders" would include authors such as Charles Chesnutt, who wrote about black American characters for an *Atlantic* readership, or even Mark Twain, who began life as a Western mechanical worker. "Outsiders" would include any author who did not belong to the ethnic or geographic community that offered the "color" within that particular fiction. The implication, of course, is that the former group would be more "ideologically sensitive" in its depictions of local life, although the audience's perception of the ethnicity of the author would also create other less polite possibilities. It is unclear whether Mason would belong to the former group, or the latter group, which further complicates the "tension between being from there and not from there" that she describes as central to her fiction.

Mason's own ethos of disposability also deserves further analysis. As an earlier part of this chapter suggests, Mason's conscious efforts to use potentially obsolescent popular culture references "date" her fictions, and create the possibility that they too will become obsolete. In addition, however, her use of those references also circumscribes her audience to individuals who are sufficiently highbrow to understand her postmodern formal gestures, and lowbrow enough to be familiar with "Donahue" and Bruce Springsteen. If Mason's individual fictions are disposable, her career is not: She simply recruits readers who follow popular culture at approximately the same distance as she does.

42 Mason, "Conversation" 143. The difference between the constraints of the short story and those in other genres is that the constraints placed on the short story writer are considered to discourage individual achievement, while the constraints in other genres are designed to display such achievements more clearly. Although a lyric poem such as a villanelle places enormous structural restrictions on the poet, for instance, poetry is nevertheless considered such a luxury good among literary forms that those restrictions become only hurdles over which an educated poet can display the sort of alienated, superior sensibility that has both the leisure time and the intelligence to triumph over voluntarily selected intellectual challenges.

43 Edgar Allan Poe, "The Philosophy of Composition," *Graham's Magazine* April 1846: 163–7. Reprinted in Edgar Allan Poe, *Essays and*

Reviews, ed. G. R. Thompson (New York: Library of America, 1984) 13–25, see especially 14–15. Poe, *"Twice-Told Tales,"* review of *Twice-Told Tales,* by Nathaniel Hawthorne, *Graham's Magazine* May 1842: 298–300. Reprinted in Edgar Allan Poe, *Essays and Reviews:* 569–77.

44 See Chapter 2. Prescott 14: "The point I think is worth considering is that alone among literary forms, the short story is the one at whose creation Americans were present . . . to be sure, foreigners tried to invent the short story and may even have thought that they had . . . the thing itself is ours, invented by us a century and a half ago and dominated by Americans ever since."

45 See Chapter 2. This canon persists, especially with the use of the short story as a teaching tool in contemporary creative writing workshops. John Knowles, in the introduction to *New Generation: Fiction for Our Time from America's Writing Programs,* ed. Alan Kaufman (New York: Anchor Press, 1987) writes that "it is unfortunate that the short story is the vehicle for the apprenticeship of these neophyte writers . . . and yet this difficult form, the short story, must be used in writing courses because in a relatively short period of time the students need to produce something which can be discussed, analysed, dissected" (xv–xvi).

46 See, for instance, Cleanth Brooks and Robert Penn Warren, eds., *Understanding Fiction* (New York: Appleton-Century-Crofts, 1943). Susan Lohafer, introduction, *Short Story Theory at a Crossroads,* eds. Lohafer and Jo Ellyn Clarey (Baton Rouge: Louisiana State University Press, 1989), writes that the "litany of New Criticism . . . proved to be the charter of professional short story criticism. . . . More accessible than poetry, more managable than novels, it was just the right size for a demonstration" (4–5).

47 Walter Pitkin, *How to Write Short Stories* (New York: 1923) 46.

48 Mason, "Residents" 103.

49 Elizabeth Spencer, "Experiment is Out, Concern is In," review of *Best American Short Stories 1982,* eds. John Gardner and Shannon Ravenel, *New York Times Book Review,* 21 Nov. 1982: 7.

50 Brander Matthews, *The Philosophy of the Short Story* (New York: Longmans, Green and Company, 1901; New York: Peter Smith, 1931). Charles E. May, "The Unique Effect of the Short Story," *Studies in Short Fiction* 13 (Summer 1976): 289.

51 Poe, "Philosophy" 15.

Postscript

1 Paul Engle, "The Place," *The Program in Creative Writing* (Iowa City: University of Iowa, 1964). Actually, Paul Engle's introduction to this application brochure says that Paul T. Chase "prepared" the booklet, so it is not entirely clear who wrote the text. Pages are not numbered. The year 1964 is an educated guess based on information provided in the text's contents.

2 Stephen Wilbers, *The Iowa Writers' Workshop* (Iowa City: University of Iowa Press, 1980). See Chapter 2 especially.

3 There have been two such maps, in 1963 and 1987. See L. Rust Hills, "The Structure of the American Literary Establishment," *Esquire* (July 1963): 41–3; Rust Hills, *"Esquire's* Guide to the Literary Universe," *Esquire* (Aug. 1987): 51–9. In the first map, Iowa is in the "hot

center"; in the second map, it is a "planet," around which other writing programs revolve as moons. In the second map, reference is made to the program "slipping," but it is not clear whether, in the shifting iconography of the *Esquire* guide, the shift from hot center to planet is intended as demotion.

4   This list was compiled piecemeal, and it is possible that some of the writers listed as teachers may have been students, or students as well; I have tried to avoid making the opposite error. The major sources were: Ed Dinger, ed., *Seems Like Old Times* (Iowa City, 1986); and Connie Brothers, ed., *The Iowa Writer's Workshop Cookbook* (Hollywood, FL: Frederick Fell Publishers, 1986). B. C. Hall, the student who refers to Norman Mailer's invasion, is quoted in Brothers 29. Similar lists can be found in Stephen Wilbers, *The Iowa Writers' Workshop* (Iowa City: University Of Iowa Press, 1980) 121; Maureen Howard, "Can Writing Be Taught at Iowa?" *New York Times Magazine* 25 May 1986: 34.

5   Dana is quoted in Brothers 19 (copyright *Iowa City Press-Citizen*, 1981). Jonathan Penner, who describes the 1966 fiction staff, is quoted in Brothers 61.

6   See Engle, "Comments from the Press." See also Hills, "Structure." These are mid-1960s figures; it is likely that, with the rise of other workshops, Iowa's numerical dominance has declined.

7   Stephen Voss, ed., *Let's Go: The Budget Guide to the USA 1992* (New York: St. Martin's Press, 1992) 333.

8   Franklin and the other *Junto* members banned "all expressions of positiveness in opinions, or direct contradiction." See Ben Franklin, *Autobiography*, introduction by Daniel Aaron (New York: Library of America, 1989) 57. See also: Robert Stepto, "Storytelling in Early Afro-American Fiction: Frederick Douglass' *The Heroic Slave*," *Black Literature and Literary Theory*, ed. H. L. Gates, Jr. (New York: Methuen, 1984) 175–86. For a description of the writers' clubs, see Wilbers 19–31. The best discussion of the aesthetic and social properties of the Puritan conversion narrative is Patricia Caldwell, *The Puritan Conversion Narrative: The Beginnings of American Expression* (New York: Cambridge University Press, 1983).

9   This is, to some extent, how Caldwell portrays the Puritan conversion narrative. More specifically, she attempts to displace the narratives from their reputation as "mere recitation and/or assent" (54) of certain morphological guidelines, and argues instead that they constitute a varied and open-ended body of literature. Her research also suggests that although many people feared the narrative test (50, 79), many others were inspired to deliver extraordinary narratives that spoke for both personal and public experience.

10 Harold Ross is quoted in Theodore Peterson, *Magazines in the Twentieth Century* (Urbana: University of Illinois Press, 1964) 236.

INDEX

―――――――

O'Connor, Flannery, 5–6, 126
O'Connor, Frank, 42, 43, 52, 75
O. Henry, 2, 3, 65, 123
"O. Henry and the Theory of the
   Short Story" (Eichenbaum), 28, 35
O. Henry short story anthology, 1
On Writing the Short Story (Burnett), 80
Orvis, Mary, 90, 97
Outsiders, 41
"The Overcoat" (Gogol), 42, 75

Pain, Barry, 89, 96, 98
Paley, Grace, 126
Paris Review, The, 109
Pattee, Frederick Lewis, 35, 46, 58, 99
Pease, Donald, 21
Peden, William, 28, 38, 51, 56
PEN/Faulkner Award, 108
"Penn Magazine" prospectus, 14–16
Periodical Publishers Association of
   America, 27
Perloff, Marjorie, 7
Perry, Bliss, 84, 85, 89, 98, 99, 101
Peterson, Theodore, 20, 40, 45
Phillips, H. A., 79, 95, 97
Phillips, Jayne Anne, 117, 126
"The Philosophy of Composition," *see*
   Poe, "The Philosophy of
   Composition"
"The Philosophy of the Short Story,"
   see Matthews, "The Philosophy of
   the Short Story"
Pioneer, 19
"The Pit and the Pendulum" (Poe),
   102
Pitkin, Walter, 28, 86, 87–8, 89–
   90, 91, 92, 94, 95, 96, 98, 99, 123
Pizer, Donald, 77
Plot of the Short Story (Phillips), 79
"The Plural Organized Worlds of the
   Humanities" (Veysey), 80
Poe, Edgar Allan
   Anthon, Charles, letter to, 14–15,
      17, 18
   "The Black Cat," 12, 23
   campaign against international copy-
      right laws, 18–19, 32
   class issues, 19, 20–21, 24, 124–5
   "A Descent into the Maelstrom," 102
   Graham's Magazine, 12, 20
   Godey's Lady's Book, 12
   Hawthorne's *Mosses from an Old
      Manse*, review of, 12, 13
   Hawthorne's *Twice-Told Tales*, review
      of, 3, 9, 10, 12–14, 17–18, 21, 23,
      25, 26, 34–5, 36, 58, 68, 75, 99–
      101, 102, 122

influence, 10, 12, 24–6, 28, 32, 34–
   6, 50, 54, 68–9, 80, 84, 85, 90, 96,
   99–102, 103, 122, 124–5
"Ligeia," 101
magazine project, 11, 14–21
Mason, relation to, 124–5
Matthiessen, response to Poe, 44
"Penn Magazine" prospectus, 14–16
"The Philosophy of Composition,"
   13, 23, 58, 99–102, 124
"The Pit and the Pendulum," 102
poverty, 2, 18, 24
"The Raven," 10, 13, 100–1
self-abnegation and "perversity," 11–
   12, 23–5
Southern aristocracy, relation to, 15–
   17
"The Tell-Tale Heart," 12
"unity of effect," belief in, 13, 21,
   23, 80, 90
Wharton, relation to, 58–9, 68–9,
   74–6
"William Wilson," 12
Poetics (Aristotle), 23, 87
Popular Book, The (Hart), 66
Porter, William T., 41
Prescott, Peter, 27, 38
Pritchett, V. S., 38
Professional Short Story Writing (Mow-
   ery), 92
*Publication of the Modern Language Asso-
   ciation (PMLA)*, 81
Puritan conversion narrative, 130–1

Quaker testimony, 129
Quinn, Arthur, 17
Quirk, Leslie, 95, 96

Ransom, John Crowe, 126
"The Raven" (Poe), 10, 13, 100–1
regionalism, 42, 49, 79, 120, 125
"The Rise of the Short Story" (Harte),
   38
Robinson, Marilynne, 127
Rohrberger, Mary, 35, 103
"Roman Fever" (Wharton), 72–4
Romantic literary theory, 59, 69
Rosenfeld, Isaac, 38, 54–5, 57
Ross, Andrew, 62
Ross, Harold, 132
Roth, Philip, 126
Ruffin, Edmund, 16

Sacred Circle, A (Faust), 16–17, 19
Saturday Evening Post, 32, 44, 48
Saturday Review of Literature, 49
Schramm, Wilbur, 88
Scribner's, 31, 76, 84

Continued from the front of the book